THE
QUEEN

ANN MORROW

THE QUEEN

William Morrow and Company, Inc.
New York   1983

Library of Congress Card Catalog Number: 83-61366
ISBN: 0-688-02136-0

Printed in the United States of America

First U.S. Edition

1   2   3   4   5   6   7   8   9   10

Acknowledgements

My thanks are due to members of the royal household and to those friends and relations of the Queen who helped so much but would like their contributions to be off-the-record.

I should like to thank particularly the following people for their guidance and help: Ronald Allison; Lady Elizabeth Anson; Eric Bean; Franta Belsky; Dr Bevan; Mrs Pat Blake; David Boddy; Eric Burdeck; Maurice Camachio; Willie Carson; Sir Hugh Casson; Sir Barnet Cocks; Peter Colmore; Brigadier Stewart Cooper; Major R. A. G. Courage; Bill Curling; Alban Davies; Mrs Stevie Day; Roy and Sandra Dickens; Charles Douglas-Home; Lord Drogheda; John Dove; Sir Roger du Boulay; Chunky Dukanovich; Andrew Duncan; Barry Evringham; Jane and Terry Fincher; Grania Forbes; Maj-.Gen. Fursden; Nick Garland; Lord Geoffrey-Lloyd; David Gentleman; Lord Gibson; Peter Goodwin; John Grigg; Paul Healey; Lord Home; Kenneth Hughes; Ruth Inglis; Bob Jennings; Thomas Joy; Barbara Kenny; Stella and Nell Kenny; Brigadier R. J. Lewendon; Lord Lichfield; Peter Lumley; Rosemary Lyne; Hilaria McCarthy; Michael McKeown; Rita Marshall; June Mendoza; Jonathan Miller; John Money; Richard and Dermot Morrow; Dr David Owen; Major Dione Parker; Leif Petersen; Henry Porter; Lord Porchester; Geoffrey and Marcia Rollstone; Elizabeth Royle; Jeannie Sakol; Tom Sandrock; Richard Stone; Douglas Sutherland; Stella Treanor; Trevor Turner; Edward Vale; Her Excellency Mrs Jean Casselman Wadds; Lord Wigg; Malcolm Williamson; Sir Harold Wilson; Pearce Wright.

I owe the *Daily Telegraph* my thanks for giving me the oppor-

ACKNOWLEDGEMENTS

tunity to travel with the Queen on her tours abroad. In particular I should like to thank the Editor, William Deedes, who helped me at the paper and with the book; Andrew Hutchinson, Night Editor, for inspired guidance; the Managing Editor, Peter Eastwood, who hired me in the first place; George Miller, formerly a subeditor with the paper, who did so much research on the book; racing expert Howard Wright on the Sports Desk, who gave up so much of his time to check and advise on the Queen's horses; and Terry Keeler, foreign sub-editor, who made valuable changes to the proofs.

My thanks also to Denis Judd, historian, for his apt comments; to Janice Robertson for her editing of the manuscript and for making only painless changes; to Marianne Taylor at Granada for her choice of photographs; and to Roger Schlesinger, also at Granada, for his buoyant attitude to the book. Thank you to Mrs Adrienne Cowin, who typed much of the manuscript, and her husband John, who delivered chapters back no matter how late the hour; to Laura Tanham, who gave up her Bank Holiday weekend to put the manuscript on the word processor.

Finally my greatest thanks are to Richard Johnson, Deputy Editorial Director at Granada who commissioned the book in the first place; and to Mike Shaw, Managing Director of Curtis Brown. For both of them it was an act of faith.

And to G.F.S. more than thanks, for being unfailingly supportive; reading everything step-by-step and adding sleek and subtle changes. As this is a first book I never appreciated before the meaning of acknowledgements which say 'without whose help this book would never have been written'. But I do now, and my thanks to his children too.

Contents

CONTENTS

List of Illustrations

LIST OF ILLUSTRATIONS

In Edinburgh (BBC Hulton Picture Library)
Managing four corgis (Popperfoto)
In Nigeria, 1956 (Hardy Amies)
Sketches of dresses (Hardy Amies)
The Queen in Paris (Keystone)
With King Khaled (Photographers International)
With Queen Margrethe (Keystone)
On the Gulf tour (Photographers International)
Opening the Festival of Sri Lanka (Keystone)
In New Zealand, 1977 (Press Association)
In the 'Tunnel of Love'
Resisting the elements (Keystone)
Miss Margaret MacDonald (Fox Photos)
Visiting the Pope (Fox Photos)
The Jubilee walkabout (Keystone)
At the Cadet Training Centre (Keystone)
A muddy horseshow (Photographers International)
Confronting journalists (Photographers International)
On the Berkshire Downs (BBC Copyright)
About to take a photograph (Keystone)
On Mustique with Princess Margaret, 1977 (Press Association)
Visiting the first grandchild, 1977 (Fox Photos)
With the Princess of Wales, 1982 (Press Association)
With Prince Andrew, 1982 (Press Association)

CHAPTER 1

❈ ❈ ❈

How Very Reassuring

TWO WOMEN IN headscarves and those green quilted jackets known as 'Husky's' were about to leave a teashop in Norfolk when they were stopped by another customer at a nearby table, who craned forward, her elbow almost in the cream, to say to one of them, 'Excuse me, but you do look awfully like the Queen.' 'How very reassuring,' the Queen smiled, exiting with her cake for the drive back to Sandringham.

At Buckingham Palace the Queen looks forward to her 'half-day', when she finishes early on Fridays to go to Windsor. When the Garden Gate opens at 2.30 pm the Queen will be at the wheel of an ancient Vauxhall Estate or Rover, wearing flat shoes, an old green coat and headscarf. As the traffic slows down at the lights, passengers in taxis look casually into the car alongside and turn away. Very seldom is there that unbelieving second look and by the time the lights have changed the moment is lost, leaving a nagging doubt in the mind of office workers on their way back from lunch. If they looked a bit more closely they might see a few corgis dozing on the back seat, though the dogs are meant to be on the floor, where there is lino laid specially for them.

The corgis – Smoky, Shadow, Spark, Myth, Fable and Diamond – can do no wrong in their mistress's eyes. Nor can her two 'dorgies', Piper and Chipper, two pooches bred from one of the Queen's corgis and Princess Margaret's frisky stud dachshund, Pipkin. There is no official Palace view on whether these 'dorgies' happened by accident or not; the Kennel Club says they are an exclusively royal strain. There is no royal 'moggy' at the Palace because the Queen does not like cats.

The Queen's sense of humour is hidden by a fairly solemn face, which is what you expect of the monarch – 'HM' or 'the Sov.' as they call her at Buckingham Palace. She is 5 foot 4 inches tall, has dark brown curly hair and thoughtful grey-blue eyes, a tiny waist, slim legs, a generous mouth and a brightness and interest perhaps surprising in someone who has been absorbing facts for three-quarters of her life. It is this quality which makes people tell her extraordinary things. An old lady in hospital in New Zealand said, 'I keep cycling my legs round and round, Your Majesty.' 'Now mind you don't overdo it,' the Queen replied.

But you never forget for one second that you are in the presence of the Queen – the poise of her head made Annigoni lyrical. She does not like people to be too clever; sees straight through the pompous; can smell social climbers miles off and has demandingly high standards. But she is warmly forgiving and, above all, has a deliciously dry sense of humour. When Prince Michael of Kent was about to become engaged to the glamorous divorcee who had been Mrs Tom Troubridge, the Queen sniffed, 'She sounds much too grand for us,' and she still finds Princess Michael rather talkative and a bit too flashy.

The success of the monarchy today in Britain stems from the Queen's intuitive feeling of what is right. Her clothes are pretty but never too flamboyant, which might arouse feelings of envy in the crowd; she has a tonic quality so that when people have been with her they feel elated, although they may not remember one word of the conversation, which is not fluff by any means. If she does not come across in public as a funny sparkly lady, that is deliberate; the Queen is not an entertainer; she does not want to be a star; she wants to do her duty. A shrewd, compassionate woman who feels things very deeply, she did not allow distress to show when Prince Andrew, her second son, was in the middle of the Falklands crisis flying helicopters as a sub-lieutenant in the Royal Navy.

The most foolish assumption was that she might feel shaken slightly out of gear by the public adoration of the Princess of Wales, but a well-informed member of the Household is confident that 'The Queen has never been fazed by Diana.' The Queen is in a position above jealousy; she is delighted with her daughter-in-law and has welcomed her in a warm and reassuring way. There is a sort of wry acceptance of the adulation. At the Albert Hall a few months after the royal wedding, as the photographers clustered round the Princess of Wales, the Queen watched, waited for a second and then said to Ron Bell, a favourite photographer with the Press Association, 'Well, I think I might as well be going on upstairs – they don't want me, do they?' It was said with a tongue-in-cheek smile, almost with relief.

The Queen was fiercely supportive when the Princess of Wales, emerging shakily from the chrysalis, was distinctly upset by the photographers' attention. Watching the metamorphosis, listening to her daughter-in-law's complaints – 'Oh, Ma'am,' the Princess pleaded, making it sound almost like 'Mum', 'they are everywhere. I find it so off-putting' – she decided she must act. She has never been one to hoist storm-cones but she had known Diana from childhood, watching her grow up at Sandringham and under-standing her sweet but emotionally vulnerable nature – tears one minute, smiles the next. She had been impressed by the way in which Diana had coped with the pressures before and during her engagement to Prince Charles and was confident she was not a silly, inarticulate creature – as described dismissively by Raine Spencer, stepmother to the three girls, who is reported to have remarked: 'If you said "Afghanistan" to Diana, she'd think it was a cheese!'

She took her stand as leader of the family, and summoned Fleet Street editors to Buckingham Palace for the first meeting of its kind for twenty-five years. 'My daughter-in-law's peace of mind comes first,' she commented calmly, pointing out that the Princess of Wales felt harassed; she was pregnant and if she did not have some peace might take up a permanent Greta Garbo attitude towards publicity. The Duke of Edinburgh or Princess Anne would have flown off the handle and been irascible in the face of such frenzy. Instead, the Queen, steady and controlled, made a graceful appeal; but she knew too, deep down, that if there had to be a choice between the royal family and the newspapers there would not be much doubt where public loyalty would lie.

There was a pleasant chat over dry martinis – said to be as good as those at the Ritz – with heat from a one-bar electric fire, as the Queen explained, in all reasonableness, 'Diana can't even go to the village shop to buy wine-gums in peace,' to which the Editor of the *News of the World*, the bluntly-spoken Mr Barry Askew, coun-tered, 'Why can't she send a servant to get her sweeties?' The

Queen gave him one of her sharp looks – hers can be an impatient glamour – and said icily, 'That, if I may say so, is an exceedingly pompous remark,' while the rest of the little group shuddered at the gaffe and at the echo of Queen Victoria's famous 'We are not amused' in the royal reply.

The Queen believes in the mystical character of royalty. It is not something to retire from even if one's health is bad (and she remembers how her father, George VI, put up with debilitating sickness). Yet there are times when she looks so strained and unhappy that one wonders what misery she may have been through – she can look so weary and drawn. Never a mistake in more than thirty years; she is surefooted and confident, and her own view of monarchy has contributed to this radiant credibility. 'The Queen looked radiant' has become a terrible cliché, but she does have an aura about her which is nothing to do with expressive eyes and a sensational smile. A courtier who has worked for the Queen for more than half a century speaks of 'a sparkling quality about her which is a hundred per cent gold.'

'What about all that kissing and clapping then,' the Queen said when one of her Household returned from the enthronement of the Archbishop of Canterbury, Dr Robert Runcie. The ceremony had been lushly ecumenical with incense, Buddhist monks, Evangelists, Roman Catholic cardinals, Russian patriarchs and Jewish rabbis, and there was a great deal of kissing on both cheeks and applause which had not been heard at the more sedate enthronement of Dr Coggan.

With his mellow vocabulary and actorish style – 'Here is the stuff of which fairy tales are made' in St Paul's on the day of the royal wedding in July 1981 – the Archbishop has found favour with the Queen. But there was a slight conflict before his appointment, when another candidate was strongly pushed by the Government. The message from the Queen to her Prime Minister was quite clear: You may run the country but I run the Church.

She takes her duties as Defender of the Faith very seriously, and will speak occasionally to the General Synod of the Church of England in her constitutional role as their Supreme Governor, urging them to realise the joy of a Christian faith (13 November 1980). On a more ecumenical note, she spoke at another Synod of how much 'we might learn from Christians in other lands'. The Queen's feminine eye for detail and immovable views on what is correct can earn even the Dean and Chapter of a cathedral a royal rebuke. Raising her eyes from her prayer book, the Defender of the Faith was not pleased to notice that scarlet cassocks were being worn. Only the royal clergy and the Bishop of Bath and Wells (Right Reverend John Bickersteth), Clerk of the Closet of the Queen, can wear scarlet without obtaining the Queen's consent. Bishops and Church officials got a letter from the Lord Chancellor, Lord Hailsham, pointing out the Queen's observations and suggesting that cassocks be dyed blue, black, episcopal purple or navy blue. The Queen, he said, did not want to put people to expense but the situation had got out of hand. The Queen, showing a catholic taste in films, remarked slyly that the erring canons all looked like 'something out of a Fellini film'.

Even if the Queen and her family were not royal, merely leading an upper-middle-class life in Norfolk or Wiltshire, the Church would be important and the men in the family would read the Lesson in their crafted county clothes. On Christmas Day at Windsor members of the royal family are expected to attend two church services and have drinks with the Dean before lunch. The Roman Catholic Church has interested the Queen Mother and, at times, Princess Margaret; they are more than nodding acquaintances of the Papal Nuncio to Britain, Archbishop Bruno Heim, whose Swiss background influences his table; he serves theology with salmon and green sauce and rather fine champagne cocktails. Princess Alexandra is another guest who has enjoyed this stimulating mix.

Nobody could fail to be moved by the Queen's exquisite manners when she visited the Pope in 1980 – by that gesture she healed so many years of tension. She has always been intrigued by a belief which is so uncompromisingly strict in its moral attitudes. It was a far cry from her first unofficial visit to the Vatican, when she went as Princess Elizabeth from Malta in April 1951. No photographs could be released so enraged was the anti-Popery faction of her father's people, although over four million of them are Roman Catholics. Meeting Pope John XXIII in the early sixties was easier – it was a happy audience. When it was over, the Duke spotted a paratrooper who had a black eye and stopped to ask, 'What happened to you? Did you meet a Protestant then?'

All this paved the way for the historic occasion when the Pope went to Buckingham Palace on 28 May 1982. The Queen did not wear black, but long, white gloves as a gesture of formality, and the Pope held her hands in his for almost a minute. 'I will pray for your son in the Falklands,' he told her, waving from his white Pope-mobile. The meeting lasted for thirty-five minutes and the Queen and the Pope were alone in the 1844 Room off the long marble hall with pink velvet sofas, red carpet, statues and eighteenth-century French clocks. She could not have been warmer – walking out to see him go – and he turned to her, giving another craggy wave to all the Household gathered in the court-yard, clapping and moved by this momentous, 'most cordial' meeting. The Queen gave the Pope a leather-bound facsimile of a fifteenth-century Sobieski Book of Hours, named after a Polish king, from the library at Windsor. The Pope gave her a bas-relief in silver of Christ on the Cross.

Her Household marvels at the Queen's ability to use her time economically, with a spectacular self-discipline which, at the end of the day, when everyone else is exhausted, leaves her with some-thing still in reserve. There is a warm expansiveness and a solid central strength. A friend of many years has said, 'She is herself and, of all the people in that age group, less of a mess – the Queen knows herself.' She has survived emotional loneliness. If you are not royal you can pick up a phone and ask friends round to share a Chinese takeaway and an emotional burden, but not if you are the monarch. For a start, security would have to be alerted if she wanted to go as far as Knightsbridge. Can even the close friends such as the Abergavennys, the Morrisons and the Porchesters hear about depressions and doubts?

Luckily she is extremely well supplied with both curiosity and an acquisitive intelligence. So much so that members of her Household find it much wiser to adopt a cautious approach to public engagements; it would be foolish to say, 'Ma'am, I think you are going to enjoy the Lord Mayor's skipping contest on Fri-day,' far wiser to suggest an engagement might be 'absolutely bloody'. If it is, the Queen will be interested – charming – but later the release of tension will not be a stiff drink but a sturdy long walk with the dogs. Trudging around in 'wellies', prodding beasts in the yard and then watching their form may well keep the Queen's sanity and judgement intact. It protects against highly-strung, excitable decisions and above all innately appeals to the English character. The stability we have we may owe partly to this institution of monarchy, which somehow is set apart from the very rich. Nobody begrudges the Queen her Gainsboroughs and Zoffanys – she is hardly ever at home to enjoy them. Even the choice of the Princess of Wales to continue the royal line is a cunning one, not altogether a question of Prince Charles's falling in love one day. The Princess is absolutely right for the 1980s, decorative, kind, gentle and not terribly intellectual. The Queen's affection for the Princess of Wales was seen by all the guests at the party given by Lady Elizabeth Anson at Claridges on the evening of the wedding. She hurried in high spirits to a small television set in a corner of the ballroom, which had been decorated with silver birch sprayed blue and bunches of green apples hanging from a canopy of Maypole ribbons. 'Oh, Philip, do look, I've got my Miss Piggy face on,' she said with a nudge just as her husband was about to go off and dance again with Princess Grace of Monaco, and her eyes lit up every time 'Diana' was in camera. It was on a royal visit to Canada almost a year later that a member of the Household let slip the 'Miss Piggy' nickname, when a Toronto journalist asked why the Queen looked so unsmiling. But the Queen, who has a great gaiety about her, did not feel the need to smile inanely while she was worrying about the Canadian constitutional changes. Friends of the indiscreet courtier were worried about him but, far from doling out one of her rare icy rebukes, the Queen thought it very funny. In fact, 'we were extraordinarily amused' by the Canadian disbelief at her private link with the Muppets.

Although the Queen was deeply happy on the day of the wedding, it was not allowed to show but at the family party she could relax. Prince Philip was wearing a 'Charles and Diana' boater and he and the Queen bopped like teenagers to a band from New York until she reluctantly left at 1.30 am, saying 'I'd love to stay and dance all night.' Joe Loss, who has played at most of the Queen's parties and dances over the years, says that at first musicians do a double-take when they see the Queen on the dance floor having fun.

Once, when there was a ball at Windsor, the Queen Mother, who was dancing with a young subaltern, was called to the telephone. When she came back, all beams and sequins, her partner was nowhere to be seen. Needless to say, there was no shortage of young officers fretting to be given the nod from her Equerry or

Private Secretary. It was duly given and, in minutes, the Queen Mother was swirling graciously on the dance floor again. Then, seeing her original dance partner now with the Queen, she waited for her moment and, when the two couples were close, whispered in his ear, 'Snob!'

The royal sense of humour, which is not allowed to peek out in public, was at its best at the royal wedding breakfast. There were 180 guests, helpers, staff and servants in the grand Ballroom. As Prince Edward and Prince Andrew announced the arrival of each guest, the Queen was busy clicking away with her gold Rollei camera ... 'One King of Norway,' Prince Andrew intoned as MC and whirled a rattle, and in came King Olaf's massive figure, beaming at the Queen. 'One King in Exile' – this was King Constantine of Greece – the Princes shook their rattles. 'One Earl-in-waiting,' until the bride and groom were convulsed with laughter.

When the newlyweds returned, brown and sparkling from their honeymoon on the royal yacht *Britannia*, the Queen got Prince Edward to take photographs for her. She wanted to be with Prince Philip and the team of estate workers at Balmoral pulling Prince Charles and the Princess in a landau decorated with heather through the grounds with four pipers ahead. The normally lugubrious Crown Equerry Lieutenant-Colonel Sir John Miller gave a terrific blast of his hunting horn, which was the signal for the Queen to run ahead. She wanted to be on the steps to kiss her first daughter-in-law as she got out of the landau and make her feel she was home and welcome.

But the Queen can also be distant. A relative used to say, 'It is always hard to tell with Lilibet whether she is happy or not . . . Is it one of her chin or chinless days?' And the royal family will impersonate a chinless day when the Queen tucks in her chin and looks forbidding. Prince Michael of Kent is a brilliant mimic and takes off most of the family, in particular the Queen, which he does hilariously well.

It is sad that the Queen is not able to show in public this highly developed sense of fun. A friend says that 'there is a strong streak of impishness about her humour; this shows itself at mealtimes and in the presence of the corgis. The Queen is a serious person, but at a country house party I would not put it past her to make up an applepie bed.' Once, when she was being taken round an artificial insemination unit by the urbane chairman of the Milk

Marketing Board, Sir Richard Trehane, they came to an object
which prompted the Queen to ask, 'What is that?' Trehane replied,
'It is a vagina, Ma'am,' and the Queen looked up at him without a
flicker of the eyelids, 'Ask a silly question ...!'

The Queen has never complained about her destiny. If she feels
angry about something she will vigorously pull up ragwort from
the royal gardens – not that there is a lot of it about. She says that
seeing the milk bottles at Windsor marked EIIR really brought
home to her that her life sentence had begun in 1952. In the first
thirty years of her reign she was to make more than a hundred overseas journeys and State visits. She has soothed Heads of State at
prickly Commonwealth conferences and she played a significant
part behind the scenes at the Lusaka Commonwealth Conference in
August 1979 when the Rhodesian problem was resolved.

It is easy to forget now how fragile she was when she came to the
throne at the age of twenty-five, and how quickly she learnt, never
acting in any way untrue to herself but with instinct and judgement,
dealing with eight wily Prime Ministers – even more than her
great-great-grandmother, Queen Victoria. She loves the job and,
with those expressive eyes, uses her charm like a weapon to win
over recalcitrant statesmen. Her courage is a refusal to accept too
much embarrassing and costly security; it is flying in a helicopter in
Northern Ireland in 1977 – something which made her pale; it is
giving Prince Andrew her blessing to fight like any other young
man of his age in the Falklands; it is going to Lusaka when everybody was frightened for her sake – and it is being Queen.

If a member of the Household is asked about the threat of infiltra-
tion by anti-monarchists, the answer, they say, is simple: 'In a very
short time they would be convinced.' There is no profligate, extra-
vagant living at the Palace. The royal family has a work schedule for
eighteen months ahead which any outsider would find infinitely
depressing. When a member of the royal family sees someone on
television who is harshly critical of them, he or she may cry, 'To
the Tower with the bugger!' And the Queen also has her little joke.
'We'll go quietly,' she says, if Britain ever wanted a republic. She
stands as a symbol of values which some might not openly admit
are theirs – duty, decency, morality – but as long as she is on the
throne there is a comforting, warm, secure feeling, even if the
monarchy is a bit old-fashioned.

There is about her an immense goodness which is in no way

pious, and she has made sacrifices. When she first came to the throne she deliberately chose to postpone having the other children she and Prince Philip very much wanted after the birth of Prince Charles (1948) and Princess Anne (1950). It was not until 1960 that Prince Andrew was born and, soon after, in 1964, Prince Edward. The Queen had felt that she could not be both a good mother and a dedicated monarch at the same time, so for nearly a decade her own happiness was put to one side. It is a very loving, close family, but the Queen can still be lonely. This may explain her attachment to her maid – her dresser – 'Bobo' MacDonald, a small old lady immaculately groomed with wavy grey hair, bent and shrinking but still in command. Bobo has cared for the Queen since she was a child, with the devotion of the old nurse to Shakespeare's Juliet, and is probably the only person the Queen can really talk to outside her own family. The old woman will listen but will never volunteer a contrary opinion unless it is about the weather or if she thinks the Queen is being frivolous and not wearing enough warm clothes. It is the age-old mistress-maid relationship and that subtle way the servant can take over the dominant role behind the scenes; but only in things that do not matter a lot. And for someone like the Queen – how comforting to be the little girl when you have had to be a paragon of strength and serenity, even with your own mother.

The Queen is a vulnerable, sensitive woman who minds and feels but does not wear her feelings on her sleeve for daws to peck at. Whatever the emotion of the occasion, she will always be very royal, very restrained. 'I would,' said an aristocratic courtier, 'lay down my life for her. I would lie down at her feet.' The Queen, he said, is 'an absolutely splendid person.' It is her honesty, her integrity and that tremendous dedication to duty which inspires such loyalty. She knew her destiny before she was a teenager, when her uncle, the Duke of Windsor, abdicated. On her twenty-first birthday she dedicated her whole life 'whether it be long or short ... to your service'. She heard that she was to be Queen at a hunting lodge in Kenya, where, after a little time withdrawn, 'she adapted to Majesty' in about ten minutes. The King was dead. Long live his daughter, now on the throne for more than thirty years.

CHAPTER 2

❁ ❁ ❁

A Wanted Child

THE WEATHER HAD been evil for a week when the Queen was born early in the morning of 21 April 1926 in Mayfair at 17 Bruton Street, the home of her grandfather, the fourteenth Earl of Strathmore. The baby was a 'wanted' first child for King George V's second son, 'Bertie', Duke of York, and the twenty-six-year-old Duchess. Advice from eminent international gynaecologists and obstetricians had indicated even then a small family, which was ironic as the Duchess of York came from such a large one. Born in 1900 when her mother, Lady Strathmore, was already thirty-seven years old, Lady Elizabeth Bowes-Lyon (now the Queen Mother) was the ninth child. Two years later a son, David, was born who was to be very close to his elder sister.

The doctors in attendance – the surgeon Sir Henry Simson and Walter Jagger, Consultant at the Samaritan Hospital for Women – told the Duchess that she had a daughter, just what she had hoped for. Downstairs in the drawing-room the Duke of York had been forced to share his 'tremendous joy' with the Home Secretary, Sir William Joynson Hicks. The Duke of York, a shy, highly-strung man, had been annoyed by the archaic custom which demanded the presence of the Home Secretary at the birth of a royal child. When he became King George VI the memory of the intrusive presence still rankled, and the irksome custom was abolished before the birth of Prince Charles. On this evening, however, the Home Secretary had been put at ease, the Duke of York being kindly and hospitable enough. Coffee and sandwiches were also sent out to the waiting reporters stamping up and down on the wet pavement and keeping their voices low in the

residential street. The London papers received the message in time
for late editions to tell the world: 'Her Royal Highness the
Duchess of York was safely delivered of a Princess (at 2.40 am)
this morning. Both mother and daughter are doing well.'

In a robe of cream Brussels lace which had been used for Queen
Victoria's children, the baby was christened at the private chapel at
Buckingham Palace, which was bombed during the war but today
houses the Queen's Art Gallery and is open to the public. Water
from the river Jordan was put in the gold lily font; Dr Cosmo
Gordon Lang, Archbishop of York, christened the child Elizabeth. 'It is such a nice name and there has been no one of that name
in your family for a long time,' the Duke of York wrote placat-
ingly to the King, smoothing over the absence of the usual Victoria, his great-grandmother's name. His happiness in his
marriage had given him the confidence to defy his father and he
got away with this first modest challenge to George V. The King's
bearishness was often a mask for the sensitivity inherited by his
children.

From the time of his marriage on a wet April day in 1923 to
Lady Elizabeth Bowes-Lyon – he had proposed to her at least once
but had persisted – Bertie became the King's favourite son. Queen
Mary, stilted and shy and with a dedication to duty inherited by
her granddaughter, did nothing to stop the King from thinking his
sons were rather wet. In any case his view was: 'My father was
frightened of his mother, I was frightened of my father, and I am
damned well going to see to it that my children are frightened of
me.' Indeed, his sons were petrified of him and did not immediately develop confident, relaxed manners, unlike the Queen's sons
today, who, from the age of sixteen onwards, have been allowed a
good deal of discreet freedom. In those days there were terrifying
scenes at Buckingham Palace. The old King so intimidated his
sons that when the Duke of Gloucester, Harry, known affection-
ately as 'Potty' or Glossipops, was late by a minute for breakfast,
he could not bear to catch his father's eye and fainted in front of
him. Even so George V had a keen sense of humour, which was
enjoyed by his favourite sister, Victoria. She rang to cheer him up
when he was dying of bronchitis in January 1936. The elderly
Princess called Sandringham and hooted down the line, 'Is that
you, you old fool?' to hear the operator reply carefully, 'No, your
Royal Highness, His Majesty is not yet on the line.'

Queen Mary found it hard to be outwardly warm and maternal even when faced with the awkwardness and stuttering speech of her frail second son. But cold, indomitable in those terrifying toques, old Queen Mary became devoted to her daughter-in-law 'the pretty Strathmore girl'. Virginia Woolf described the Duchess of York as: 'A simple, chattering, sweet-hearted, round-faced young woman in pink. Her wrists twinkling with diamonds and her dress held on the shoulder with diamonds' when she saw her in the royal box with the Queen at a performance of Edgar Wallace's *The Calendar* in December 1929. Lady Diana Cooper called the Duke and Duchess 'a sweet little couple ... so fond of one another.'

The King and Queen were charmed by their first grandchild, lavishing on her affection held back from their own children. Most uncharacteristically, Queen Mary would cry, 'Ah, here comes the bambino' as the rigorous nanny, Mrs 'Clara' Knight, carried the baby into the drawing-room at Bruton Street. The house has gone now and instead there is a thirties style bank with no trace of the tall Georgian windows. But there is an unobtrusive plaque in the doorway telling businessmen, messenger boys and visitors to the Lombard North Central Bank that the Queen was born there. The nursery was at the top, overlooking neighbouring mews and the chimney pots of Grafton Street.

In October 1926 the King insisted that the Duke and Duchess of York should go on a Commonwealth Tour, which was to mean a lengthy separation from their daughter. Miserably they set sail, leaving behind a coral necklace for the baby as a Christmas present. 'The baby was so sweet playing with the buttons on Bertie's uniform that it quite broke me up,' the Duchess of York wrote to Queen Mary, using a phrase extraordinarily ahead of its time. 'We always wanted a child,' the Duke added, and now they were not to see her again for many months.

It seems almost to have been a premonition of the King's, to send the young Duke and Duchess on such a tour. He argued that the Prince of Wales had recently been to Australia, so it was not appropriate for him to return so soon for the opening of the new Parliament building in Canberra in May 1927. They were home again on the 27 June 1927. The Duchess held her fourteen-month old baby in her arms on the balcony of their new home, 145 Piccadilly, where they were to live for nine and a half years before moving down the hill to the Palace to take up 'This intolerable honour'.

At 145 Piccadilly, a graceful nineteenth-century house of Portland stone four storeys high, now bulldozed, the Duke and Duchess of York came closest to a reasonable family life. The house, close to Apsley House with its stone balconies and balustrades, was nicely placed for the royal nannies to walk their charges through the back door into Hamilton Gardens. The Duke of York could hear them going out from his study on the ground floor near the hall with its dark brown carpet, tusks of elephants shot by the King of Buganda and pictures of wild horses in gilt frames. The window boxes were filled with pale blue hydrangeas, showing the Duchess of York's love of blue, and setting a fashion for town house ledges. As Princess Elizabeth grew old enough to cope with binoculars, she used to watch her grandfather, the King, having a crusty walk in the Palace gardens.

On 21 August 1930, in Lady Strathmore's pleasant bedroom at Glamis Castle, Princess Margaret was born. The King refused to allow the Duchess to call her 'Ann', perhaps getting his own back for the omission of his grandmother's name with the first baby, though he had gruffly given in at the time.

'I shall call her Bud. You see she isn't really a rose yet,' Princess Elizabeth said. Even in childhood the 'Bud' was to be a spirited sibling who often tormented her gentler sister, teasing her and prompting her to say irritably one day, 'Oh Margaret, with you it's always what *I* want ...' But doughty Queen Mary confessed that Princess Margaret always made her laugh and was so frightfully '*espiègle*' or high spirited.

Sometimes when the two Princesses were taken to play in Hamilton Gardens on the dusty grass, other girls of the same age, between six and ten, were invited to join them. Shirley Temple curls were all the rage and regulation soft blue coats with velvet collars, white ankle socks and button-down shoes were worn by all these 'suitable' little girls. The nannies sat on benches, hands folded on ample laps and watched one another's charges with professional eyes. One afternoon Princess Elizabeth, dressed like her sister in Fair Isle sweater and velvet beret, was skipping on a strip of grass behind a small rhododendron hedge. Her doubleskipping and 'salt, mustard, vinegar, pepper' could hardly be matched, and when she was asked to come out from behind the bushes and give a demonstration for the audience of nannies and little girls, she skipped rhythmically and with style to the discreet admiration of the onlookers at the energy of their Princess 'Betty'.

Then a voice with a strong, Scottish rolling of rrr's called on Princess Margaret to come out and do her turn. It was the redoubtable Miss MacDonald, who earned her nickname 'Bobo' from games of hide and seek and the high piping cries of 'Bo' from her charges. 'Your turn now, Marrrrgaret Rrrose,' the nanny requested; but Princess Margaret ignored the instruction and went on bouncing a ball at a furious pace. There was a grim nanny warning about the fate of girls who did not do as they were told, a long pause and, eventually, the younger princess appeared – but acting like a mad horse, throwing her head up and down in the air, plunging and cavorting before the open-mouthed spectators. A shudder ran through some of the nannies. One observed comfortably that it was always the high-spirited children who were crushed in the end. You could, another nanny said afterwards, have ridden to Balmoral on Princess Margaret's lower lip.

When Prince Philip was engaged to the Queen, a naval friend suggested that he had proposed to the wrong sister. 'Margaret is much better looking,' he said, as if selecting a fine mare. Philip replied that he was marrying the nicer person. Margaret was better looking, but she was always precocious. When they were moving to Buckingham Palace at the time of the Abdication, the younger Princess remarked crossly, 'I *was* Margaret of York, now I'm just Margaret Nothing.'

The King had refused to allow the Princesses to be sent to boarding school. There were lessons at 145 Piccadilly, in a garden room on the first floor filled with maps and books. Princess Elizabeth, grave and considerate, was not all sweetness and light. She tipped a silver inkpot over her ash-blond curls when exasperated by her French mistress, but it was typical of her training even then that the ink should be poured on herself: thoughtful good manners again, and she was very good at French. But it was a lonely childhood and the two princesses learnt how to be self-reliant from a very early age. The Queen's love of animals may stem from these years. Like so many women she finds the company of her pets comforting, their affection unchanging. The first corgi came into her life when she was seven years old. A breeder of corgis, Mrs Thelma Gray, was invited to bring a basketful of puppies to 145

Piccadilly. The Duke of York chose one which eventually was called Dookie, an inexplicable abbreviation of the name Rozavel Golden Eagle. The Duchess selected one called Jane and not long afterwards Princess Elizabeth had a corgi pup to walk over the railway bridge at Ballater, setting a fashion for these short-legged dogs from Pembrokeshire. There were only nineteen registered with the Kennel Club in 1925. Over the years these snappy little creatures have formed a group of dwarf guards round the Queen as they herald the arrival of 'Elizabeth and her dogs'. At Buckingham Palace lunches guests wait around making idle, nervous small-talk and then hear a rustling and scurrying along the corridors. It is a little like a circus act as the Queen and Prince Philip come in preceded by a flurry of dogs, who fan out whirling and hopping and home in on every gentleman in the room who is trying to engage in studiedly informal conversation. At the threat of attack the men put down their dry sherry and clasp their hands over vulnerable areas, rather like footballers lining up in front of an indirect free kick!

The Duchess of York, full of the old-fashioned graces herself, taught her daughters the right way to behave, saying to them, 'Now I am the Archbishop of Canterbury ... Now I'm Grannie,' so that they could learn how to meet people. Her own mother, Lady Strathmore, drummed into Elizabeth Bowes-Lyon the sensible dictum, 'If you find somebody or something a bore the fault lies in you.' The Queen Mother, standing for hours in the mud and rain at a Garden Party at Knole, in Sevenoaks, to mark her eightieth birthday, or inspecting a housing estate, gives the impression that there could be no more appealing way of spending her time; and gives a wave of such sweet reluctance at having to leave as she is driven away. Often the press are blamed by some members of the royal family for portraying them in an unsympathetic light; but it would be impossible to find an unflattering published picture of the Queen Mother. Photographers edit the pictures they take themselves and throw away any they feel might be unkind.

For the two Princesses it was a childhood short on company of the same age, although there were occasional visits from cousins such as the Elphinstones or the Lascelles, but in every other way it was secure and loving, without too much emphasis on study or grand events. It was a small household. There were lots of dinner parties; the Yorks liked to eat at about 9 pm and loved dancing afterwards. At Glamis and at weekends at Royal Lodge, Windsor, there were games like Snap and Happy Families after tea. The Princesses had one hundred and fifty dolls to play with and some had belonged to Queen Victoria's children; only in royal circles could a doll last so long without being pulled apart. Two French dolls, Marianne and France, had ten sets of gloves, beaded bags, fans, sunshades, tortoiseshell hair brushes, monogrammed writing paper and made-to-measure shoes, accessories still on view at Windsor which make a nice vignette of those royal, pre-war years.

Holidays were simple picnics or paddling on the sands at Dunan Bay, near Montrose in Forfarshire, with their parents. Princess Elizabeth loved being with dogs and horses and had a serenity about her. She enjoyed her sister's gift of mimicry, and developed her own, which is of a high standard, particularly when the unctuous, the pompous and the pretentious have turned their backs at the end of a tedious day. Christmas was often spent at Sandringham. Archbishop Lang saw George V on the floor being led by the beard by his grandchild, the 'sweet little Lilibet' as they played horse and groom. Then in the New Year of 1936, the King, known to the Princesses as Grandpapa England, took to his bed at Sandringham and confessed to feeling 'rotten' in his diary of Friday, 17 January. Most of the house guests disappeared though the few who were left sat through a film which the King had ordered. The Queen took the Princesses out to walk in the light, fragile snow and explained that their grandfather was very ill. Princess Elizabeth was taken in to say goodbye to him as he sat propped up in his favourite Tibetan dressing gown, given to him on an early tour of India. It was a first experience of the approach of death, and Princess Elizabeth looked very unhappy when she left for home with her younger sister. The King died five minutes before midnight on Monday, 20 January.

Correct as always, even in her moment of grief, Queen Mary had risen to her feet at the moment when her husband's life had moved 'peacefully to its close' and kissed the hand of her eldest son. At five minutes to midnight on 20 January 1936, Edward, the Prince of Wales, aged forty-one and carefree enough, was now Edward VIII, the new King. He was to reign for 327 days and then abdicate for the woman his mother had called an 'adventuress', a description of Mrs Wallis Simpson which, in his own phrase, was to come between his mother and himself like a 'coiled malevolence' for the rest of his life.

When his brother abdicated, the Duke of York was appalled.

'This can't be happening to me,' he cried in a state of shock when a servant correctly addressed him as 'Your Majesty'. He had gone to bid his brother goodbye at his home, Fort Belvedere, at the edge of Windsor Park on the evening of 11 December 1936. The new King said miserably to Lord Mountbatten, 'This is terrible, Dickie, I never wanted this to happen. I'm quite unprepared for it ... I've never seen a State paper. I'm only a naval officer. It's the only thing I know about.' He wept when he went to see his mother later.

After her initially robust remark on the Abdication: 'Well, Mr Baldwin, this is a pretty kettle of fish all right,' Queen Mary remained as straightbacked and imperious as ever. She felt for Bertie but could not show her feelings, although she did say, 'My second son, he is the one making the sacrifice.' An inability in royal circles to talk about really private things has endured to this day and is a shield against any breakdown or show of emotion. In those days, they would talk about shooting, the weather, 'a friend's marriage, the shocking behaviour of the French, but never a word about what was gnawing their souls', a friend of the Duke of Windsor's remarked at the time of the abdication crisis. It may be a royal coldness. The Duchess of Windsor said that when she stayed at Buckingham Palace for the Duke's funeral in 1972, sur-rounded by all that 'dreadful damask', the royal family were 'polite and kind, especially the Queen'. The Queen thoughtfully arranged that traffic on the Duchess's route from Heathrow to the Palace should be blocked off at intersections so that the widow would not be stared at while her car was at a standstill. But though the Queen was welcoming, and tried to ease things, and was as friendly as possible, the atmosphere was chilly and formal. The Duchess of Windsor remarked afterwards from the safety of her home in Paris: 'Royalty is always polite and kind, but they were cold. David always said they were cold.'

As the Queen gets older, those near her often see a growing resemblance to Queen Mary, particularly in repose or when she is bored or vexed. Queen Mary hardly ever laughed openly in public or showed her teeth, she merely allowed her lips to move a little to the left and right if there was a particularly good joke in *Punch* or *La Vie Parisienne*. Yet she was full of surprises, loved sending comic postcards and was meticulous about learning the words of the song 'Yes, We Have No Bananas'. She visited antique shops

regularly and had a keen eye for silver trifles, and she did not hesitate to admire them in other people's homes in the sure knowledge
that they would feel bound to offer them as gifts. Ladies-in-waiting
would graciously accept and often send them back later. But these
were peccadillos, the main preoccupation for Queen Mary was
duty and this she passed on to her granddaughter, Princess Elizabeth, who was to learn a great deal from Queen Mary and still
quotes her often, and who wrote on a piece of writing paper that
December, in capital letters, ABDICATION DAY.

The Duke of York became King George VI three days before his
forty-first birthday on 14 December. Born at Sandringham in 1895,
he was bedevilled by early stomach problems, a nervous stammer
and being left-handed. In those days the ignorant belief, shared by
the King, was that it was a habit which should be broken. But he
became an excellent shot, better even than his older brother, and
with five other guns once killed 495 duck in a New Year shoot. He
even overcame the speech defect.

The Duchess had her own problems in readjusting; fighting
resentment against her brother-in-law and the distaste she felt as
stories from his below-stairs staff seeped back. A footman was
asked why he left the employment of King Edward VIII at Fort
Belvedere, when applying for a job in London, and said, with all the
hauteur of a servant disappointed in his master's behaviour, 'Well,
madam, the butler, Mr Osborne, sent me down to the swimming
pool with two drinks. When I got there what did I see but His
Majesty painting Mrs Simpson's toenails. My Sovereign painting a
woman's toenails. It was a bit much, madam, I gave notice at once.'

The move to Buckingham Palace took place on 15 February
1937. The new Queen tried to make it more relaxed; the four-poster
bed, kidney-shaped dressing table with its satin skirt, books and
gramophone records were all moved to the royal suite. The
Princesses arrived from Royal Lodge, Windsor, two days later and
were dismayed by the bleak corridors. The bond between Princess
Elizabeth, soon to be eleven years old, and her prim Scottish
nursemaid, Margaret MacDonald, stems partly from that time.
Inevitably she saw less of her parents, although each evening the
King tried to set aside time to initiate her into the subtleties of
monarchy, and there was an altogether more formal atmosphere.

CHAPTER 3

❊ ❊ ❊

Setting an Example

WHEN THE QUEEN takes guests around Windsor Castle after dinner and shows them a painting of her parents in their Coronation robes, she says her memory is of the artist who kept coming back day after day for more sittings.

'He didn't seem to have any sense of perspective; he kept rubbing bits out and starting again and we thought we would never see the back of him.'

On the day of her father's Coronation she wore a long dress of lace and silver, the pearls that 'Grandpapa England' had given her and a purple cloak lined with ermine. The Princess's passion for neatness never had more justification than on that morning of 12 May 1937, the date set for Edward VIII's Coronation and unchanged by his brother. Awake at five in the morning to the sound of the Royal Marines Band almost outside her window, Princess Elizabeth checked her silver slippers, to be worn with the white ankle socks suitable for an eleven-year-old and a coronet. When the Princesses were photographed by Marcus Adams, their good manners were noted, but so, too, were their well-darned white socks.

On that grey, raw morning of the Coronation, Princess Elizabeth wrote, 'Bobo made me put on an eiderdown,' exactly what Miss MacDonald would do today, forty-five years later, if she caught the Queen not being sensible.

'We crouched in the window looking on to a cold, misty morning. There were already some people in the stands and all the time people were coming up to them in a stream ... At six o'clock Bobo got up and, instead of my usual time, I jumped out of bed at half past seven.' This simple account, written for 'Mummy and Papa in Memory of their Coronation as a gift from Lilibet By Herself', is preserved, tied in pink ribbon, at the Royal Library at Windsor. There are few people left today who know the Queen as Lilibet – except for the Queen Mother and those of the vintage of the Dowager Duchess of Gloucester. But Princess Margaret always uses her pet name. Contained and considerate, almost too aware, Princess Elizabeth was anxious about her young sister, whom she thought 'very young' for a Coronation and feared she might 'disgrace us all by falling asleep in the middle'. But even then, aged six, Margaret carried her cloak with style, occasionally drawing attention to herself with the extravagantly loud turning of the pages of a prayer book. The light, though, was on the King and Queen. 'Bertie and Elizabeth,' said Queen Mary, now Queen Mother, 'did it all too beautifully'. Uncharacteristically, allowing herself to be moved by the Coronation and, particularly, by the Princesses, 'who looked too sweet in their lace dresses and robes, especially when they put on their coronets.'

The first time the children had curtseyed to their father was when he came home from the Accession Council at St James's Palace on Saturday, 12 December 1936 and they had gathered in the sombre hall at 145 Piccadilly. These curtseys, although correct, distressed him, for, unlike his father, he could not bear the stiffness of royal formality being imposed on his two daughters. He had doted on them since they were tiny, with curly blond wisps of hair; they were often 'strange' to him, but always 'wonderful' and he found the curtseys only added to his anguish. The new King and Queen tried to see as much as ever of their daughters, prompting a rebuke from Queen Mary who disapproved of the Princesses' late nights, complaining about their 'yawns in the morning'. It was a cloistered life at the Palace; and attempts to form a Girl Guide troop, the 1st Buckingham Palace Company of Girl Guides with two Brownies included for Princess Margaret's benefit, hardly got off to the rough and tumble start a Brown Owl could normally expect.

War found the royal family at Balmoral, where, when they were younger, Princess Elizabeth and her sister used to march up and down the drive with a few cousins singing Souza's 'King Cotton', their first and favourite record, absolutely at the tops of their voices. After Christmas at Sandringham, the Princesses were moved away from the vulnerable East Coast to Royal Lodge, Windsor Great Park. At the time of Dunkirk they moved to Windsor Castle for greater safety. Princess Margaret recalls, 'We parked for the weekend and stayed for five years. We were not allowed to go far from the house in case there were air-raids; there had been a pathetic attempt to defend the castle with trenches and some rather feeble barbed wire. It would not have kept anyone out, but it did keep us in.'

They missed Buckingham Palace, which they thought very cosy apart from the corridors and where they had particularly enjoyed watching the Changing of the Guard. But all this was now different, the sentries were in khaki and the Palace bleak and cold, for the King insisted on only using one bar of any electric fire. Setting an example made the King and Queen almost relish their deprivations. There they sat, in the draughty dining-room, some of the windows blown out by bombs, eating Woolton Pie made of nothing more fleshy than wholesome root vegetables, parsnips, carrots, turnips and potatoes under a thin pastry crust, on elegant Sèvres or gold plate. Although most of the aristocracy had managed to send their children across the Atlantic, setting an example demanded that the Heir to the Throne should stick it out in Britain. So the Princesses went to sleep in the cellars at Windsor each night, carrying their French dolls' trousseaux in blue and pink suitcases. The Palace was hit nine times and a V bomb destroyed the royal chapel. 'I'm glad we've been bombed; it makes me feel we can look the East End in the face,' the Queen said, stepping over the debris and insisting on remaining in London. The only concession the King and Queen made towards their own safety was to try and sleep at Windsor in the same cellar as the children. This unrelenting sense of duty of the King and Queen was passed on to their eldest daughter. Old Queen Mary trumpeted that 'This fellow Hitler was a most ghastly bore.' The young Queen, with that sweet way which was never saccharine, helped out with the Voluntary Aid Detachment, the VAD, and was affected deeply by the wounded soldiers. She found their charm of manner and sardonic humour, above all their niceness to each other, their 'best of luck' to the outgoing ones, 'gave her such a lump in her throat'. This frivolous girl, who had turned down five other proposals of marriage and loved dances and parties, and who had unexpectedly become Queen, could never again be called 'a simple, sweet-hearted little thing'. During the war the young Queen even practised self-defence with a .303 rifle and a .38 revolver in case the 'beastly, boring Hun' should land in the flowerbeds at Buckingham Palace. The war took such a toll of the King physically that he confessed to feeling 'burnt out' by 1945. He was forty-three at the outbreak of the war; afterwards, though physically drained, his personality had changed, become resilient and more confident, so that the Queen could step to one side and leave all decision-making to Bertie.

The Princesses came to London only for dental appointments during the war. One outing which they could have done without was when their mother took them to a poetry reading by Edith Sitwell in aid of the Allies in the spring of 1943. They looked fearfully bored and a bit sulky as the bejewelled, turbaned poetess held her audience with formidably assertive reading. But mostly the children stayed in the icy Castle, scampering about substituting Mother Goose and the Ugly Sisters in the empty frames which had held generations of Stuarts and Hanoverians, the original canvases being stored in Wales for safe-keeping. 'How do you like my ancestors?' the King would laugh as he joined guests for a pantomime put on by his daughters, a light relief which sometimes moved him to tears. Nervy and given to irritation if there were any delays or slapdash planning, he was moved equally easily at the sight of Princess Elizabeth as Prince Charming and 'Bud' as Cinderella.

The King's expertise as a horseman – he was the best among the brothers – was passed on to his eldest daughter, giving them another bond. In the early thirties the slump forced him to sacrifice a stable of fine hunters and it hurt him deeply. Princess Elizabeth had riding lessons at Royal Lodge, Windsor, with Henry Owen – the man who had been her father's groom. Chunky, in a bowler hat and with correct gaiters, he was quoted so constantly by the Princess at home that the King joked he had little influence over her any more. 'Ask Owen, don't ask me; who am I to make suggestions?' Apart from the pleasure of being a good horsewoman there was that marvellous feeling of solitariness cantering at Windsor early in the morning, when shyness and reserve do not matter; and the skill learnt in childhood of judging fences and highly-strung animals helped to train the mind subconsciously for hurdles and dangers in adult life.

Talking to horses was a pleasure cultivated early on. Staff in the Royal Mews remember the two Princesses asking, 'Please may we go and talk to the horses?' in any moment they had between lessons or before tea. Lonely children become protective of their pets – dogs, cats, budgerigars and gerbils. The corgis got some of Princess Elizabeth's affection, but the horses got most. The man who taught her the real subtleties of good horsemanship – which she was to pass on to her daughter, Princess Anne – was Horace Smith, who had a riding school at Windsor called Holyport. His assessment of Princess Elizabeth's riding ability said much about her character and qualities – conscientiousness, thoroughness, taking pains and not shirking difficulties. There were few silly questions but a great deal of adult interest in the cost of feeding and training horses.

While Mr Smith may have taught the Princess to ride side-saddle expertly, he must be held responsible, too, for the popular notion that the Queen would like nothing better than to live a comfortable 'county' existence: a JP, perhaps, with a modest, crumbling country place where the labradors are more welcome on the sofa than even the vicar, and the horses more cherished than the children; taking her turn with the church flowers, organizing the village fête and making sure she gets the right couple occasionally for tennis. This nonsensical suggestion stems from a polite, passing-the-time remark made by the Princess to Smith when she was thirteen, a typical schoolgirl ambition that she would like 'to be a lady living in the country with lots of horses and dogs.' It is absurd because, although people like to represent the Queen as a middle-class woman, she is, in fact, nothing of the sort. The Queen is a confident upper-class, grand, landowning figure.

The King had pretended he could see no reason why he should not send his eldest daughter to Eton. She went along with the joke. The next best thing was to get the Vice-Provost of Eton, Sir Henry Marten, to teach her history, which he did, twice a week either at Windsor or Buckingham Palace, and he corrected weekly essays, sent by post from Scotland. He was impressed by her writing style but occasionally he marked her work with an 'N', which did not stand for Nonpareil, but Nonsense. He was an engaging, jolly man of some eccentricity who, after years of teaching boys, never thought it odd to call the two Princesses anything but

'Gentlemen'. His puckish manner once led him to produce a globe from a fake umbrella. He would set homework on *English Social History* by Trevelyan and *Imperial Commonwealth* by Elton, from which the Princess graduated to studying the national exchequer in war and peace, the laws of freedom, the British Commonwealth, Church and Parliament. Government Ministers may sometimes curse the excellent teaching of Henry Marten, as they can be disconcertingly put on the spot by the Queen on a question of Constitutional Law.

'Poor darlings, they've never had any fun yet,' the King said on VE day, standing on the Palace balcony with the Queen. He could not see his daughters – Elizabeth, then nineteen, and Margaret, fifteen, having a marvellous time dancing in the crowds with a favourite uncle who, as Princess Margaret said, was 'very jolly and gay'. It was to remain one of their most enchanted memories, their first experience of being close to their father's people. Princess Elizabeth was surprisingly mature – she had got her wish to 'do as other girls of my age do' and been allowed to join the war effort, being gazetted 2nd Subaltern Elizabeth Windsor in the Auxiliary Territorial Service. Like other girls of her age, she had also fallen in love.

CHAPTER 4

❀ ❀ ❀

Romance and Mr Oldcastle

THE FIRST REALLY aware meeting between Princess Elizabeth and Prince Philip was in the summer of 1939. She was a sheltered thirteen-year-old, wise enough about the role of the Commonwealth and the performance of the King's racehorses, but a child still. The galling fact irked the Princess when she was sent to bed early on the royal yacht after that first meeting with Philip. In those days before 'permissiveness' and co-education, most well-brought-up girls were naïve until marriage but had terrific crushes on gym mistresses, head girls, and then boys who were athletic and competitive.

Prince Philip of Greece, on the other hand, aged eighteen, had not known the secure comforts of a stable home. Joining the Dartmouth Royal Naval College as a cadet that year symbolized achievement and the beginning of an outwardly confident personality. But, behind the outspokenness, the macho flamboyance, there is an inner sensitivity reflected in his painting, even though he feels the art world insists on seeing him as 'an uncultured, polo-playing clot'. Emotional deprivation in childhood stemmed partly from an early separation from his father, Prince Andrew of Greece, who left his son two suits and an ivory-handled shaving brush when he died in exile in France in 1944. The Prince describes his childhood as 'not necessarily particularly unhappy'. The occasional meetings with his father were like dreamland to the boy, coming, as he did, from the bleak household of his mother, the ascetic Princess Alice of Battenberg, older sister of Lord Mountbatten, himself another formidably strong character.

Princess Alice was the eldest daughter of Prince Louis of Battenberg. He was the First Lord of the Admiralty when World War I began, but because of his German birth he was forced by public opinion to resign in 1914 though he had served in the Royal Navy with distinction for forty-six years. During World War I he renounced his royal title and became the first Marquess of Milford Haven.

Prince Philip's parents were married at Darmstadt on 9 October 1903. The bride was eighteen years old, delicately striking with a fine bone structure and an intriguing seriousness. Her appearance – she was said to be the prettiest princess in Europe – and her character had attracted Prince Andrew of Greece, a younger son of King George I of the Hellenes, and grandson of King Christian IX of Denmark. After the wedding, as the newlyweds left in their honeymoon carriage, the last Tsar of Russia ran through the crowd and hurled a white satin slipper at the bride. She caught it neatly and tapped the ill-fated Nicky on the head with the good luck symbol.

The early days of the marriage were spent in the Old Palace in Athens with the bridegroom's father. The young couple kept warm by cycling and skating in the corridors and Princess Alice, who had been deaf from birth, went on perfecting her lip-reading in several languages.

In 1917, this frugal lifestyle was interrupted when the King was exiled and the whole Greek royal family fled to Switzerland.

In exile, the couple drifted apart. Their characteristics became more developed: Princess Alice, always dedicated to good works, became even more religious. Prince Andrew settled uneasily first in Paris and then in Monte Carlo where his extrovert personality helped him make new friends who enjoyed his style and laughter. The early days in Paris were modest. All their possessions had been impounded. Prince Philip was very fond of his father, sharing his intolerance of inefficiency or stupidity. He complained some years ago to Basil Boothroyd, 'I don't think anybody thinks I had a father. Most people think that Dickie's [Earl Mountbatten] my father anyway ... I grew up very much more with my father's family than I did with my mother's. And I think they are quite interesting people. They're the sort of people that haven't been heard of much.'

Prince Andrew died on 3 December 1944 but Prince Philip had not seen him since France had been overrun in June 1940. The

funeral service was held at the Russian Orthodox Church in Nice.
Two years later his body was taken by Greek cruiser to the port of
Piraeus and then to Tatoi – once the country house of the Greek
royal family. In the gardens there is a gravestone which says:
'Andrea Vasilopais [Vasilopais means son of a king], Prince of
Greece, Prince of Denmark, 1882–1944.'

Prince Philip wound up the estate in Monte Carlo and it showed
a debit balance at the end. His mother, who became known as
Princess Andrew, had long since gone back to Greece – Monte
Carlo would never have been her sort of place. She sheltered refu-
gees from the Nazi SS in Athens during World War II and had
refused to flee in 1941, preferring to nurse the wounded. In 1949
she founded her own order, the Christian Sisterhood of Martha
and Mary, and nearly always wore the grey, full-flowing robes
and coif of the order. She died at Buckingham Palace in December
1969 aged eighty-four. She had endured exile and poverty and the
mud-slinging which hurt her father so much during the Allied
propaganda aimed against 'German Greeks', though she was a
great-granddaughter of Queen Victoria (her father Prince Louis
had married Queen Victoria's granddaughter). But she was resilient and in her final years at Buckingham Palace she had the peace
in which to enjoy her spirituality and solitariness. Nobody could
ever say the relationship between Prince Philip and his mother was
cloying but he was a caring son. Once when she was very ill in
Munich, he heard that she wanted to come home to Buckingham
Palace. He had been at Balmoral but immediately flew to Aberdeen then to Munich where he organized her stretcher and flew
back to London leaving the controls of the aircraft occasionally to
come back and cheer her up.

The Prince today likes to joke that he is just 'a discredited Bal-
kan prince of no particular merit or distinction', but this tendency
to put himself down is only seen by those close to him and, of
course, really draws attention to what he has achieved. His
life began on a dining-room table in Corfu, where he was born
on 10 June 1921. Christened Phillippos Schleswig-Holstein-
Sonderburg-Glucksberg, of Danish stock, he was soon bundled
away from Corfu in an orange box. For as if in a bad fairy story
his father was banished and unable to provide a home for his only
son. Nothing could have been less like the gossamer-cosseting of
the Princess's childhood at Hyde Park Corner. Princess Alice was

concerned that Philip might become 'cissified' with four sisters spoiling him, and this brought her brothers Lord Mountbatten and the Marquess of Milford Haven into the picture early on. Occasional visits to his father in Paris did not provide enough manly influence for the boy, and he was indeed adored by his sisters, the youngest of whom was seven years older than himself, though even they found him a bit pugnacious and aggressive. Prince Andrew was witty and delightful and visits with him to restaurants such as Le Tout Paris made a lasting impression on his son, who remembers that 'there was always a silver bucket of something on ice'. But this did not suit Princess Alice, who, as she lacked money for school fees, turned to her eldest brother, George, the second Marquess of Milford Haven. He sent his nephew to Cheam with his own son David, who was two years older, and later to Salem School near Lake Constance on the border of Bavaria and Switzerland, under the influence of its demanding founder Kurt Hahn. As a result Prince Philip's early life was influenced by rather elegant but threadbare Almanac de Gotha royalty. Whereas Princess Elizabeth was served wholesome greens by Bobo and made to finish her semolina and jam in comfortable nursery surroundings, Philip mixed with the Countess of Milford Haven's languid, aristocratic friends with high cheekbones, thin legs, Fabergé eggs and no money. The Countess was the daughter of the Grand Duke Michael of Russia and survived in crumbling elegance where nannies sat down to tea with bowlfuls of caviar. Even today Prince Philip sometimes seems more at home with the carelessly indolent European royalty, deposed though most of them are. As he greets a Greek royal cousin, for example, there is sometimes a look of 'now we are really talking the same language'. He was a naturalized British citizen before his marriage but remains in his bones a European.

The Queen does not surround herself with slightly dotty, inbred aristocrats – but with solid, tweedy advisers, squirarchal figures with their farms and their fields, hunting landowners in tune with their Anglican church and keeping the wilder excesses of revolution at bay. There is an air of settled decency about this strong English Protestant element that is also benign, and quite unlike the world of European aristocracy, with nostalgic longings for an *ancien régime* that hints of fascism.

Lord Mountbatten, the uncle who took a father's care of Prince

Philip after his brother George's death from cancer in 1938,
remarked that Princess Elizabeth was in love with Philip from the
beginning. That day at Dartmouth he was pleased with his
nephew, except when he showed off, rowing dangerously near
the royal yacht *Victoria and Albert* as it sailed away with the
Princesses on board, after an 'amusing' day with them and a
decent helping of banana split and trifle.

'The colour drained from her face and she blushed,' Lord
Mountbatten noticed, which was rather perceptive for a senior
naval officer more used to reading a chart than human emotions.
'She stared at him and for the rest of the day followed him everywhere.' His own daughters, Pamela and, particularly, Patricia,
were two of Princess Elizabeth's best friends, and he was to be
influential later in smoothing out any problems which might prevent his nephew marrying into the royal family, almost as if it was
part of a contrived plan. The girl who shared lemonade and ginger
nuts with Philip at Dartmouth was at an 'awkward and leggy age,
rather large-mouthed', according to her governess; while he was
like a *Woman's Own* hero, with Viking colouring and Greek-god
physique. It was a quarter of a century before sex-appeal focused
on a much thinner, weedier style of man, rolling his own cigarettes with hair to the shoulders and avoiding anything more out-
doorish than playing a guitar at a festival. That sort of young man
would hardly go down well in royal circles even today, though
Princess Margaret fell in love with, and married, a far from
chunky figure – the photographer Lord Snowdon, who is said to
be surprisingly diffident at photographic sessions.

During the war, when Prince Philip was at sea and on active service, he and Elizabeth wrote to each other intermittently. When he
visited Windsor a few times on leave Princess Elizabeth was quite
open in her attraction but this fact was not taken seriously by the
King, who was more interested in hearing about the use of pom-
poms on Philip's ship, HMS *Valiant*, at the Battle of Matapan off
Crete in 1941.

In 1944, Prince Philip's cousin, then King of Greece, quietly
nudged George VI at a family wedding about the possibility of the
young couple's getting engaged. The King was rather shocked.
Fathers are always protective of their daughters and there is rarely
a young man whom they consider suitable. In this case, the King
replied, 'Lilibet' was far too young for marriage at just eighteen

and anyway it would be quite inappropriate while the war was still on. He diplomatically added that there was nothing wrong with Philip; he was intelligent, he went about things the right way and, indeed, made him laugh. This ability to make people laugh was characteristic of Philip's father and is a talent which has endured. It was invaluable in the early years of the marriage, when sometimes the shy Princess needed drawing out. He used to chase her along corridors wearing a huge set of false teeth; offer her nuts from a tin holding a joke snake, or bread rolls which squeaked.

Prince Philip's background was quite suitable, for he, too, was a great-great-grandchild of Queen Victoria and, by 1945, their love was mutual. But the King thought his eldest daughter should meet other men. To this end he arranged a constant series of dances, tea-parties and weekends at Windsor and Sandringham at which the Princess was surrounded by what old Queen Mary, who knew perfectly well what was going on, disdainfully referred to as 'The Bodyguard'. This was chiefly composed of 'Hooray Henries' drawn from the conveniently located Household Brigade in Birdcage Walk, Chelsea and Knightsbridge.

During these years, too, Prince Philip was embroiled in the sensitive matter of becoming a British subject at a time when the Greek royal family was involved in the civil war in Greece. So the question of getting British nationality for Philip was not just a simple matter of answering a few questions, swearing an oath of allegiance before a Commissioner for Oaths and paying £10 to the Home Office. Lord Mountbatten himself became involved and, from his South-East Asia Command office in Whitehall, set about organizing his nephew's naturalization, stressing that Philip 'has been brought up as an Englishman who rides well, shoots well and plays all games such as football with more than usual ability.' He pointed out that his nephew had entered the Royal Navy before the war with the intention of making it his life's career. At that time, as a cadet and midshipman, it was not necessary for him to have British nationality but, when Philip was made a sub-lieutenant in 1941 and wanted naturalization, the war had suspended all applications. Later, a further problem arose because, in peacetime, commissions could only be granted to British subjects and Prince Philip, quite naturally, wanted to pursue his career.

Behind the scenes, Mountbatten was paving the way for good publicity. He used his influence to talk to politicians and diplomats, pointing out that Philip had spent most of his life in England – making his home with Mountbatten – and that he had been in the Royal Navy since before the war.

Meanwhile, the Prince, while not yet quite British, was being initiated into native royal customs on the grouse moor. For a strong-willed young man – who had been independent by force of upbringing and used to racy company – it was a novel experience to go stalking and to be constantly under the eye of the King, who was still not persuaded about his suitability as a son-in-law.

Going to Balmoral with just a small suitcase containing a dinner jacket passed on by Lord Mountbatten, a pair of flannels and a few jerseys, Philip was ill-equipped for a weekend of royal outdoors. He had no tweeds, no formal clothes and his shoes had to be repaired quickly at Crathie after a tramp over the heather. He never wore pyjamas and never bothered with slippers. Far from doing his image any harm, it was just the sort of frugality which appeals to the royal family. He borrowed what Princess Margaret thought were 'frightfully inelegant' plusfours from her father, and was seen by Princess Elizabeth, who still loves stalking, to be acquitting himself well. Philip loved this outdoor life, and about the only thing he and the King did not have distinctly in common was landscape gardening. King George loved shrubs, and Prince Philip remembers their first meeting after the war when the King emerged out of a rhododendron bush at Royal Lodge, Windsor, wearing a quirky rabbitskin cap. Gradually the two grew closer, and eventually in the late summer of 1946 the King gave way and agreed to an informal engagement.

At Balmoral there was often Highland dancing in the evenings, and even after the marriage, when the King had grown very fond of his son-in-law, he was to tick him off for being irreverent about the kilt. Philip, as a member of the family, had to wear one and could not resist a mock curtsey to the King, who was most displeased. It says much for Princess Elizabeth's character that, once committed to a course, she rode the obstacles, particularly when she knew that the King could easily be upset by Philip's cavalier behaviour. She was in love and could bear with all the waiting, the doubts of the King and the delay with the naturalization papers; indeed, anything but enforced separation. So, in February 1947, it was a very reluctant princess who took part in the royal tour to South Africa. She pined for ten weeks and nothing could cheer her up, not even a whole new wardrobe by Norman Hartnell, who had worked like a beaver designing clothes which, by today's standards, have an outlandishly dated ring and were appropriately coloured 'Pale Mealies' and 'Rhodesian Gold'. She moped, looked glum, and nothing could make her laugh much. The King was to explain to her later that he had been terribly anxious that she should go with him to South Africa and felt badly about the separation. If he had wanted proof that theirs was an adult and serious romance, this was it. Yet still he found it hard to believe that his elder daughter had really fallen in love. He relied on her more than he imagined. Margaret made him laugh; but Elizabeth was an appealing, intuitive companion. She now knew even more than his wife about the practice of monarchy, and often worked with him at the Red Boxes learning about the problems of the day.

The South African tour was an exercise in royal public relations and it marked the first ever twenty-first birthday celebrations by an heir to the British Throne in one of the Dominions. Her eyes glistening with tears, Princess Elizabeth made her dedication speech, offering her whole life, 'whether it be long or short, to be devoted to the service of my people'.

It had been a time of strain for both of them, but on 28 February 1947 Prince Philip of Greece became a British subject, Lieutenant Philip Mountbatten, RN. The College of Heralds had first suggested the name 'Oldcastle', being their version of one of his ancestral names, Oldenburg. Not very royal, it was not favourably received, perhaps because it sounded more like a family brewery in the Midlands, and so he adopted the anglicized form of his mother's maiden name, Battenberg. The announcement was made in the *London Gazette*, alongside the names of eight hundred other newly adopted British citizens. It was the final hurdle. Well, almost, but there were one or two stray echoes. Lord Mountbatten was agitated when he heard there was to be a question in the House asking why Philip had been given British nationality, and did not hesitate to write to a press lord, hoping it could be made abundantly clear that he had always wanted to be British and that his first application had taken place years before the rumours about his engagement started.

The engagement was officially announced on 10 July 1947. Princess Margaret, who was losing her older sister's indulgent company and seeing her in the limelight, said at that time, 'Poor

Lil. Nothing of your own, not even your own love affair.'

On the eve of his wedding Philip was created His Royal Highness. At the time he was earning eight guineas a week in the Navy
but, on the day of the wedding, 20 November 1947, he was allocated £10,000 a year State salary. He was also given some very
grand titles – Baron of Greenwich, Earl of Merioneth and Duke of
Edinburgh. It was, as the King said, 'a great deal to give a man all
at once.'

CHAPTER 5

I Remember Your Wedding

IF THE KING had misgivings about his daughter's happiness when she married almost forty years ago, they were soon dispelled. Before his own marriage, Prince Charles said he hoped that he would be as lucky as his parents. Today, friends of the royal family see a closer bond between the Queen and Prince Philip than ever before. He is more philosophical, calmer and more indulgent; the Queen is softer, more flexible and more confident. They laugh a lot together. On tour, he often calls the Queen to see things she has missed; one sees him pointing out something on the royal yacht – and she will turn and look and then look back at him. There is a little-girl quality about her devotion to him which is perhaps old-fashioned but endearingly feminine. When the Queen married, wives were dutiful, loving and restrained, mothers calm, wise and quiet; the husband was the boss. That was their relationship in the early years: 'Oh, ask Philip, he'll know.' To this day she enjoys relying on him, unlike her daughter, Princess Anne, who has a much more abrasive attitude towards her own husband, Captain Mark Phillips.

But Prince Charles, who is close to the Queen, has chosen a wife who seems to have those old-fashioned attitudes of sweet dutifulness. 'With Charles by my side, how can I go wrong?' the Princess of Wales said on her engagement day as the Queen hid behind a curtain watching the couple being interviewed for TV. Both Princess Elizabeth and Prince Philip were comparative innocents when they married, but they grew together, understanding each other more. 'The Queen quite simply adores him,' according to a friend who sees them in private. She calls him 'darling' in

private moments and 'Philip' in public, or when she is cross. He
calls her 'darling' privately, and 'the Queen' when talking about her
socially; sometimes he gets round this at parties. '*We* thought the
Bantu originated in the Kalihpong desert,' he might say, but he
never slips up and says 'my wife'. He is still extremely attractive to
women, even his lurking impatience and challenging hawkishness.
The marriage has had its turbulence: he has compensated by travelling all over the world alone. Constitutionally he may have to be
one step behind but, in the marriage, he is ahead, protective and
considerate. Today it is a relationship of friends who have been
through a lot together but still find each other amusing and good
company – and he always sings the national anthem!

On the morning of the wedding the bride was alarmingly pale.
One of the three dressers from Norman Hartnell helping her into
her wedding dress thought her 'so solemn'. There were of course
the usual last-minute panics: finding her spray of orchids which had
been put in a 'fridge by a nursery footman; a jeweller mending the
frame of her mother's sunray tiara and her double string of pearls
having to be fetched from St James's. Her satin wedding dress was
dotted with thousands of raised pearls scattered in garlands of York
roses and crystal ears of corn. Prince Philip had overslept, was a bit
brusque, and quickly had some toast and coffee. He walked out to
the waiting car, but was too early. The policeman on duty shook his
head and he went back in again. He had a quick gin and tonic.

Possibly remembering his nervousness at his own wedding,
Prince Philip was full of jokes on his son's wedding day, chivvying Prince Charles during that long, almost interminable wait in
St Paul's as the bride came up the aisle on the arm of her ailing
father, Earl Spencer; the Queen Mother smiled at Prince Philip, 'I
remember your wedding,' she seemed to say. The Queen, in pale
blue, tried to pray; she could not bring herself to look at Charles
and put on her gloomy face to hide her thoughts: although, later,
as Charles and his bride drove away after the wedding, she stood
on the steps of St Paul's, bit her lip, and shook her head slightly as
if to say, 'Well I never!'

But there was very little family support for Philip at his wedding. His sisters, now only three, Margarita, Theodora and
Sophie, since Cecilie had been killed in an air crash in 1937, had
married Germans and the King was advised not to invite them. It
would be 'unwise' and perhaps inflammatory, which was hard on

Philip as well as his mother. Yet if Philip was coping with the
strictures of royal life, his wife had to get along with an unusual
mother-in-law. Her devotion to Philip was seen early on in this
willingness to get on with his mother. With the sweetness of character Philip had spotted a long time before, Princess Elizabeth
tried harder to get on with Princess Andrew than many a
daughter-in-law might. Often putting out her hand to Princess
Andrew, she talked about her solitaire diamond engagement ring
set in platinum: this had originally been given to the older woman
by her husband and had been re-set. Princess Andrew was not a
troublesome mother-in-law in the music-hall sense. But neither
was she a cosy granny figure. She had strong ideas and made them
known. Philip was like her in many ways. There was a great
respect for her views, ascetically clear-cut until the day she died.

The wedding ring was made from Welsh gold; the same nugget
that had provided the Queen Mother's ring and was to be used for
Princess Margaret's in 1960 and Princess Anne's in 1973. In the
summer of 1981 Collingwood, the sleek, royal jewellers, made the
Princess of Wales's ring with almost the last of this North Wales
gold. In Westminster Abbey, the marriage register records that
'Elizabeth Alexandra Mary Windsor' married Lieutenant Philip
Mountbatten on 20 November 1947. The King wrote to his
daughter while they were on honeymoon to say how proud he
had been of her. 'Your leaving has left a great blank in our lives,
but I can see that you are sublimely happy with Philip. Your
ever-loving Papa.'

As early as their wedding day, Prince Philip was to realize the
importance of corgis in the Princess's life. Susan, the most beloved
corgi, had been tucked cosily into the going-away carriage by a
Palace servant, and hidden under some rugs. The corgis had their
own Christmas stockings made up by the Princess, and the honeymoon itself was interrupted by a return visit to Buckingham
Palace, to get a special dog lead. The first part of the honeymoon
was spent at Broadlands – the home of 'Uncle Dickie' – with its
airy elegance, pink and blue chintzes, wide lawns and views of the
river. Lord Mountbatten was delighted to offer them the privacy
of his home which he loved so much. Sitting on a pink sofa he
once described how visitors came to see him long after he had
retired. 'Why, one day, this Maharaja fellow came to see me,
obviously wanted a look at his last, beloved Viceroy. We had a

spot of lunch, came back into the drawing-room and the fellow dropped down dead at my feet,' he said, as if describing the death of a faithful labrador.

The Mountbatten influence in India brought a wedding present from Gandhi, and a shriek of horror from Queen Mary when she went to see the 3,007 gifts. 'What a horrible thing,' she said, peering at what she was convinced was a loin cloth, crocheted personally by the Mahatma, as it lay amongst the diamonds, the furniture, the gold cigarette cases and the silver one with a cabochon sapphire.

Even in those days Prince Philip was not frightened to speak his mind, and he was quick to defend the champion of the Untouch-ables, who had himself spun the thread for the piece of cloth at Mountbatten's suggestion. 'I don't think it's horrible; Gandhi is a wonderful man, a very great man.' To Queen Mary, Gandhi was a curiously unsavoury person who wore inadequate clothing. The next day, when she went to look at the presents again, Princess Margaret darted ahead, hid the homely crochet cloth and drew her grandmother's attention to more suitable gifts, such as her own present of a little picnic case with engraved champagne glasses. There was the good taste of a mahogany round-top mantel clock by Gudgeon of Bury from the Earl and Countess Spencer; a Siamese kitten from two district nurses in Corsham; a complete cinema from the Mountbattens; and 500 cases of tinned pineapple from the Government of Queensland, a great treat in those post-war days – the bride joked, 'You open that one, darling' – among some less practical foodstuffs such as a piece of condensed soup from the stores of HMS *Victory* at the Battle of Trafalgar and some chocolate sent by Queen Victoria in 1900 to her troops in South Africa.

The Golden Arrow boat train carried European royalty to the wedding. Crowned and uncrowned heads emerged daily from the train with its mahogany panelling and gold lamps in the dining car casting a glow in the November gloom. It had been a reunion of royals as they swopped confidences, languid heads resting on lace anti-macassars during the long journey across Europe. For Queen Mary it was a nostalgic gathering of the clans: 'Saw many old friends. I stood from 9.30 till 12.15 am. Not bad for eighty,' she wrote in her diary. Even Princess Andrew put away her grey nun's habit and allowed herself the frivolity of a lace dress for her son's wedding.

After the ceremony in the Abbey came the wedding photographs, which today hold their own in glamour even alongside those of the Prince and Princess of Wales: Philip looking fair, heroic, a bit bemused, with much more hair and that quizzical look which has stood him in such good stead over the years; the bride, slow to smile, but pretty – small-waisted, naturally curly hair, that amazing skin and air of fragility.

Pelted with rose petals, the newly-weds left for Broadlands. The King and Queen watched the carriage – an open landau with four hot-water bottles and lots of rugs – until it was out of sight along the Mall. The Queen put her hand on her husband's arm and they went in through the archway at Buckingham Palace.

CHAPTER 6

❀ ❀ ❀

The Sagana River

IT IS HARD enough adjusting to marriage even after a trial run. How much more difficult it must have been for the Duke of Edinburgh and Princess Elizabeth, a girl who was sheltered, unworldly, a little bit prim and a Daddy's girl. Even today the Queen remains passionate about neatness; only once has she ever been seen in public with a ladder in her stocking, but she has been spotted lining up coffee crystals by shape and size. Meals are served on the dot, the corgis are fed at 4.30 pm and a superstitious streak insists on spilled salt being thrown over the shoulder, candles all being lit from the same spill and never thirteen sitting down to dinner; their salvation was a shared sense of humour. Once the Duke had injured his leg at a polo match and the Queen Mother had hurt her knee; so when the Queen saw them both getting ready to join a royal garden party, she started dragging her leg too.

As young marrieds, the friends who came to wedding anniversary dinners, a posy of white flowers from the Duke always on the table, were typically the Nevills: good company and informal. Lord Rupert Nevill, who became the Duke of Edinburgh's private Secretary in 1976, slightly florid, with white hair, was easy and witty. His wife, Lady Anne Camilla Wallop, known as Micky, was daughter of the 9th Earl of Portsmouth, and their style was always relaxed. The newly-married Princess loved summer evenings on their terrace having dinner by candlelight and the American chintzy comfort of the Nevills' home in Uckfield, Sussex. Lady Anne had an American mother, and so her flair for decorating a house had a certain flamboyance and she was not frightened of rich colours, mirrors hanging by broad ribands and bright floral wall-paper.

They themselves entertained, as well. When the Princess and her husband had a first tentative cocktail party there was a famous inquiry afterwards. The Princess wanted to know what the exact alcoholic content had been of the drinks served. She has never enjoyed alcohol particularly and once primly rebuked her husband when he enjoyed three champagne cocktails, saying, 'What kind of speech do you think you're going to make now?' Lady Elizabeth Anson the sister of Patrick Lichfield and a planner of wonderful parties like the one she gave at Claridges on the evening of Prince Charles's wedding day will receive a kindly handwritten note from the Queen to thank her for arranging a party, 'But I am sure it cost much more than you said.' Once a cook, Mrs Alma McKee, suggested grouse for dinner. 'Nonsense,' Prince Philip said, and went out and shot a couple of pigeons, saying the Queen would much prefer the dry little birds.

When expecting her first baby, in 1948, the Princess, dressed as a Spanish Infanta in a black lace dress with black mantilla and large comb, danced flamboyantly until dawn. Chips Channon, remembering that party, at Coppins, the Duchess of Kent's home near Iver in Buckinghamshire, wrote in his diary, 'The dance was really for the Edinburghs, who were enchanting ... and danced every dance until nearly 5 am ... ' remarking how supremely happy they were. Later this sort of flair had to be severely put down, in dedication to duty, but the gaiety, so often masked nowadays, is sometimes allowed an elusive flutter. At a party given after a banquet on a royal visit to Luxembourg in November 1976, champagne flowed and the Queen was in marvellously high spirits, playing the drums, keeping the rhythm and shaking her head.

Prince Philip was quite philosophical about that first pregnancy. His view of the baby was, 'People want the first child very much when they marry. They want the second child almost as much. If a third child comes along they accept it as natural, but they haven't gone out of their way to get it.' Much more recently, he has become exercised about the population explosion and is sharply critical of the numbers of 'females of breeding age who are either ignorant or irresponsible and so many men to encourage them in their irresponsibility.'

Prince Charles was born on a misty, bleak, Sunday evening at 9.14 pm at Buckingham Palace on 14 November 1948. Sister Helen Rowe, with the sharp features of a seabird, was the midwife. Years later, when she was being whisked to the Palace to help with the delivery of another of the Queen's children, the old lady with white hair and demure black coat was grappling in the back of the limousine with a collapsible umbrella. As the car got nearer and the gates swung open, she suddenly snapped, 'Oh f— the thing!' and then smiled sweetly at the policeman. Sister Rowe and a medical team led by Sir William Gilliatt, the gynaecologist, delivered the baby in the Buhl Suite after a quick labour. The Buhl Room, on the Mall side of the Palace, had been fitted up as a surgery a few days before for a medical examination of the King and was now equipped as a labour ward. Curiously Prince Philip had occupied it when he first stayed there. Now the 'enormously proud' mother came round from the anaesthetic and sleepily saw a great arrangement of roses and carnations with, behind it, her husband. He was kissed by the Queen, and the King for once forgave his son-in-law's casual clothes – sweatshirt and sneakers. Philip had been working off tension with a vigorous game of squash with his equerry, Michael Parker.

When the baby, who was breastfed, was christened Charles, Princess Margaret thought wryly, 'That makes me Charley's aunt.' Prince Philip, with typical salty comment, said the baby looked to him like a plum pudding. Princess Elizabeth thought she had never seen a baby with more interesting hands, such long, fine fingers. The photographer Cecil Beaton noticed the Princess's total absorption in the baby as, intrigued and amused, she looked at him through white dotted muslin. In the early months, Prince Philip had dinner in his wife's bedroom and the baby was in an adjoining dressing-room.

The King had not been at all well. In the spring of 1949 he had an operation, again in the Buhl Room; afterwards he seemed stronger, cheered perhaps by his first grandchild. Prince Philip took an appointment in Malta as first lieutenant and second-in-command of the destroyer, HMS *Chequers*. Happy days on long visits to Malta as a young naval wife, driving round the island in a small car, going to the hairdresser and spending sparkling evenings with other naval couples in crenellated villas peeking above orchards of white blossom on the orange trees, were to be some of the most carefree for the Princess. The royal couple swam and picnicked together in secluded coves.

A second baby, Princess Anne, was born at 11.50 am on 15 August 1950 at Clarence House and was described by her father, in a phrase not often used by photographers later, as 'the sweetest girl'. Like her brother, she adored her father and subconsciously modelled herself on what she thought he would like, becoming slightly tomboyish and sporting. She would turn to Prince Philip over the years, particularly when, as an adolescent, she and her mother were going through a difficult time. When there was an attempted kidnapping of Princess Anne in the Mall in 1974, she telephoned her father who was with the Queen on a State Visit to Indonesia. Princess Anne reassured Prince Philip but did not speak to the Queen. It is no secret that the Queen threw up her hands one day and said to one of the younger ladies-in-waiting, Lady Susan Hussey, 'Can you do something with her? – I can't.' Lady Susan took Princess Anne in hand. There were shopping expeditions to Susan Small for the sort of tailored clothes she liked herself; sleek, classic, wild-silk dresses and coats and evening clothes which were never flamboyant or flippant.

Prince Philip had to complete the formality of registering Princess Anne's birth. He was given an identity card and ration book for her and a bottle of orange juice and cod-liver oil. Princess Anne was born on the day that Prince Philip was promoted Lieutenant-Commander. The King was delighted by the double event and insisted that his son-in-law should join him at Balmoral to shoot, for a celebration.

In that upper-class way the babies were taken care of by staff, while the parents, once the five or six months' nursing was over, did not feel the need to see their children all the time. So much so that the Princess was able to return to Malta with her husband when he got his first command, the frigate HMS *Magpie*, and leave both children behind. 'Charles is too sweet, stumping around the room. We shall love having him at Sandringham. He is the fifth generation to live there and I hope he will get to like the place,' the King wrote to his daughter in Malta, reassuring her about his own uncertain health, glad she was able to relax and that he could enjoy the grandchild he would not know for long.

When the Princess and the Duke did have time with the children, they were sometimes surprised. Prince Charles produced a

child-size working model of a muck-shifter, a present from work-
men digging up the road outside Buckingham Palace. He was
crazy about this and had to be given a part of the gardens at the
Palace where he could use it to dig trenches or make piles of earth.
Prince Philip liked the toy too, and when he was there one day
asked his son if he could 'have a go'. Prince Charles, who was then
about seven, chirruped in a Cockney voice, 'Make us a cup of tea,
mate.'

In Malta, there were more dreamy days for Princess Elizabeth,
sometimes just leaning against the steep, terraced, yellow rocks of
the Barrack Heights watching the *Magpie* steam out of Valetta
Harbour with the Marine Band playing as she searched for a familiar, brisk figure on the bridge. But unlike other young wives,
proudly wearing their naval crowns pinned to collars of summer
dresses and holding babies in their arms, the Princess was allowed
to live on board the Commander-in-Chief's despatch vessel,
HMS *Surprise*. Instead of being lonely in Valetta she had the privi-
lege of sending cheeky messages from *Surprise*, and the dreamy
look in her eye was often the result of trying to think of another
religious text to fox her husband. She would signal 'Isaiah 33:23'
which says 'Thy tacklings are loosed' – very disconcerting to the
new captain of *Magpie*. But quickly a reply would be flashed, 'I
Samuel 15:14' – 'What meaneth then this bleating of the sheep?'
These messages made light relief for Prince Philip from the formal
exchanges about weather conditions, navigation and radar. Often
today, if things are glumly faltering on royal tours or the Duke
feels the Queen needs to smile a bit more at the crowds, he has
only to quote a biblical text to get her laughing. He reads the
lesson often enough to know the texts by heart, and the Queen,
unlike many churchgoers, is not admiring hats or looking at the
threadbare kneelers, she does actually read the Prayer Book and
concentrate.

'Whatever we did it was together; I suppose I naturally filled the
principal position,' Prince Philip said later of those early years. He
was amusing, unstuffy, informal and abrasive and the Princess
blossomed with the confidence of a good marriage. For four years
he was very much the 'master in the house', full of commonsense.
His ex-Headmaster, Kurt Hahn, said that he was a born leader and
that his best at anything was outstanding. Unlike Queen Victoria,
Princess Elizabeth enjoyed the stability of being a wife and a

mother before becoming Queen. People close to her stress her determination that Prince Charles should have ten years at least, to bring up a family and to enjoy the psychological comfort and maturity it gives before even thinking about the responsibilities of the monarchy.

By the early summer of 1951, when he opened the Festival of Britain, George VI was in noticeably low spirits. Cancer of the lung had been diagnosed and everyone in the family, except the King himself, knew. He was operated on and seemed to make a slight recovery, enough anyway for the planned visit by Princess Elizabeth and her husband to North America. Breaking a rule which seems extraordinarily old-fashioned now forbidding the Princess Elizabeth to make any long-distance flights, it was decided that she should fly across the Atlantic and became the first heir to the throne to do so. The King had come through the operation but Queen Mary was to outlive a third son: Prince John in 1919, George, the Duke of Kent, in 1942, and now, shortly, the King. She knew with a mother's instinct that he would not pull through but said publicly that he was progressing satisfactorily; he was 'very thin, but very plucky'. The Princess spent some time in the King's sickroom the night before she left London in a British Overseas Airways Corporation jet for the seventeen-hour flight to Montreal. That time together was almost unbearably poignant and as Princess Elizabeth left for Canada there was a sealed envelope in her luggage which held the draft Accession Declaration which would be needed should the King die during the tour.

In Canada the Princess often looked drawn and preoccupied. She was worried about her father and exhausted by the constant travelling. It was all Prince Philip could do to get her to smile. One evening she did perk up enough to go square-dancing. Bobo, much nimbler then, rushed out to a local chain store and bought a casual shirt and folksy skirt, for there had been nothing informal enough in the royal luggage.

In America, the Princess was a great success. President Truman wrote a cheery letter to the King complimenting him on his elder daughter's poise. From one father to another, the President wrote, 'We have reason to be proud of our daughters ... you have the better of me because you have two!' The President's elderly mother, deaf and a bit absent-minded, congratulated the Princess on the results of the recent general election in Britain. 'I'm so glad your father has been re-elected,' the old lady quacked. Actually, the general election results were worrying the King, who felt that his new Prime Minister, Sir Winston Churchill, was a bit elderly at seventy-five for the new challenge. And perhaps he knew intuitively that the old man would be shouldering the task of guiding his daughter as well as a new government.

Returning to London late in 1951, the Princess found her father in good spirits and apparently much improved. The country had celebrated his recovery with a Day of Thanksgiving on 2 December 1951. The King was worrying about a promised visit to East Africa, Australia and New Zealand and asked the Princess to go in his place. The royal family had an eve-of-trip celebration and went to Drury Lane to see *South Pacific*; the young pair knew the Rodgers and Hammerstein music by heart. On 14 December the King celebrated his fifty-sixth birthday at Buckingham Palace with his family around him and on the bleak, cold morning of 31 January 1952 stood hatless waving goodbye to Princess Elizabeth and her husband as their plane arrowed into the clouds bound for Kenya.

By a strange irony the weather in Kenya on 5 February was much the same as in Norfolk, blue skies, cold, crisp, inviting air, when the breath spirals. The King felt so well that he joined the relaxed end-of-season hare shoot and chatted to his tenants and all the people who worked on the estate at Sandringham. He went from beat to beat, keeping his hands warm with heated gloves. Lord Fermoy, the Princess of Wales's maternal grandfather, remembers how he was in good spirits and shot a few hare and wood pigeon. That night the King had hot chocolate brought to his room by his valet and read for an hour before having a last breath of Sandringham air as he fiddled with the window latch, turning the light out at midnight. He died in the early, lonely, hours of the new day, 6 February 1952.

On the 5th, the Princess had been relaxing at a game sanctuary called Treetops, by the Sagana River in Kenya. Jim Corbett, the celebrated big game hunter, had been invited to meet her and, on her arrival at Treetops, said he hoped the King had not caught a cold at the airport as he waved her off. 'That was so much like him,' the Princess replied softly. 'He never thinks of himself.' She said, with a smile, that the turning-point for the royal family had been when the King had lifted his walking stick to his shoulder and said, 'I believe I could shoot now.'

When the Royal party arrived at Treetops the Princess showed cool nerve as a herd of forty-seven elephants, including a furious-looking bull, were right in the royal path, trumpeting and stamping with rage. But instead of scampering back to the cars, the royal party continued on foot, Lady Pamela Mountbatten, Commander Michael Parker, and, as Corbett described it later, 'the small figure which, from her photographs, I recognized as Princess Elizabeth, walking unswervingly toward the elephants'. Treetops was perched in a big tree and the herd was within ten yards of the foot of the ladder the Princess had to climb to reach its balcony. Without hesitation, although with her knowledge of animals she realized that they were frightened and angry, she led the party towards them and up the ladder. There was more furious trumpeting as the elephants crashed away through the bush while the Princess filmed them from the safety of the balcony. 'I have seen some courageous acts, but few to compare with what I witnessed on that fifth day of February.'

Dressed in a bright yellow shirt and tan slacks, the Princess was loving the atmosphere as she stood on the wooden observation platform of the hut perched high in the tree. It was still daylight and at dusk the early moon would shine onto an oval clearing in the forest and the tiny lake with its tall grass where the animals would drink when it got dark. Looking back it was as if she had a sixth sense, for she savoured every minute. She watched through binoculars and filmed the purple blue flowers on the Cape chestnuts and the colobus monkeys with feathery, white, silky fur and tails. The branches sprang as they chased one another, while below a rhinoceros looked churlishly at a delicate snow-white heron perched on a spindly leg at the water's edge. The Duke enjoyed seeing one elephant being annoyed by a couple of doves, hopping about him as he scooped up a trunkful of dust, blowing it at them and then waggling his cabbage-leaf ears. 'Watch this,' the Prince said and the Princess filmed the doves, which were foolish enough to return.

'Oh, look, it's going to drive the baby away,' the Princess said, absorbed, as a cow elephant suckled a calf near the balcony and a four-year-old scampered up and started a practice it should have long given up.

When tea was produced in the little dining-room the Princess asked if it might be served on the balcony. 'Oh, please may I have it here? I don't want to miss one moment of this,' as she watched a grisly fight between two waterbucks at the salt-lick. 'Oh, is that blood? Do you think it will die?' Later, Corbett went back to rejoin the Princess and found she had hardly moved her field glasses from the wounded waterbuck. 'I think the poor thing is dead,' she said and made a note. All her film and all the animals seen were catalogued in that distinctive hand.

Dinner was served to the party sitting round an unpolished table on hard benches with cushions only for the women. The hosts were Eric Sherbrooke-Walker and his wife Lady Bettie, a relative of Olive Baden-Powell, and the seventh at the table was Jim Corbett. Everyone was hungry and the only mishap was that the spirit lamp caught fire as coffee was being made. The African servant who had served the simple meal from a cubbyhole behind the stove sauntered out with a wet cloth and flapped out the flames. Afterwards, the Princess and the Duke returned to the balcony to watch nine rhinoceros on the salt lick until the moon set, when they went to bed. Corbett, despite his eighty years, felt romantically impelled to act as guard to the heir to the throne. He spent the night on the top step of a thirty-foot ladder keeping vigil with the animals in the stillness of the forest.

Before dawn the Princess was up with her light meter, anxious to catch two rhinos sparring by the salt lick, and barely stopped to take the hot tea brought out. The time difference between London and Kenya was three hours, so it is highly likely that Princess Elizabeth was Queen by the time the first tentative light of dawn struck the balcony where she was sitting. The old gamehunter, more interested usually in the sheen on a leopard's fur, thought that morning that the Princess had 'eyes sparkling and a face as fresh as a flower'. After breakfast of scrambled eggs, bacon, toast, marmalade and coffee, the royal luggage was lowered on a manila rope to the ground. 'I will come again,' the Princess waved as she drove away. It was a minute after 10 o'clock on 6 February. Corbett later wrote, 'For the first time in history a young girl climbed up into a tree one day as a Princess and down from it the next as a Queen.'

The royal couple drove back to Sagana Lodge, Nyeri, to the cedarwood house given to them by the people of Kenya as a wedding present. The Duke went fishing for trout in the cold Sagana river, the Princess caught a few fish. After an early lunch they went for a siesta.

At 1.30 Nyeri time, while Bobo MacDonald and John Dean, the Duke's valet, were sitting on the steps cleaning shoes, Sir Martin Charteris, the Princess's Private Secretary, left for lunch at the Outspan Hotel on the opposite side of the valley. He was walking to his car when he was touched on the shoulder and told of a Reuter's News Flash announcing the King's death. It was officially confirmed in London at 10.45 am. There was then an extraordinary half hour or so when the people around the Princess knew that she had become Queen while the Princess, unaware, was relaxed and in sparkling spirits. Prince Philip's attention had been caught by Parker, who beckoned mysteriously to him from the garden, with its tropical red flowers, in the shadow of Mount Kenya's snowy peak against a bright sky. The Prince thought it a bit odd but went out.

As he told Prince Philip the news, Michael Parker said afterwards. 'I never felt so sorry for anyone in all my life. He looked as if you'd dropped half the world on him.' On the pretext of looking at the horses they would be riding next morning, Prince Philip persuaded his wife to walk outside with him. And by the banks of the Sagana River he told her the news of her father's death. They walked for an hour together. At 2.45 pm, Kenya time, quietly dry-eyed and tautly composed, the Queen appeared before her household, a small band now relieved of a dreadful confidence.

A press conference was given by Sir Martin Charteris about 'the lady we must now call the Queen'. He had asked what name she would like to be known by and she answered without faltering, 'Oh, my own name – what else? Elizabeth. Elizabeth II.' That evening, shortly after 5.30, the car took the new Queen at speed over rough roads with clouds of red dust snaking out behind like a fiery trail on the forty-mile journey to the small local airport at Nanyuki. The bush telegraph had spread the news and Africans stood by the dusty roadside, heads bowed. As she got out of the car, her chauffeur threw himself down on the ground and kissed her shoes. The Queen, still in a beige and white dress, walked towards the Dakota and all the photographers lowered their cameras and held them at arm's length – making a personal sacrifice in response to the request that the Queen, in her grief, would prefer not to be photographed. The BOAC plane Atlanta bore the Queen home from Entebbe, landing at Heathrow just one week after the take-off for Kenya, on the late afternoon of 7 February.

Black clothes for mourning are always included in the royal luggage. The Queen asked, 'Shall I go down alone?' and went down the steps of the aircraft to where Winston Churchill, Anthony Eden and Clement Attlee stood like three black ravens, their heads bowed low. The Queen shook hands with them and with each member of the Privy Council and then turned to thank the crew who had carried her on the 4,127-mile journey.

Her grandmother, Queen Mary, called on her half an hour after she returned to Clarence House. She insisted on curtseying and kissing the Queen's hand, and although the old lady, now eighty-five, said briskly that she was just being the Queen's 'Old Grannie and subject', for the Queen, at twenty-five, there could not have been a more painful reminder of the traumatic changes in her life and in relationships to those close to her. It had been a super-human effort for Queen Mary, who was not even strong enough to go to the King's funeral; she died the following spring.

For the Queen, her father's funeral was a special strain; in broad daylight and unable to cry she remembered their final parting only ten days before. Her flowers for him said simply: 'To darling Papa from your sorrowing Lilibet.' At the Lying-in-State the previous evening she had stood in the shadows in Westminster Hall as some 300,000 of her subjects filed past to pay their respects. Her Accession Declaration was short, promising that she would always work for her people as her father had done. She then excused herself, saying, 'My heart is too full,' and wept on Prince Philip's shoulder. There had been a Privy Council meeting in her absence on 6 February; the Accession Declaration was at 10 am on the 8th at St James's. The formal Proclamation was at 11 am.

The Coronation was on 2 June 1953. For weeks beforehand the Queen rehearsed. In front of the two children, Prince Charles and Princess Anne, she practised moving about with the five-pound weight of the Crown of St Edward on her head. Even trying it on at rehearsals the Queen, now twenty-six, was tinglingly aware of what it meant and, when her husband was mildly skittish, he was briskly told, 'Don't be silly, Philip. Come back and do it again.' He had given the Crown a desultory touch and his wife a light brush on the cheek, treating the Oath of Fealty rather irreverently, she thought, so they both rehearsed again.

On the morning of the Coronation there was a grey sky and fallen cherry blossom was sent swirling along the London streets

Above Princess Elizabeth, just
eleven months old in March 1927,
is taken for an airing by her
nanny, Clara Knight.

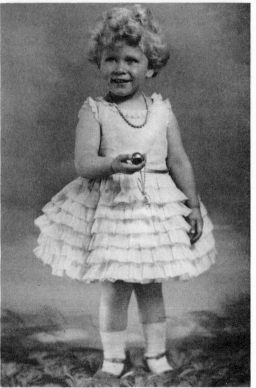

Right Blonde and pretty, Princess
Elizabeth, aged two and a half,
looks like her daughter Princess
Anne at the same age. Quite
chubby and wearing a frilly
confection with satin ribbons, the
Princess has been given the
photographer Marcus Adams's
crystal watch to keep her amused
during the session.

EXHIBITION HALL

above left Princess Elizabeth walking in Hyde Park with one of the first corgis owned by her parents.

left Princess Elizabeth was always a great favourite with her grandfather George V and called him 'Grandpapa England'. This picture, taken in the summer of 1935, shows Princess Elizabeth, her parents the Duke and Duchess of York and George V on the way to Crathie church in Scotland.

above Princess Elizabeth and Princess Margaret in their neatly tailored coats, white socks and gloves have a day at the Zoo in 1939. Princess Margaret is apprehensive about goings-on at the tea table!

right The two princesses, who both became accomplished pianists, practise at Windsor Castle in June 1940 under the gaze of some elegant ancestors.

Right Amateur theatricals gave the princesses a lot of fun in what could otherwise have been a lonely childhood during the war years. This is the programme for their production of *Cinderella* at Windsor Castle, Christmas 1941.

Christmas 1941

PANTOMIME

CINDERELLA

written and produced by H. I. Tannar

Characters

Jemima Blimp -	-	- Anne Crichton
Agatha Blimp -	-	Alathea Fitzalan Howard
Dandine -	-	- Elizabeth Hardinge
Buddy -	-	- Cyril Woods
Buddy's Aunt -	-	- Rose Turner
Baron Blimp -	-	- H. I. Tannar
Cinderella -	-	Princess Margaret Rose
Prince Florizel -	-	Princess Elizabeth

CHORUS

Band	No. 1 Coy. Training Battalion, Grenadier Guards
Sketch -	Guardsman Fearinside, Guardsman Goodwin
Baritone - -	- Guardsman Godwin
Accordionist - -	- Guardsman Thomas
Quartette	Sergeant Richards, Corporal Cooper, Guardsman Hathaway, Guardsman Bilson

WINDSOR CASTLE
19th December, 1941

Below Another Christmas pantomime, *Old Mother Red Riding Boots*, staged by the two princesses for Christmas 1944. Princess Elizabeth is the scene stealer here.

Left Princess Elizabeth as Prince Florizel and Princess Margaret in the pretty clothes worn by Cinderella in the final scenes. The two princesses are photographed here with H. I. Tannar who played the part of Baron Blimp and also wrote and produced the pantomime. George VI always enjoyed his daughters' theatrical evenings.

Left The two princesses were enthusiastic Girl Guides. Here, in 1943, Princess Elizabeth writes a message on the occasion of "Thinking Day", marking the birthday (22 February) of the late Lord Baden-Powell, founder of the Boy Scouts, and of his wife. Princess Margaret holds the waiting pigeon in a container. All messages went to Lady Baden-Powell at the Girl Guide Headquarters in London.

Below A delightfully girlish moment when Princess Elizabeth appeals to Lieutenant Philip Mountbatten to take her coat as they go to the wedding of Lady Patricia Mountbatten at Romsey Abbey in 1946.

Left George VI had asked Princess Elizabeth to refrain from announcing her engagement until after the tour of South Africa in 1947. Queen Elizabeth and the two princesses had elaborate new clothes for the tour but often Princess Elizabeth was a bit abstracted.

Right Princess Elizabeth on her wedding day, 20 November 1947, at Westminster Abbey, flanked by the Guard of Honour. The title Duke of Edinburgh was conferred on Lieutenant Mountbatten by George VI on the eve of the marriage.

Below Windswept in white overalls, the princesses ride on the footplate of one of the engines hauling the Royal Train during the 1947 tour of South Africa. The South African Minister of Transport, the Hon. F. C. Sturrock, accompanied the princesses. Here Princess Elizabeth is sounding the whistle.

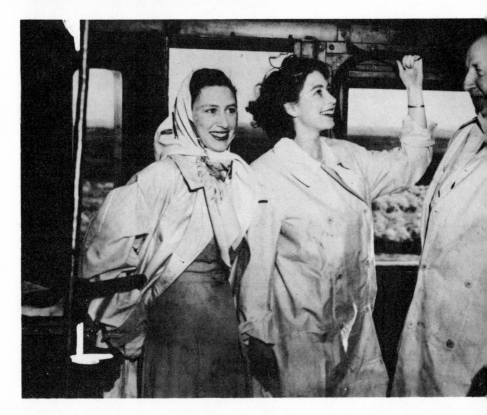

Above The newlyweds on honeymoon at Broadlands, the home of Lord Mountbatten near Romsey, Hampshire. The house and grounds have always been great favourites with the royal family and the Prince and Princess of Wales went there after their own wedding in 1981.

Left Princess Elizabeth and the Duke of Edinburgh had some of their most carefree times in Malta staying with the Earl and Countess Mountbatten at their villa, Guardamangia. This was a study of Princess Elizabeth on the eve of her 24th birthday, the first she spent away from home.

by an icy wind. The Queen's grand dress was created by Norman
Hartnell, who was not overwhelmed by the task. His creation was
a flowing white satin robe studded with flowers and emblems –
the thistle, the lotus of Ceylon, the wattle of Australia, the fern of
New Zealand, the Tudor rose and the shamrock. In Westminster
Abbey during the ceremony the Queen was, according to the diar-
ist Chips Channon, 'quite perfect', and Prince Philip like a
medieval knight. Cecil Beaton, the photographer, thought the
peeresses were the 'most ravishing sight', like a bed of auricula-
eyed Sweet William in their dark red velvet and foam-white,
dew-spangled with diamonds. Lady Haddington and the Duchess
of Buccleuch in huge diamond 'fenders', the Duchess of Devonshire, sister of Nancy Mitford, with her hair dressed wide to con-
tain the Edwardian cake-like crown, were, he thought, the most
beautiful of all, in the eighteenth-century robes of Georgiana,
Duchess of Devonshire. Channon described the thirteen duchesses, raising their pale arms like swans' necks as they curved
upwards to put on their strawberry-leaved coronets and cry 'God
Save the Queen'.

In the gold State Coach of George III, drawn by eight Windsor
greys, the Queen was driven back to Buckingham Palace, pale,
contained and with the cries of 'Vivat, Vivat' ringing in her ears.
Beaton realized that she was back from the Abbey when he heard
piping girlish voices at the end of the Picture Gallery – the high
voices of the Queen and Princess Margaret above the others as
they chatted. 'Oh, hullo! Did you watch it? When did you get
home?' From the mirror doors of the Green Drawing-Room he
could see the Queen in her purple robes and her crown, Prince
Charles and Princess Anne running around the Queen Mother's
purple train and Princess Margaret, as Beaton described, all pink-
and-white make-up and 'a sex twinkle of understanding in her
regard'. The Queen had tired eyes and her hands were white with
cold as she stood for pictures, admitting, 'Yes, the Crown does
get rather heavy.'

Beaton was uneasy because he felt the Duke of Edinburgh
would have preferred his old friend Baron, the photographer, to
have been chosen for the Coronation pictures. Certainly Beaton,
tall, sensitive, with darting movements, wrote later in his diary
how 'The Duke of Edinburgh stood by making wry jokes, his lips
pursed in a smile that put the fear of God into me. I believe he

doesn't like or approve of me. This is a pity because, although I'm not one for "Navy type" jokes and obviously have nothing in common with him, I admire him enormously and think he is absolutely first-rate at his job ... ' Beaton, like any good photographer, was nervous of the moment anyway, but he also misunderstood the Duke's chivvying way of jollying along tense, formal occasions.

Patient and uncomplaining, the Queen, who had been wearing her crown for three hours, went out on to the balcony at Buckingham Palace to watch the RAF Fly Past with Prince Philip and the children. Beaton and his assistant thankfully seized a glass of champagne which had been the Queen's but from which she had barely taken a sip. Everyone was having a better time that day than the monarch – the crowds, the rest of the royal family, even Princess Marina looking elegant and withdrawn, Princess Alexandra joking with her brothers Prince Edward and Prince Michael, all in irrepressible high spirits. The Duke of Gloucester told Beaton he could not stand with his ceremonial cape open because, 'As a matter of fact I've got on the wong wibbon.' Beaton inquired sleekly, 'Which ribbon, sir?' and the Duke rather tremblingly replied, tapping his chest, 'This wibbon wight acwoss here.' The Queen suddenly reappeared and Beaton was given a few more seconds to take pictures of her in her robes. She sat at a table with flowers which he had brought from his garden in Wiltshire, by that time 'rather sad-looking' Etoile d'Hollande roses and wilting Jackmanii clematis. She had, he thought, about her 'a certain humility and slow shyness, but at the same time innate dignity and one senses a quality of kindness.'

On that same day the news that Everest had been conquered by Hunt, Hillary and Tensing seemed like a symbolic gift for the young sovereign. 'Long Live the Queen!' the crowds shouted in the Mall until they were hoarse and when it got dark the wise ones went home, to save their voices to cheer her over the next thirty years.

CHAPTER 7

�֍ �֍ ✖

Frugal and Abstemious

THE QUEEN IS abstemious, self-disciplined and frugal. Her weight stays at about eight stone, which is right for her height, and she has a clearly-defined waistline which shows no sign in its mid-fifties of letting go. She has excellent health and a lack of interest in alcohol, pills and rich food. The royal routine, like the way of life of old-established aristocratic families, is really a continuation of 'nanny's regime'. In the Queen's case, this is not just a memory. For there is Bobo, always there, always solicitous and nagging about woollies and wellies for her charge, as she has done for the last fifty-three years.

The Queen's day starts early with a cup of tea served by Bobo at 7.30 am, and she is at breakfast by 8.30 in the small, family dining-room on the first floor of Buckingham Palace. At 9.00 each day, the Palace echoes to one of the sounds the Queen likes best: Pipe-Major Brian Macrae of the Gordon Highlanders plays the bagpipes for fifteen minutes, drowning the sound of nothing more calorific than a boiled egg having its top sliced off. Pats of butter with specially imprinted coats of arms are about the most fattening items on the modest breakfast table.

The Queen eats sparingly. Recently a visitor to the Palace saw her lunch go by and was shocked by its ascetic simplicity. 'It was simply a stick of celery and a few lettuce leaves.' Wholesome, well-cooked English food is the order of the day when she is in London. Nothing fancy, just salmon from Scotland, game from Sandringham and milk, vegetables and cream from the farm at Windsor. Garlic is forbidden. 'We never eat it,' was the message for one enterprising cook, and there are no puddings for the

Household at the Palace when the Queen is away. Favourite dishes are simple grilled haddock, chicken casserole with a creamy mushroom sauce and economical stuffed cabbage. But chicken, game and fish must always be boned, because dissecting them takes time and leaves the guest with cold food as well as a pile of unsightly debris. Tomatoes are deseeded, to avoid embarrassing old ladies and gentlemen whose false teeth may not be a perfect fit. There is a distrust of dishes gingered-up with exotic spices or flavouring.

A glass of pink vermouth with soda or a tonic with ice and lemon can last the Queen through a cocktail party; glasses of wine are hardly touched during a banquet. She drinks a great deal of Malvern water for its gentle properties; the Duke of Edinburgh prefers the effervescence of Perrier. After a long public lunch he may have a brandy and soda at the end of the speeches.

Sharing her dislike of smoking and alcohol, Dr Nigel Southward is exactly the right 'Apothecary' for the Queen and her Household. The title dates back to the days of a more excitable monarch – George III. Sir Nigel's father, Sir Ralph Southward, has always looked after the Queen Mother.

Exuding that glow of good clean living and regular habits, Dr Nigel Southward has been going to the Palace every day for the last eight years. It is one of the perks that, quite often, his Rover is cleaned before he leaves the Royal Mews to drive back to his consulting rooms in Devonshire Place, studded with warnings like, 'Beware the End is near ... if you smoke or drink'. A member of the personal staff explains, 'This is the first port of call, so he will be summoned to the Queen if she wakes up with spots. But, after that, John Batten, the Head of the Medical Household, takes over.' Dr Southward is the sort of no-nonsense outdoor person the Queen likes. He loves sailing, skiing and golf. Robust and with Scandinavian colouring and physique, he has always been interested in psychological reassurance. He is astute about depression and has seen at least one royal patient through a bad bout of what is known to be a Hanoverian encumbrance. Princess Margaret is a more relaxed and contained person these days, but may not always share her apothecary's Methodist views. The Queen is a much more balanced woman; her training and time-table, anyway, hardly allow too much introspection. Advice can be given, and the Queen will always listen.

In the Queen's case, apart from conventional illnesses like flu, mumps or chicken pox, only sinus trouble has been a problem.

If she has to cancel an engagement, it may well be because of sinusitis, described by the Queen once as 'a cruel stroke of fate', when she was prevented from visiting the sensitive Principality of Wales. Instead, the Duke of Edinburgh pressed a button and the Welsh people heard the Queen's recorded message and her nasal promise to 'create my son Charles, Prince of Wales today ... and when he is grown up I will present him to you at Caernarvon.'

Stress, that modern illness, is never allowed to make a public appearance. Even at the time of the Silver Jubilee in 1977, when she travelled 8,000 miles and shook more than 5,000 hands in a hundred days, the Palace only admitted a dent in her stamina, 'Yes, the Queen is fagged-out.' The pace had been almost too much but the remedy was one Dr Southward thoroughly approved – a climb up three-hundred-foot cliffs on Lundy Island and then a three-mile walk.

The royal family, believing in restrained living, have been attracted to homeopathy since George V's time, and the late Dr Margery Blackie, a homeopathist, was the first woman physician to the Queen. Her successor is Dr Charles Elliott. Sinusitis became less of a bugbear thanks to simple white pills containing deadly nightshade as one ingredient. A horror of sneezing in the middle of a speech no longer haunts the Queen. A homeopathic mix including a little arsenic taken with Malvern water has been the sinister-sounding remedy. Prince Charles keeps his throat clear by sucking cloves.

Before 1969 Sir John Weir was physician to the royal family and the first representative of the Homeopathic School of Medicine at Buckingham Palace. He loved to recall how he wrote five prescriptions for three kings and four queens on the day of George V's funeral. Each prescription had Nelson's, the homeopathic chemist in Duke Street off Grosvenor Square, bustling in their white coats on that gloomy January day in 1936.

The Queen is full of commonsense, with little time for fey attention to spooky doings, but her appointments with a spiritual healer and manipulative therapist show a far from rigid outlook. On a high and windy rooftop overlooking Harley Street, that bleak parish of unwanted confidences, Miss Kay Kiernan runs about in a tracksuit calling her patients 'darling' and 'love' before she applies her psychic powers. The daughter of a Broadmoor prison officer, she wanted to be a psychiatric nurse but there was not enough money for her training. Her mother died when she was fourteen; she went into service and then joined the ATS as a driver mechanic. It was much later, in New York, that Kay Kiernan realized that she had special powers, and time spent at the Mind and Body exhibitions confirmed this gift. Doctors have always been rather sniffy about her ability, though her clinic is full of Swiss-made electro-magnetic high-pulse frequency machines.

In 1970 the Queen was having a lot of pain from a tendon which she had pulled when chopping wood. Princess Margaret had recommended Miss Kiernan and the Queen had two sessions on one of the Swiss-made pulsed high-frequency machines. These deliver pulsed electromagnetic energy to the site of a wound or injury. The heat sent directly to the muscle tissue can reduce the swelling and relieve the pain quickly. The healing process is speeded up in some cases by forty per cent. For some years these machines were regarded with caution by the orthodox in the medical profession though these healing waves had benefited patients suffering from sinusitis, bursitis, rheumatoid arthritis, osteomyelitis and disorders of tendons and muscles.

If the Queen slipped off furtively for these appointments her physician and Head of the Medical Household at the time, Sir Richard Bayliss, would probably have been happy so long as the wiring was secure. Those old-fashioned plugs and electric fittings at Buckingham Palace almost gave him heart failure on more than one occasion. Explaining to another doctor why he had not answered a letter sooner, Sir Richard wrote, 'Sorry I have not replied to your letter, but I have been on my hands and knees crawling round the floor of the Palace with the heir to the Throne, looking for a plug for some ENG equipment. Fortunately The Young Man is pretty knowledgeable about electricity – the wiring at the Palace is frightful.' He trained at St Thomas's and became Dean of Westminster Hospital Medical School. Appointed physician to the Queen in 1970, he was awarded the KCVO in the New Year Honours List seven years later and retired from royal duties in 1981.

While some of the Household may not get enormous salaries, there are discreet bonuses. The Queen's health is usually so undemanding that Dr Southward has time to see her staff at surgeries held in the Palace. It is all rather different from the days of Queen Mary, though the old Queen could be quite skittish at times and enjoyed throwing cake, cut into cubes, in the air at afternoon tea. To the delight of the younger guests, she would catch them in her mouth with the precision of a juggler. But a young Welsh GP was not to know this as he dug his garden one weekend in Hampstead.

Queen Mary had been taken ill. The Head of the Medical Household was away; so was his deputy. Dan Davies, a modest but reliable young doctor, was eventually contacted. His wife had answered the telephone and shrieked, 'It's the Palace.' Davies, thinking she was joking, took the call and then, in a shocked voice, explained, 'But I have no morning dress.' 'Come as you are' was the order, and off he went to the Palace in his gardening clothes – still shaking. A lady-in-waiting showed him into the presence and described the Queen's symptoms. The doctor asked the lady-in-waiting to remove the Queen's clothing. Nothing happened. He asked again, waited and asked once more. When, eventually, he had examined the Queen, he asked the lady-in-waiting to leave, for he did not consider it medical etiquette to give his diagnosis to anybody but the Queen herself.

The lady-in-waiting tensely left the room. When she was summoned back, Queen Mary sat up straight and, in her most commanding way, said to the little Welshman, 'Never before have I been asked to remove my clothes like this. I have never been subjected to such an examination.' Standing quaking, his hands behind his back, Davies could scarcely believe his ears when she peremptorily commanded, 'In future you will be my physician.' His integrity later earned him a title and money enough to buy a bigger garden.

When Queen Mary had to have a tooth pulled by a stand-in dentist the occasion was less happy. James Snarey Wright was in partnership with Mr Toomes, who always wore a frock coat when he went to the Palace. Once again, both were away and the 'duty' dentist was called to the Mall to do an extraction. 'Everything will be in order; all the equipment will be at the Palace,' the locum was told. Those were the days of pedal-pushing dentistry. As he tried to extract the royal molar, in his nervousness he damaged a tooth on the lower jaw, but the Queen could not have been kinder.

It was unthinkable, then, that the King or Queen should go out to a dentist. As a result, after years of such old-fashioned care, the present Queen's teeth were in a 'right old mess' when she eventually went to a Harley Street surgery. Loyalty, as ever, prevented her from changing to a more up-to-date dentist until her own retired. Now the Queen goes to Nicholas Sturridge in Harley Street. Her smile is a credit to him.

By Appointment, Mrs Tessa Seiden is corsetière. A dying breed, she reckons there are only about nine left. Driven out of Hungary at the time of the Russian invasion in 1956, her discreet work takes place in a first-floor office of Rigby & Peller in Mayfair. Outside, leaving behind that faintly depressing pale pink and oyster of corsetry, the vibrant glossy fashion in the South Molton Street walkway smartly revives the bra-less twentieth century.

After the birth of the Queen's third child, Prince Andrew, Mrs Seiden was called in. It was a time when the Queen had never looked happier, though afterwards she was said to be suffering from a deeper depression than the usual post-natal blues. Laughing off innuendo about a rift in the marriage, the Queen remarked, 'Well, if you read the Continental papers, apart from all this I am apparently not even talking to my mother or Princess Margaret.' The first order was for a riding girdle to be worn under a full coat. Others followed for several one-piece white or peach swimsuits. The Queen loves swimming but, unlike her daughter-in-law, never contemplated bikinis. Suspender belts and stockings are always preferred to the freedom of tights. The employment of a professional corsetière was a godsend to the designers, who had always had difficulty because of the Queen's particularly narrow back. The Queen's bosom, too, had created problems in the early years, when she wore hopeless brassieres, like a 'couple of hammocks', which did nothing for her shapely figure. Support was subtly built into evening dresses, but day clothes were often top-heavy.

'Speak more,' Mrs Seiden was told after her first tentative visits to Buckingham Palace with her tape measure, when she had conformed by wearing black but remained virtually silent. Her confidence grew. She measured deftly and with tact; she learnt to chat to the Queen with graphic stories of her own 'rotten capitalist background' before her escape from Hungary. Later she earned an apt message thanking her for 'her support'. These days there is less for Mrs Seiden to do at the Palace and it is suggested that cosmetic surgery may be blessed for this happy state.

The Queen's creamy and supple complexion is an example to any woman who likes to think that expensive cosmetics are the secret of a good skin. The royal secrets are early nights, barley water and a few quality skin products. The barley water, taken by itself on two consecutive days for two weeks running, promises a weight loss of up to eight pounds. 'But I have to go out such a lot,' the Queen wails, if she is reminded about this forecast. Nevertheless when the recipe was published in the *Sunday Express*, shops all over the country sold out of pearl barley.

Trends in make-up are all serenely ignored. On her wedding day she wore only a little mascara and a lipstick called Balmoral, and she stays steadfastly with her own uncompromising pale powdered face and bright red lipstick. Yet even through that unhelpful layer, a soft skin of natural beauty all its own shines out. The bright red lipstick is quite deliberate. The Queen will never be seen in public wearing anything other than a pillarbox red when chestnut, coral and berry shades might be more flattering. The hard red colour is for the sake of her people. 'To see and be seen,' the Queen never tires of saying. Her eyebrows are not subjected to the tweezers very often and were not thinned even when the thirties pencilled arch came back. Sometimes she will take out a compact in public and put on more lipstick, even at a banquet. In Wellington, on the 1981 tour, while the New Zealand Prime Minister Mr Muldoon was speaking, the Queen was checking her lips. This is not rudeness, but for the ever-present photographers, and also a relic of days when women such as the Duchess of Argyll constantly checked their make-up in restaurants and night clubs, dreading a hint of that get-up-and-glow sheen that became so fashionable in the sixties and seventies.

During the Silver Jubilee tour of the South Pacific in 1977 a roof collapsed in Fiji in the middle of some local dances for the royal visitors. Nobody was hurt but, as the crowd ran to the scene, the Queen seized the moment to whip out a lipstick and add another streak of rich red.

Several times a year Cyclax, which earned the royal warrant in 1961, will make up jars of skin preparations especially for the Queen and deliver them to the Palace. Founded in 1896 by an elegant beauty, Mrs Frances Hemming, who learnt her trade in Vienna, the emphasis is on diligent skin care. The brightly-coloured young things at Annabel's may never have heard of these Viennese potions, but what will their skin be like at fifty-six? Suitably respectful packaging, purple and silver with the 'By Appointment' symbol embossed, holds a magical All Day Face Firmer which keeps make-up cool and matt for hours; just the thing for a steam heat walkabout in the tropics. Pure milk and honey cleanser, flower-fresh balm, and milk of roses moisturizer exude integrity.

Happily there is no evidence of porphyria, an error of metabolism which makes the skin hypersensitive to the sun and which began with Mary, Queen of Scots, in any of the members of the royal family. Just as well, because, as a well-informed royal relative said, 'Frankly, my dear, it turns your pee purple.' However, the Queen never gets suntanned and Prince Charles confided once to an Indian Tea Board official that his metabolism prevented his enjoying hot drinks; so he asked for iced tea – Darjeeling, naturally.

The Queen's hairdresser is a most amiable and gentlemanly soul, but in about an hour he can add twenty-five years to a client's age. He favours the set look and so does his most undemanding customer. Charles Martyn is sixty-three, tall, rather severe-looking with a white toothbrush moustache, but gentle and courtly. He has been doing the Queen's hair for years – to the regret of those who think she could look more striking with a softer, up-to-date style like Princess Margaret's. But the Queen loves her hair the way it is, and who is Charles Martyn to change things? This mild-mannered man originally worked with Emile of Sloane Street and those great characters in hairdressing, the Boudon Brothers. When Emile's shut down, the enterprising Neville Daniel in Sloane Street offered Charles Martyn a job. He has the discreet use of an upstairs salon, while fashionable, trendy styles are created by bronzed young men with medallions on their chests for a young clientele below. But now this one of many good salons in Sloane Street has earned itself a 'By Appointment'.

Every Monday at 4 pm, Charles Martyn can be seen on his way to the Palace, cutting through by the Carlton Towers Hotel, round Belgrave Square and then discreetly into the tradesmen's entrance with 'the box of tricks'. The Palace has special dryers, but Charles Martyn likes to carry his own plugs with him and, on foreign tours, insists that sockets are checked as part of the recce. He feels it is a tribute that the Queen never wants to change her hairstyle. Her theory is that she must be easily recognized, so highlights, henna or fancy styles are out. It is strong, springy hair, demanding at times 'brute force and lacquer'. It is permed through the year in sections, because the top stays firm while the back sometimes becomes a little unmanageable. When this happens, Mr Martyn heats up Carmen rollers in warm water, because that way they are easier on the royal hair, and a protection against faulty electricity.

Unlike many a hairdresser today, Charles Martyn is not likely to entertain you with the flamboyance of his conversation. He wears nondescript, grey and white shirts with grey trousers, and combs hair as if it were silken strands, revealing cufflinks that discreetly say ER. He always wears a tiepin given to him in 1974. When he is not going on royal tours he likes to holiday in Italy. A single man, he says, 'I travel such a lot I find it nice to go to the same place each year where I am known.' At home, he enjoys gardening and cooking at his North London flat.

The Queen dislikes bending her head backwards over the washbasin. Instead, wearing a gown, she goes into the vast bathroom off her bedroom on the first floor and, as she has always done since childhood, puts her chin over the basin under the massive spray and taps. At one time it was Queen Mary's bathroom; it is carpeted, with the bath in a recess, has a big bow window, a chandelier and a table with *objets d'art*. The ladies-in-waiting have even better arrangements with three basins – one for face, another for teeth and the third for hands. Mr Martyn uses an especially effective egg and lemon shampoo. It is specially made up, and the Queen asks anxiously 'Have you got enough for another year?' It is not easy to obtain, but Mr Martyn has a secret store.

The Queen has no time for blow-drying; is as unaccustomed to it as Mr Martyn and has confessed to him, 'Once I burnt my cheeks with electric tongs.' Her hairdo takes an hour and a half. The hair continues to be a warm brown colour, a few grey wisps are visible only occasionally. A rinse called Chocolate Kiss is said to be the secret, but all knowledge of this is denied in royal crimping circles. However, on a trip to Canberra some years ago, a young hairdresser at an hotel salon described the look of desperation on the face of the Queen's hairdresser when he rushed in for some of the rinse with the edible name. Once done, the Queen manages her hair perfectly and plonks on top tiaras or hats which must stay on all day. It has been the same for fourteen years, so why change now?

In Balmoral and at weekends the Queen does her hair herself; she gives it a good brisk brush and a whoosh with the lacquer and frankly finds it hard to imagine why other women take so long with their hair. A few years ago an old woman in Balmoral, now dead, and who mainly did men's hair, would pop in and put a few rollers in, with the Queen instructing her.

The Queen could never be described as a vain woman. While her hair is being done there are no anxious looks in the mirror; she sits with correspondence on her lap working all the time, looking up only occasionally to say, 'What a nice letter.'

'Will this lipstick do?' she may ask as she slaps make-up on in about five minutes and hurriedly fixes a tiara on the freshly-set hair.

The Queen always wears hats in the daytime for official functions but, for some unknown reason, she thinks of her afternoon visits to the Chelsea Flower Show as an 'evening event' and therefore goes hatless. It is at the Flower Show – or, better still, during the Christmas broadcast – that you can see Charles Martyn's work best.

CHAPTER 8

Before the Music Starts

NOTHING HAS CHANGED much in the style of the courtiers surrounding the Queen today, though the Palace will irritably deny this. Recently a member of the Household tried to suggest that the courtiers were not all chosen from the landowning squirarchy or the aristocracy. They were, he said, ordinary folk. This is fair nonsense and the examples given hardly support the argument. The Queen has people round her with background and private money, although talent and academic distinction alone can occasionally be enough.

'Look at Billy Fellowes – the Clerk at Sandringham – everyone knows old Billy.' This immediately conjures up a picture of an old Norfolk varmint, shuffling about in loose corduroys tied below the knee with string, heavy boots, a torn shirt and ruddy cheeked from days with his root vegetables. In fact, Sir William is a distinguished figure who ruled the Queen's estate at Sandringham for twenty-eight years with a mixture of benevolence and discipline. The wife of a retired head gardener at Sandringham remembers how, 'We always had to ask the 'Captain' if we wanted to do anything special like give a party on the lawn of the house for charity.' Now himself retired, he is still very much a part of the Household as his son Robert is the Queen's Assistant Private Secretary and married to the Princess of Wales's sister, Jane.

Robert is in the classic mould for a courtier, tall, earnest, black hair brushed smooth, pinstriped suits, often carrying bundles of papers, and has a walk which is brisk with a hint of courtly reticence. But he is authoritative and will say, 'Look here, we really must insist that the Queen's car moves off at seven minutes past eleven and not ten past, as the Lord Mayor suggested.' Very much the sleek Palace servant, he has a sense of humour and the courtier's fetish about shoes. One can nearly always tell a royal courtier by his gleaming polished shoes; old they might be, but preferably hand-made, coming often from Lobb in St James's. Being a courtier is not a job which pays well, so finding £350 (£415 including VAT) for a pair of new shoes is a decision not to be taken recklessly. Courtiers tend to wear crisp white shirts, occasionally blue ones but never flamboyant stripes, and usually navy or dark grey suits. Leisure wear is faintly old-fashioned for the men, flapping short-sleeved bush shirts and baggy trousers. Not many jeans are worn.

'Take Sir Philip Moore; well, his daughter is married to the pop singer, Peter Gabriel.' Here again, this proved a flimsy part of the Queen's Private Secretary's formidable background. Granted he does not have quite the aristocratic lightness of Sir Martin Charteris, his predecessor, whom the Queen liked for his talent and wit; they were great friends too. Charteris had guided her from 1950, when he became her Private Secretary as a young major who had served with Intelligence in the Middle East. The classic courtly Englishman, Sir Martin is said to have apologized to fellow castaways when he was seasick on a raft after being torpedoed in mid-Atlantic. His background was romantic and intellectual, and the coterie of friends who rallied round his mother when his father, Hugo Charteris, was killed in World War I were people such as the Asquiths, the Horners, the Grenfells and the Herberts, 'The Souls' as they called themselves. 'I'll see you, my dear, in Pago Pago,' he said before the Silver Jubilee in 1977 which was to round off his time with the Queen on a perfect note of dazzling, comforting achievement. He retired in 1977 and became Provost of Eton. At the Palace it was felt that now it was time for something completely different. The world was changing, the Commonwealth was being threatened and the Queen needed an adviser who was a working civil servant, an experienced 'eyes and ears' for her. The Queen's advisers should be worldly men, truly in touch and not leaving an estate in Norfolk or Northumberland on an occasional summons to the Palace to fill in the diary for Ascot and Badminton.

Sir Philip Moore is in his sixties, clean-cut, firm-jawed, decisive and at times rather frightening. He is feared by some of the

Household and lives up to his Civil Service reputation of saying, 'I am going to be ruthless,' if things go awry. But he is a skilled diplomat and had 'a good war', being shot down while in Bomber Command and a POW for three years. He was Deputy High Commissioner in Singapore; then, amidst much controversy, he took over as Director of Public Relations at the Ministry of Defence, at what was in 1965 thought the princely salary of £70 a week, going from that job, a year later, to work for the Queen as an Assistant Private Secretary. The Queen's speeches have been changing subtly over the last five years and Sir Philip is said to be the influence here. His office is below the Queen's pale bluey-green sitting-room/study on the first floor of the Palace.

For some hours each day the Queen is at her desk, sitting on the mahogany Chippendale elbow-chair with a hand-embroidered seat that was given to her by her father. When she calls one of the Household to her office they know immediately from the intercom who it is. A red button simply marked 'The Queen' lights up and the well-known voice will say, 'Can you come up for a moment please, Philip?' The Queen is said to dislike Prince Charles's liberal use of Christian names, but she herself uses them with staff close to her. Once in the office, the men do a neck bow and remain standing. It is a warm room and on the elegant chairs there are usually piles of papers, books and magazines. There are silver-framed photographs of the royal family, a gold-framed miniature of an eighteenth-century Countess of Strathmore, two telephones and an intercom, always fresh flowers and fruit for nibbling. There is a painting of her favourite corgi, Susan, the one which was sneaked into the carriage after her wedding, and the study has pretty touches such as a Fabergé spray of buttercups and a Hepplewhite mahogany breakfront bookcase. If the Queen is away from the Palace all her papers are locked into a satinwood chest of drawers. 'I like my rooms to look really lived in,' and she loves to have roses in the summer and narcissi in the spring on the sofa table.

The Queen is disciplined, informed and cannot stand inefficiency. 'She does not like people to be too clever or too cheeky – on the other hand she hates pomposity,' one of her staff said. If the Queen is displeased she will put on one of her cold looks; or if a silly mistake has been made she may remark, 'Well, that was a fair-to-average stupid thing to do.' The gracious atmosphere of the Household's offices on the ground floor, usually rather splendid rooms with elegant furniture and draped curtains over the French windows leading into the gardens, conceals a tough efficiency; on some desks there will be memos from the Queen – in her own handwriting, which we rarely see except as a large scroll E – pointing out some mistake. But she will be kind to anyone who makes a real mistake. One of her staff had behaved erratically and the Queen said, 'Oh, let's give him another chance.'

Sir Philip Moore has often conveyed royal pleasure, praise or disapproval. For a man with a weighty and important job, he will go to extraordinary lengths on royal tours to rebuke a journalist he thinks may have gone too far, and will bustle that burly figure along a remote strip of desert or through cheering crowds to make his point. He is fit – was an excellent rugby player – and loves hockey and cricket. He has a jazzy wife, who likes flamboyant colours, and two children. He is the foreigner's idea of the courtier, clean-cut and striding a few paces away from the Queen with feet at ten to two. His critics feel that Sir Philip can at times be rather like a self-satisfied commissar.

Sir Martin Gilliat is a Private Secretary who is a real friend. Now seventy, he joined the Queen Mother's staff when he was forty. He keeps a check on the up-to-date racing information in the Private Office which he relays instantly to Clarence House.

Prince Philip's office is also on the first floor but is completely different, rather modern and very functional. It is full of press buttons, maps and gadgets; he designed it to suit himself. His Private Secretary was Lord Rupert Nevill, an old family friend. He was one of George VI's 'Body Guards' and a member of the Stock Exchange who advised the Queen on her private finances.

Edward Adeane, small, portly and bald, whose spectacles make him look a little like Mister Cheeryble in *Nicholas Nickleby*, is Prince Charles's Private Secretary. He is a bachelor in his forties and the only son of Lord Adeane who was the Queen's Private Secretary for nearly twenty years. His great-grandfather was Lord Stamfordham, who was Private Secretary to Queen Victoria and then to George V. Edward Adeane gave up a good practice at the Bar, where he specialized in libel. This experience was valuable at the time of the alleged phone calls from Australia between Prince Charles and Lady Diana Spencer. He is correct and clear-headed but conservative.

In appointing Oliver Everett to the Princess of Wales's office,

Prince Charles showed a wish to change from the conventional advisers. Everett was formerly with the Foreign Office in Delhi and Madrid. He is an excellent polo player, has an unconventional way of dressing, a dry humour and a wise head. When he was going on holiday to India with his wife and their latest baby, William – they have four children – the Princess, agreeing to the time off, scribbled in the margin, 'Oh, poor William, so many awful injections.' He is much younger than most of the Palace advisers. At a Buckingham Palace garden party he was seen following the Princess of Wales dutifully, but in his upturned top hat there was a bouquet of flowers which he was carrying for her. The Princess – dashing in and out of the private offices – often complained to girls of her own age, 'Oh, everybody is so old round here,' but finds in Oliver Everett the ideal person to take the chill out of ceremonial.

There are portraits of the Private Secretaries along the Privy Purse Corridor, darkly formal eyes fixed on each other on opposite walls. And there is one rule which is pretty inflexible; that nobody in the Queen's Household should be divorced. Bachelors are fine, widows and widowers too, but you will find that royal advisers have long-standing marriages which endure; they must.

Amongst the Household there are always a few Commonwealth appointments. As one member of the royal family said, 'I do like these Australians and Canadians – so fresh.' The man tipped to succeed Sir Philip Moore is Sir William Heseltine, the deputy Private Secretary, the son of a schoolmaster, he was born and brought up in Australia. He is stocky with brown curly hair, light brown eyes and full lips, but it is a firm mouth. He is appreciated by the Queen and gets away with innovative ideas more easily than perhaps a more conservative, homegrown Deputy Private Secretary might, and has been responsible for much that is imaginative and modern about the Palace. He can be icy but he is a courageous and cultivated man who was highly regarded, too, when he worked as Private Secretary to the former Australian Prime Minister, Sir Robert Menzies. He enjoys music and is helpful to artists from home; even musicians of the calibre of Malcolm Williamson and Joan Sutherland appreciate his presence at a concert. His first wife was killed in a car crash and he has since remarried. Sir William wears a sports jacket and cavalry twills when he wanders through the Tachbrook Street market on Saturdays in

Pimlico, having a lively chat with Danny Ralph about the price of the lobsters on his stall. Many of the Palace staff live in Pimlico because it is so near the Palace and has a 'village' atmosphere without the pretensions of Belgravia. One of the Queen's Women of the Bedchamber, the Hon. Mary Morrison, lives in Cambridge Street and drives an estate car with the apt registration, Mam; but she says it is a pure coincidence and only because she bought the car in Dorset.

While there might be a slim sliver of truth in the suggestion that not all the Queen's advisers are aristocrats, there is not one lady-in-waiting who is not of impeccable background. 'Well, yes, the ladies-in-waiting are aristocrats, but then they are not decision-makers.' If you were in their circle, you might know some of the ladies-in-waiting as 'Mossy' for Mary Morrison, the forty-six-year-old unmarried daughter of Baron Margadale, 'Kath' for Mrs John Dugdale from Shropshire, or 'Fortune' for the Duchess of Grafton, who is Mistress of the Robes and really the boss of all the ladies-in-waiting. But it is unwise to call her 'Fortune' unless one is absolutely sure of one's ground. She is extremely grand – and not the sort of person ever to throw her head back and laugh in public, though apparently she can be great fun. Now in her mid-sixties, the mother of two sons and three daughters, the Duchess with a grown-up family can take on more royal duties and is probably one of the Queen's closest confidantes.

The Graftons are Norfolk people with a stately eighteenth-century house, Euston Hall, set in parkland with a river, a lake and an impressive collection of paintings, including a Van Dyck of Charles I. The title Mistress of the Robes has of course nothing to do with the Queen's clothing and is quite honorary. The Queen's clothes are looked after by Bobo, her maid. The Duchess of Grafton will go with the Queen to the splendid occasions such as the State Opening of Parliament but does not accompany her on simpler engagements such as inspecting needlework by Girl Guides, when a Woman of the Bedchamber like Lady Sue Hussey or Lady Abel Smith will attend. Originally fair-haired, the statuesque Duchess was a lady of the Bedchamber in 1953–6, and it seemed, as one of the Household put it, 'as if Fortune had been there for ever, too straightforward for words that she should become the Mistress of the Robes.'

Ladies-in-waiting work to a rota so that school holidays, travel-

ling with their husbands or their own work as magistrates on the
Bench or in hospitals are all catered for. There is a strict hierarchy.
There are two or three Ladies of the Bedchamber, usually the
wives of peers, who attend on the big ceremonial occasions. One
of these is 'Ginny' – Lady Airlie – small and attractive; she has
great style, often wears velvet Highwayman berets with ostrich
feathers and is lots of fun and bright company. Then there is Lady
Abergavenny: her husband is the older brother of the late Lord
Rupert Nevill and looked after Peter Townsend at a critical time
during the romance with Princess Margaret. Lady Cromer was an
Extra Lady of the Bedchamber but then went to live in the
Channel Islands and found it was impractical to keep up royal
duties. During the early years, when the ladies-in-waiting were
having babies, the rostering had to be very flexible; but the Queen
was 'always terribly understanding and marvellously helpful'.
They all know their rota months in advance, working a month on
and a month off with 'Fortune doing the grandest things.' Their
wardrobes are discreet – the Queen is never outshone. When the
Princess of Wales chose her ladies-in-waiting they were not particular friends but amiable, sensible girls of good class, chosen for
their efficiency, a way with people, and the art of pleasant,
non-controversial conversation.

Women of the Bedchamber hate being called female ADCs but
that is what the job is. A lady-in-waiting must hover, be helpful,
smooth and, if the Queen wants to shed a coat or a bouquet, be on
hand to take them. If the Queen wants to powder her nose they
escort her; they will chat to nervous lady mayoresses, do personal
shopping for the Queen and deal with masses of children's letters;
they send flowers to the Queen's friends if they have been ill or are
having an anniversary or a baby; they will organize Christmas
presents and, when the Queen's children were young, arranged
dancing classes and parties for them.

When she was first invited to help at the Palace, nobody had
ever heard much about 'Sue', Lady Susan Hussey. After the birth
of Prince Andrew in 1960, when bootees, woolly toys, letters and
cards were arriving at the Palace by the sackful, the ladies-in-
waiting at the time could hardly cope. One of the inner circle
mentioned that Sue Hussey, 'that nice Waldegrave girl' now living
in Chelsea, would be just right to help out. Then in her twenties,
bright, independent and attractive with large, dark eyes and a

slightly mocking, gentle humour, she has stayed at the Palace ever since and was very much in evidence in the aftermath of the Princess Margaret/Peter Townsend affair.

The only question mark over Sue Hussey at the Palace was the fact that her husband, Marmaduke ('Dukey') Hussey works in Fleet Street; he is a director of Times Newspapers. But there has never been a breath of an indiscretion. In 1977 he was once in the middle of delicate negotiations with an intransigent union when the phone rang. Shining-eyed he put the receiver down. 'Great news,' he reported in a bullish mood, and the men thought their pay deal had come through. Their faces brightening, they were told: 'Isn't it wonderful, Princess Anne has had a son.' Sue Hussey helped a lot with Prince Charles and Princess Anne. She took them to the theatre and selected suitable girls for Charles at the dinner parties that she arranged. In a box at the opera Prince Charles was heard to say wistfully to Lady Susan, 'Will I ever be able to choose the girl I want to marry?' and give a little sigh at her: 'We'll see,' as his hand received a comforting pat. Clearly she has since become a great friend of the girl the Prince did marry, for she is now godmother to the Princess's son, Prince William. Lady Susan is popular; hers is the briskest, deepest, most correct curtsey, the taffeta of her low evening dress fairly crackles in its swift drop to the carpet. Men enjoy her company at dinner, finding the Duchess of Grafton less jokey.

'Mossy', Mary Morrison, had been a lady-in-waiting to Lady Baring when Sir Evelyn was Governor-General in Kenya. Quiet and serious, she spends much of her time in the country – in Wiltshire – occasionally coming to town to the pleasant house in Pimlico she shares with her unmarried brother, the Conservative MP Peter Morrison, rushing in with long frocks in cellophane over her arm for a spell of royal duty.

At the Palace the ladies-in-waiting do not sit around the Queen, as they did in the old days, playing the piano or the harp. Nor are they needed for chores nearly as much as they might be for a Queen Consort; the Queen Regnant has an army of Private Secretaries who deal with most of her two hundred letters a day. Like the rest of the staff at 'The Shop', as George VI used to call Buckingham Palace, they arrive for work at around 10 o'clock. One of the best perks about working for the Queen is being able to drive to work and park without any trouble. And if something went very wrong with the engine, and you had to be in Dorset that evening, they just might put the fault right in the Royal Mews, but of course nobody takes advantage of this. The cars in the Palace courtyard are a mix of battered white foreign cars with Snoopies on them and the odd sporty Saab – but no ostentation.

The ladies-in-waiting have their own sitting-room on the second floor opposite the nursery. The Queen will send up a note asking if they could cope with some task. Essentially the ladies-in-waiting are concerned with women visitors and 'tend not to look after the chaps'. The duty lady-in-waiting tends not to go out at lunchtime to the hairdresser or to a private function in case she is needed. Instead lunch is served in the Household dining-room. The food is simple and drinks are paid for. Quick trips to Sloane Square for gloves and tights – particularly those pale, ivory-coloured ones – are squeezed in: they do get a small allowance to cover expenses. Even ladies-in-waiting say they do not wear hats too often these days, but they all seem to have a huge number of suitable straws. Only Lady Airlie and Mrs John Dugdale seem to veer away much from the petals and schoolgirl boaters. They tend to wear calm colours or, particularly the Duchess of Grafton or Lady Abergavenny, a pink, pale-misty blend of pastels.

They nearly all have the sort of legs which can pick their way across any turfy surface: sensible legs in low, black, patent shoes – occasionally white. It would be mad to wear anything more frivolous. Like the Queen, lots of them do the *Daily Telegraph* crossword in their sitting-room at the Palace. In Queen Victoria's day the ladies-in-waiting held political appointments; today they have become friends of the Queen's – some more than others. They are appreciated for their stability, their easy sociable manners and, of course, their discretion, their unswerving ability to stay buttoned up about anything they might see on the first and second floors of the Palace. On royal tours, they have a lot more work to do and part of that is entertaining the press, whom sometimes they want to strangle. The Duchess of Grafton said loftily on board the royal yacht in the Gulf that it should never have been published that she found it odd to be wearing a long dress in the desert in the afternoon. The Marchioness of Abergavenny is one of the more human and at race meetings is usually off with friends, leaving the Queen to enjoy her racing in peace. The ladies-in-waiting –

kindly, earnest and solicitous – are devoted to the Queen, though their husbands may joke: 'My wife has got a part-time job' or 'My wife's employer is going to Helsinki'.

The hours at the Palace can be long and you can't have a pot of tea or coffee just when you want it. Tea is served in the Equerries' Room at about 4.45 pm with sandwiches and biscuits. One of the Household said with feeling, 'Folk don't sit around doing their tapestries. I don't think people outside know how hard we work.' If the Queen has a late engagement, perhaps at a theatre, the Master of the Household will arrange a cold snack for the lady-in-waiting, the equerry and the detectives afterwards. If a Private Secretary is working late, he can go to the Equerries' Room and pour himself a whisky which he marks up on the slate.

Equerries are equally skilled in the arts of civil behaviour and non-controversial conversation. They are usually rather pleasant, youngish men, with short back and sides and a career in the Services. They move on well-polished shoes, have wives called Helen or Patricia. The Duke of Edinburgh has a Service Equerry who is attached for two years. The Queen's Equerry at present is Squadron Leader Adam Wise, tall with oiled black hair, brisk, burly, not entirely at ease with the harmless conversation, a bachelor who lives in Chelsea and likes to give the impression that he is more of a radical than is credible. Air Vice-Marshal John Severne, who formerly was the Duke of Edinburgh's Service Equerry, has taken over as Captain of the Queen's Flight. He replaces a man of great charm, Sir Archie Winskill, who sometimes seemed to dismiss the members of the Household as 'a lot of boring old farts'. He was good at his job, talked about his crews as 'my children' and, under the pretext of seeing that they were all right, often sloped off in the evenings on royal tours to entertain them. Meticulously correct and devoted to the Queen, he was an ideal member of the Household because that charm was invaluable at stuttering receptions and long lunches in Town Halls.

Working at Buckingham Palace offers security, regular meals, not a lot of money but lots of glamorous occasions and a rare standard of courtesy. From the moment one arrives at the Palace, even the policeman on the gate is kind – there used not to be any impression of being checked over. After parking on the left of the Privy Purse door one is welcomed by a footman in dark jacket and red trousers with a quiet 'Good morning'.

Inside the Palace there is an easy atmosphere, open shiny-dark mahogany office doors. Following a page in scarlet along the ground floor one passes the doors to the back courtyard which the Queen uses. There is a blue pedal car near them. It belonged to Prince Andrew and is now kept in case Princess Anne's son, Peter, wants to amuse himself. The Queen takes her own lift to the first floor so rarely sees the Privy Purse door, or the signs which one day warned, 'Loose carpet – Beware' because somebody had obviously slipped. 'It is, after all, the Queen's home,' one of the staff will say, excusing the lack of tea and coffee. In the small sitting-room with portraits in oval frames there are two newspapers – the *Daily Express* and *The Times*. As one waits a distinguished army of people go in and out with pleasantries, one of the secretaries to the Private Secretary will be discussing the value of a second-hand typewriter with a nervous young salesman in a brown suit who is rather over-whelmed at being there at all. When one makes an appointment at the Palace, they will usually say airily, 'Do come before the music starts,' which, of course, is the ritual Changing of the Guard. In the Palace one may hear someone playing the piano, and in some of the private offices with cinnamon walls and paintings, there is a comfortable bed in the corner to accommodate any of the Household who has been kept out too late on royal duties to get home.

Members of the Royal Household do not take contacts out to lunch. Someone really trusted might be asked to lunch in the Palace – no alcohol though. The Press Secretary, Michael Shea, says: 'I do not entertain people; I am not in the PR business.' But he is not shy about promoting his books, thrillers and travel writings under his own name and that of Michael Sinclair. The Palace has long been committed to not publicizing the monarchy, believing 'We don't exist to convert or divert people. Our capital is stuffiness.' That may be the view of the Household, but there are those even amongst the Queen's own family, at the outer edges admittedly, who feel that it is not helpful to her to be surrounded by pompous people: people who will pass on masses of arid information and leave one feeling slightly depressed; people who are trained not to say anything controversial. 'How frightfully nice,' 'How awfully kind,' and 'Wasn't it a tremendously enthusiastic crowd?'

Handpicked for the job, it is not surprising that the Household tend to come from the same polished mould. They are all immensely polite, always concerned and, like the royal family, tend to talk in gushing superlatives: 'So kind,' 'Frightfully interesting.' But they do not have the careless, indolent, amused air of the really grand old aristocratic families with their deliciously eccentric ways which totter dangerously near the mark. The people around the Queen are solidly Establishment, coming from the landed families or the Household Division. These phlegmatic, unflappable, confident courtiers are attractive in their way. They belong to the vast army of tweedy men and headscarved ladies standing on the edge of windy weekend events, being capable with loudspeakers and making announcements at agricultural shows while the Royal Army Service Corps demonstrate unarmed combat on the other side of the cabbage patch.

When the Queen came to the throne she said she wanted to rid herself of all those 'greybeards in satin breeches'. But believing as she does that things were very nicely done in her father's and grandfather's day, she has seen no reason to alter things too much. So there have been no revolutionary changes in the sturdy, trustworthy, English Protestant establishment at the Palace. They are at the top of a structure which is confidently based on enormous amounts of money, lots of land, a lot of horses, based in a way on agriculture and secure in the slow turning of the agricultural seasons. As an institution, British royalty works. It provides stability and continuity for the British, representing, as it does, decent, steady humanity. It is not a heady mix of wit, elegance, even a bit of fineboned inbred decadence but, unlike most of Europe, this crown stays firmly put.

CHAPTER 9

✿ ✿ ✿

Not a Vain Woman

THE QUEEN IS a size 12, her height 5 foot 4, her weight steady and her waist still trim, although allowances are always made after the holiday at Balmoral, well known as a fattening break with all that sturdy Scottish baking: baps and oatcakes waiting after days on the moors. Before a royal tour abroad, the designers are sent an itinerary and this means clothes have to be worked on a year ahead, which is nothing unusual in the fashion world. Not that the Queen's clothes are subject to whims. Hems must be about one and a half inches below the knee: the Queen was never tempted by the mini skirt in the sixties, revealing a touch of her doughty grandmama, Queen Mary, in the reluctance to show the knee. When skirts dropped again, she could not resist an amiable dig: 'You see, I was right not to change.'

'Nothing too high or too low,' so evening dresses can never plunge to show off one of her best features. Colours must always be bright and she wears blue best. Her pearly complexion means a tolerance to all shades, even sour yellow. The Queen's own favourites are lime green, pink, aquamarine, peacock blue and red. Strong colours are chosen to stand out for the crowds and for the photographers. Though photographers may be the bane of royal lives, attention is astutely given by Household staff to what might suit the lenses for worldwide circulation.

Sophisticated dark colours are avoided, though they would suit the Queen well in middle age, and black and cerise are out. This is unfortunate because the Queen, who has been seen in black only for funerals or visits to the Vatican, wears it with the élan of the medieval Spanish Court and her wardrobe abroad will always include black day and evening outfits in case they are needed for mourning. Once, when she was trying on a black dress at a fitting, she asked her maid to 'Get out my thing, would you?' Bobo disappeared and shuffled back with a diamond clip the size of a saucer. The Queen plonked it on her dress, stood up, threw a black mink over the shoulders and looked so dramatically elegant there was a stunned silence, broken by her: 'Now if only someone would invite me to something smart.' In fact she refuses to wear anything too stylishly flamboyant in public, preferring a neat, tailored, unfussy look. Her well-cut clothes always hang perfectly; and they are shrewdly chosen. Those dresses and coats, or simple suits with easy pleated skirts and pussy bows at the neck, are not calculated to cause twinges of envy in the crowd, unlike the more stylish clothes of some of the newer members of the royal family. 'Oh, doesn't she look nice!' is what one hears in the crowd when the Queen steps out of her car to open a new housing estate. There can even be a bit of quiet identification; though the Queen, her dressmakers assert, 'is incapable of looking middle-class or suburban'.

Her approach to clothes is professional; it is a task to be done and the guidelines must be followed. 'I never wear artificial flowers,' a distraught designer was told as he tried to pin a fetching bunch of Parma violets – made specially in Paris – to the royal waist. She is strong minded and, whatever fashion is doing, unlike so many women she will not delude herself into mere extravagance. Selective and cautious, she is quite unlike the Queen Mother, who will impulsively order a dozen outfits at once as if they were brown eggs. Quite unable to resist, the Queen Mother loves to shine and it would be hard to get a knife between the clothes in her wardrobe at Clarence House. Even so the Queen does get excited about clothes and has a sensuous appreciation of silks and brocades. She is amenable to new ideas. A recent breakthrough has been persuading her to wear taffeta. Suggestions can be made, tactfully, but one should never labour the point.

'You must remember I often have only twenty minutes, at the most, in which to dress,' the Queen never tires of pointing out, and is sometimes seen pulling on a tiara as she runs down the corridor. So clothes must be easy to get on and off. There must be no awkward zips and skirts must move easily for stepping on to podiums, up aircraft steps or for that hazardous manoeuvre, step-

ping out of the royal barge on to *Britannia*. Everything is checked
for easy movement and nothing is left to chance; hems do not have
weights in them but there will be a rebuke if a close-fitting coat
fails to allow enough freedom for waving. The Queen demon-
strates how at an Investiture 'there was this enormous man. I
couldn't make him smaller so I had to reach up with the sword. I
heard a ripping noise and my sleeve got torn. It was hard to know
who was the more embarrassed.' Full-length dresses should not
have fiddly long trains in case a nervous young diplomat puts his
foot on it. Floaty evening dresses are kept for private occasions at
Windsor and Sandringham. At fittings she likes to twirl and swish
in front of the long mirrors, enjoying the frivolity.

The Queen's dressing-room, once Queen Mary's, is huge, a bit
bleak but innately grand with a simple beige carpet, professional
mirrors everywhere, a dressing-table with a skirt, and chintzy
furniture. All the hairbrushes are in solid gold; there are bottles of
scent and masses of photographs in silver frames – the Queen
Mother in cloche hats, Farah Diba, Princess Grace of Monaco
looking serene, Princess Margaret all cloudy and misty with her
first baby, all the royal children and lots of the Duke of Edinburgh. There are bowls of fresh flowers on every table. Practising
movement in a slim skirt takes the Queen to the bow window
with a view across Constitution Hill and in the spring the purple
and yellow ribbons of crocuses in Green Park.

When the designers are submitting their sketches they go to
Buckingham Palace by the Privy Purse door. They talk with the
Queen for about three hours, looking at fabrics, selecting and eli-
minating. Then there will be three fittings before the creation is
wrapped up in tissue paper and carried to the Palace like a piece of
Dresden.

Tuesdays are Palace days for the couturiers, and the appointment is always for 2.30 pm. Just before 2 o'clock a scurry of milliners, fitters and vendeuses carrying striped hatboxes, evening
dresses in tissue paper and day clothes arrive at the Tradesmen's
Entrance in the Royal Mews. The designer leads the way into the
basement of the Palace with the urgency of the White Rabbit. A
footman guides them past hundreds of pipes into the lift which
seems to shoot to the first floor. Here they are met by the Queen's
Page in his jacket of blue cloth and dark breeches. The vendeuses,
their hair freshly set for the day, go first along the corridors under

domed ceilings where immensely grand portraits of the royal
ancestors – among them Queen Alexandra with hair all wuzzed up
and a wistful look – and white marble statues gaze down at the
armfuls of tulle and satin whisking by. The small room where
they wait is rather an anticlimax after the red carpets, the paintings
and collections of lovely china. It is next to the Queen's dressing-
room and has an austere atmosphere, a one-bar electric fire and a
round table. But everyone is too busy to sit down, as every
minute is spent fussing and hanging out the creations on the rail
wheeled in by the salon staff. 'The Queen is ready,' says Bobo
MacDonald, summoning the vendeuse and a couple of fitters who
go in before the rest. The Queen is by her dressing-room mirror
for the fitting. It may have been an exhausting morning spent
mainly on her feet, but she is ready for another two hours' standing and reminds everyone that: 'My grandmother warned me I
would have to stand for hours.'

The women curtsey and the men do a neck bow when they are
allowed in. She can sometimes be in such a relaxed mood, talking
airily about 'Mummy, Philip, Charles and the family' that at times
it is almost too easy to join in. On other days, there will be an
invisible glass wall and no amusing chat about happy Buckingham
Palace lunches, like the one for owners and trainers which was
nearly perfect except the horses were missing.

The Queen's lack of vanity is striking. As hats and clothes are
tried on, she sees reflections of herself all round the room, but
there is none of the face pulling and posing which most women do
unconsciously. Wearing a minimum of make-up, just some powder and lipstick, one realizes what a pretty woman she is, with that
relaxed assurance of maturity. She wears very little jewellery, a
pin, a simple watch and pearls which are an in-between length;
they really should be either longer or shorter. The other inescap-
able fact is the constant presence of Bobo, small shoulders
hunched, rummaging for a scarf or a pair of gloves in a set of
drawers. 'I know we have lots in there,' the Queen will say, gently
pointing to exactly the right dressing-table.

There are those who blame Miss MacDonald for the Queen's
unadventurous clothes. The Queen feels the cold, so sensible
warmth is always preferred by the old lady, and stout comfortable
shoes instead of pretty ones. It is said that the Queen is mesme-
rized by Bobo. There was a time in the past when an elaborate lace

dress was turned down. 'Too heavy for us,' Bobo will have grumbled; really meaning too awful to iron. It is said that she grumbled so much about ironing cotton gloves that Hardy Amies's vendeuse, Mrs Sheila Ogdon, introduced white nylon ones made by Cordelia James, for the Queen can wear four pairs a day. Yet the two designers, Ian Thomas and Hardy Amies, have a great regard for her and for her professionalism. 'Bobo's a cracker,' says Ian Thomas; and he points out, 'After all, she has been with the Queen since Her Majesty was a baby. She has got to be efficient, get out the right jewels, the right hats, the right gloves, at high speed.' These days, Miss MacDonald has assistants to help her but they do it most tactfully, walking on eggshells.

For most women an afternoon spent with designers fussing round them, fitters with mouthfuls of pins making changes almost before they have been hinted at, would be bliss, but not for the Queen. However, the designers all come away feeling elated. The Queen has three favourites. With those innate royal good manners, they are kept strictly apart and ideally go to the Palace on different Tuesdays. But if this cannot happen they are shown into separate anterooms well apart. The Queen enjoys the rivalry between them and commissioned a long black dress from each for her last visit to the Vatican to meet the Pope. 'I believe you don't know each other,' the Queen said dryly as she introduced Ian Thomas to Hardy Amies at the original 'marvellous party' at Buckingham Palace to mark her Silver Jubilee.

Sir Norman Hartnell, 'Dear Mr Hartnell', as the Queen called him before she made him a Knight Commander of the Royal Victorian Order in 1977, could be held responsible for the royal weakness for baby blues and pinks. When the Queen was nine years old, Hartnell designed a bridesmaid's dress for her, a confection of pink silk and frills for the wedding of the Duke of Gloucester to Lady Alice Montagu-Douglas-Scott in 1936. From that moment on he was to design for all the grand occasions, despising those 'dreadful "Who's for tennis?" dresses' of his younger rivals. Beads, mother of pearl, sequins, crystal, aquamarine and topaz jewels were stitched on to pale blue, primrose and oyster satin by ninety-five girls working at a great loom behind the dormer windows of Hartnell's workshop: to be seen all over the world on the backs of pale-skinned royals. Sculptured evening dresses shimmered up to meet the real glitter of tiaras, those decorative half crowns from the court of St Petersburg which sat so easily on the heads of the Tsarinas.

Sir Norman designed the wedding dress and the Coronation dress and was cherished for twenty-five years by the Queen, until his death. He left her a wardrobe of evening dresses, doing them both credit and confirming the old-fashioned belief that upper-class Englishwomen look better in balldresses than day clothes.

Sir Norman was a kindly man who loved champagne and adored puckish gossip. He would sit in the French salon in Bruton Street under the Waterford chandeliers, watching the Queen in one of his creations on television. 'I'd think "Oh cripes" when some goofy child handed her a posy and I'd watch her bend down and into that angle the photographers love.' By the time he died in 1979 the salon, which had dressed duchesses, princesses and the glitterati of pre- and post-war years, had become a little sad. Edith Auley Read, who did 3,000 hours of hand embroidering on the Coronation dress and was by then in her seventies, went home to Stanmore in Middlesex in the evening with memories rather than a bag full of precious work.

Sir Norman's personal secretary for thirty-eight years, Mrs Ann Price, no longer sent out five hundred hand-embroidered Christmas cards, as she once did when it was 'a world full of glamour'. There was Ivy the Matcher, Flo the Packer, Miss Whistler the vendeuse and the dark, haughty-looking house model Mara, who was really a jolly northern lass. And they all used to go up to the Palace. 'Sometimes I'd be standing there with nothing on but the radio,' Mara remembers.

John Tullis, a tall man, delightfully diffident and cousin of Captain Edward Molyneux, the only British couturier ever accepted in Paris, succeeded Sir Norman at Hartnell. It was typical of the Queen that she should stay with the House, and Tullis was soon called to the Palace. As the Page led him to the Queen's apartments, he thought how wonderful it would be to have a pair of roller skates, to go speeding along the red-carpeted corridors which seem as endless as the Champs Elysées. The Queen put him at ease at once: 'It's been a long time, Mr Tullis.' She had remembered his cheery little Horrockses cotton dresses, which she was very attached to in the fifties and which Tullis had designed for twelve years. The Queen would be photographed wearing one and the next day there would be thousands of orders.

At that first meeting, Tullis says, 'The room was bright with electric lights. I couldn't speak. I was standing there like the village idiot. But I managed to stumble out, "I hope you are not going to ask for dresses which are too long."' 'Oh no, I don't like that,' the Queen replied and heard Tullis say gratefully, 'I am so glad, they are terribly ageing.' When it came to fittings, the professional in him took over. One of the first times he saw the Queen standing in a dress at a fitting was most unfortunate. The design was frantic cabbage roses and tulle. He took one look and saw a great chunk of material on her bosom. 'Poor darling. I just rushed forward and clasped the offending bit.'

Another time it was the Queen's ankles. The elderly fitter, Madame Emilienne, was creakily crawling round on her hands and knees trying to fix a hem. Tullis could bear it no longer and flung himself at the Queen's feet, saying, 'Oh, let me do it.' After an abstracted few minutes he realized the impropriety of it all. 'There I was scrabbling round and suddenly in the mirror I saw HM roll her eyes at Miss Whistler, trying to hide a smile, so I carried on.'

The Queen liked John Tullis's clothes and his score card was particularly high at the Commonwealth Conference and visit to Australia in September 1981. A fitting swansong, for he has now decided to go home to South Africa. The ready-to-wear designer and director at Hartnell, Annette Harvey, has specialized in more practical day clothes, a far cry from the days of the Master.

The man who can always make the Queen laugh is that witty grandee, Hardy Amies. His father was an architect and Edwin Hardy Amies, now in his seventies, was, happily for rich ladies, deflected from journalism. Instead he joined Lachasse in Mayfair as a designer and first made his name in the late thirties with a suit with the mocking name label 'Panic'. His clothes today are flattering and racy. He sees the Queen as: 'Simply a very grand English lady, perfectly at ease and with perfect manners.' When going to the Palace for fittings, Hardy Amies says: 'The atmosphere is relaxed, but never palsy-walsy. It is just as you'd expect with a rich upper-class lady. The Queen's attitude is that of any rich woman; a millionairess of position who does not like to be exploited. She is practical with that good Scottish sense; in many ways the same as an East Coast American Daughter of the Revolution.'

Hardy Amies first designed for the Queen for the royal tour of

Canada in 1948, when allowances had to be made for her first baby. Her figure in those days was less than perfect, and it was a time when the Queen favoured fussy crepes and fattening cotton frocks, even hand-me-down dresses from Queen Mary, which did nothing for her small waist but added inches to an already adequate bosom. There had been a discreet telephone call before the two princesses came to Hardy's salon in Savile Row with its inviting, winding, chocolate-carpeted staircase and graceful windows, giving the sort of light which makes one long for new clothes. The sisters saw the collection and had a cup of tea. Princess Margaret dropped a glove. As Hardy picked it up, he saw a hole in it and thought 'Hmm, she hasn't got a very good maid.' He was invited to the Palace and was much less nervous than his rivals.

Immensely successful, Hardy Amies was made Commander of the Royal Victorian Order in 1977. But he has always watched his p's and q's with the monarch and once had a slightly narrow squeak. A great crinoline in organdy was being fitted and Hardy had just come back from New York. 'The poor fitter seemed to be taking an eternity crawling around and I was thinking about Gertrude Lawrence and said, rather absentmindedly, "Have you seen *The King and I*, Ma'am?"' 'The King and Who, Mr Amies?' was the Queen's chilling reply.

The presence of the corgis is something designers, like Prime Ministers, Privy Councillors and Household staff, all learn to tolerate. 'Oh, do you like dogs?' the Queen will say breezily to some perspiring dignitary trying to sidestep a minimum of seven dogs at once in the royal presence. Both the Queen and her corgis, who rarely leave the room under any circumstance, have picked up so many pins from the carpet over the years that Hardy Amies gave her a satin covered magnet. Of course, there are those who would not mind too much if the corgis were to swallow something indigestible, as they roam round the dressing-room snappily waiting for their chopped liver at 4.30 pm. The bowls are always lined up punctually by a servant in the corridor outside.

One Christmas Hardy Amies gave the Queen a trendy white shoulder bag, hoping she might wear it on the royal yacht and be eventually wooed away from her favourite clumpy handbags. The present was accepted, 'How kind', but never seen in public, on land or sea, and large, sensible, square-shaped white or black bags were carried as firmly as ever on the wrist. The Queen's handbag

contains a small compact, a lipstick, a hanky and occasionally a little money and a set of car keys. Clutch bags, which would be so
much more attractive, have not been considered.

Thrift, all part of the Queen's Anglo-Scottish blood, means that
when the question is asked: 'What does the Queen do with her old
clothes?' Palace servants can look you in the eye and say, 'She
wears them.' There is another theory that they go to underprivi-
leged German relations of the Duke of Edinburgh who were so
kind to him in his early years. The ladies-in-waiting are expected
to look smart. They are given discounts at the couture houses, but
somehow for some of them, 'Poor dears, it is never quite enough.'
One of them has a model figure and does rather well with clothes
shown in the salon but otherwise perfect. Bobo gets a gift of a
couture outfit from Hardy Amies each year, but the Queen pays
for all her other clothes, which have cost many thousands of
pounds over the years.

'I wonder why that should have cost so much?' the Queen will
ask, even though it has been a great favourite and worn often. Or,
if she is shown an exotic fabric, she will enjoy it for a moment and
then put it aside, dismissing any self-indulgence. 'I really do not
need another dress.' The Queen has always resisted evening coats,
complaining jokily, 'You see they always take them away from
me.' But she weakened for one grand occasion at Versailles. Much
later, on a cold, grey morning in Edinburgh at the Synod, there
was the Queen in the Versailles evening coat. Asked about this
afterwards she said, 'I just found it in the wardrobe.' For the Silver
Jubilee, the Queen should have been wearing a new pale
lime-green outfit but, as it was a miserable looking day, out came
the cherry pink worn the previous year for the Olympic Games in
Montreal.

The 'baby' of the designers is Ian Thomas, whose clothes are
youthful and pretty. The Queen has said of his work, 'I feel happy
in these clothes. Once I put them on I can forget about them.' Formerly with Hartnell, Ian Thomas is briskly humorous and has a
passion for horses. His background is not a story of cushy times
designing beneath chandeliers and sipping Lapsang Souchong.
After years as a backroom boy at Hartnell, where he did a lot of
the creative work but was never allowed to meet the royals, he
decided to leave. 'Then, just before I left, I got a call from Miss
MacDonald who told me to come to the Palace. I thought: "Oh

my God, Mr Hartnell will be livid!" But the elderly maid was her usual sharp self and instructed, "It's a command. Be here at half past two."'

He went and was utterly terrified by the red carpets, the white marble busts and the paintings. 'And then suddenly you find yourself with this rather nice woman.' They had a 'lovely chat' for twenty minutes. The Queen asked why he was leaving and he explained that he thought the days of couture were over, and added: 'Now I am going to try and design cheaper clothes on my own.' He was then brave enough to ask the Queen how she knew he was leaving. With a smile she replied, 'Oh, we know a lot more than people think.' He was given a photograph and a pair of cuff-links and six months later was asked to submit some sketches to Buckingham Palace.

Ian Thomas opened a salon in Knightsbridge on a borrowed £3,000. The early days were tough, getting up at six in the morning and working all hours. He is a realist. 'I always tell students the rough side of designing. It is not sitting at a drawing-board dreaming up dresses for film premières. It is designing for Mrs Brown, who is a size 18 and wants a little brown dress to wear in the country, so never get too grand.' Today he has a pampering, bijou boutique, Number 14 in stylish Motcomb Street, London SW1, which is full of the sort of bright things he creates for the Queen and such clients as the Duchess of Westminster, who all love his clingy, feminine, silk-crepe dresses which flatter the hips. Now he is his own master he is not enthusiastic about beading and sequins, finding them a little coarse, 'all that tin', and prefers something more delicate. He has been given a corgi by the Queen; a rather high-spirited creature called Frisky which is constantly enquired about. 'Is he wearing a collar yet?' They share a love of horses and dogs, but the corgi was a complete surprise for Ian Thomas, who probably thought he was getting more cufflinks when the Queen said, 'I have a present for you', and handed over a warm bundle. The talk is light, of books, theatre and TV ... and horses.

Even if the Queen were the same age as the Princess of Wales is now, it is doubtful whether she would have the same interest in clothes as her leggy, coltish daughter-in-law. Studying international law and the Constitution from childhood must make fashion seem a little less relevant. For the Princess of Wales, with her model-girl potential and never burdened with trying to get to University, it has been natural and irresistible to be up to the mark in fashion. Her sister, Sarah, worked at *Vogue* magazine before her own marriage and was highly thought of there, which made a connection for the Princess of Wales.

Now the Princess goes regularly to *Vogue* and, in the Board-room, has long sessions, standing in her bra and panties, being advised by the formidable Editor-in-Chief, Beatrix Miller, and the fashion staff. She has her own flair but she gets a lot of help too. 'You want something for Ascot?' Miss Miller will say briskly. 'Yes, something different for every blessed day,' the Princess replies. A favourable arrangement is reached about the price of the clothes. Designers are only too delighted to see her wear their creations. Copies of her rather matronly blue engagement-day suit by Cojana, bought from Harrods, sold terrifically, though the girl on the staff who revealed the sale left like a rocket for being indiscreet. The Princess still nips into Fenwicks and to Peter Jones, where she likes to buy her brassieres, while one of her detectives stands outside the cubicle.

Shortly after she was married, the Princess pleaded with the designer Margaret Howell to let her have an up-to-the-minute outfit of rather severe black trousers with white shirt and braces, quite masculine with its bow tie like a waiter's outfit. The designer thought her too tall for it, but the Princess won, saying, 'It will amuse Charles.' Princess Michael wears clothes stunningly, too, and is not averse to an accommodation being reached on the price. Her husband, Prince Michael, was despatched to buy a pair of braces like those which had been seen on Diana, and were much admired. You could not imagine the Duke of Edinburgh persuading the Queen even to wear jeans – her most relaxed clothes are jodhpurs or loosely cut trousers, dating from the style when they were called slacks. But she does take notice of him and will reject a hat, or colour, saying, 'Oh, Philip wouldn't like that.' Occasionally the Duke of Edinburgh does stride in to ask 'Shall I make the tea?' or 'How long will you be?' giving a gritty look at the piles of organza, tulle and taffeta on the floor. Before Prince Charles was married he often dropped by to see one of Mother's new creations and particularly wanted to see a hat being made for the Gulf tour, hearing 'it was full of Eastern promise'.

In the old days, when the Queen was still influenced by her

grandmother, her hats were made by an elderly plumassier and the effect was a random one; a flower here, a bow there, and certainly not the co-ordinated look the Queen has today. Then the Danish designer Aag Tharup made some hats for the Queen before he retired to his native country. Hardy Amies and the Queen were learning that it should all be a 'theatrical performance', which suggested the name of an Australian milliner called Freddie Fox whose hats can make plain women beautiful. Freddie Fox, amusing but not pushy, goes to the Palace with his creations and there is always the same battle of wills, one royal and the other antipodean. The Queen will try on a hat – she likes them to be off the face, and never too large because it is difficult getting in and out of cars. The little milliner puts it on in the correct forward position, then a royal finger will creep up slyly and tilt it back. 'Photographers won't like that too far forward, Mr Fox.' The hats are tried at the dressing-table and there are two sets of triplicate mirrors at each end of the room. Once a pretty, small hat was produced which prompted the unguarded comment: 'Have we been watching too much *Edward and Mrs Simpson*, do you think, Mr Fox?' Try as he will, Freddie Fox cannot persuade the Queen to wear hats without any hair showing; a few curls are always sure to peep out at each side. It is strong, springy hair and at times a nightmare for the milliners.

Piles of stylish brown and white boxes, printed with the royal cypher, hold Fox's creations. At the time of the Gulf tour, he made some small hats with eastern scarves, which were to be worn draped in Arabian style. Photographs of the tour showed the Queen holding the scarves with her handbag, as if she were at a point-to-point in Gloucestershire. Later the Queen said, 'I really had to hang on to those scarves otherwise they would have been round a sheikh's neck.' There must be no large brims or tassels and hat scarves must never touch the face. Once Fox suggested diffidently that some fruit and flowers might be appealing on a new hat – perhaps a bunch of cherries. He thought that perhaps he had gone too far. 'Mr Fox, I suppose you will be wearing your fruit-picking gloves in your workroom in future.'

'Oh, perhaps, Ma'am, you'd be happier if I took the fruit off?'

But he was instructed, 'Oh no, I love the fruit; it's such fun.' There was conspiracy over the pink outfit which the Queen wore for the Silver Jubilee, which had a captivating hat with pink bells on it. Hardy Amies hated the bells. He was away when the final outfit was brought to the Queen so the bells stayed on – she loved them.

Simone Mirman, a dark-haired Frenchwoman who works with Hartnell, says one of her greatest triumphs with the Queen was a white stetson. 'Sometimes, when I am fitting hats, we work and watch racing on television.' 'Come and watch the 3.30,' the Queen will say, either going into her bedroom or getting the television brought into the dressing-room. There are comical moments as the race becomes exciting, when fitter and milliner do the best they can as they lean backwards and forwards to match the Queen's movements. They are trying to work with as much decorum as possible, but for the Queen, they might as well not be there.

The Queen has long slender legs which are not always shown to flattering advantage. There is firm refusal to wear anything but beige stockings; ivory is 'too much like the colour Granny used to wear'. Shoes tend to be black or white patent with chunky heels. They are all designed by Edward Rayne, who is still so overwhelmed by the appointment as royal cobbler that he does not dare to make any suggestions on colour changes, much to the chagrin of the couturiers. The Queen knows this and will say, 'Mr —— does not like my shoes', but as a big concession might wear beige. At about 4 pm, the fittings over, tea is served in the ante-room.

Going to Balmoral is much more fun. It is a lovely day out, starting with the night train or the flight up, delicious lunch with aperitifs and wine and, in the afternoon, a Mrs Beeton type tea of scones, sponges, chocolate cake and Indian tea. If there is a train journey back to London, the designers and their teams are given hampers of cold food with decent glass and silver cutlery.

CHAPTER 10

A Rich Currency

IN THE FIFTIES the monarchy suddenly came under criticism from people such as Lord Altrincham – now John Grigg since renouncing his title in 1963 – and Malcolm Muggeridge. Their main charge was against the Queen, who they thought had surrounded herself with 'tweedy advisers' who were out of touch. Writing in *The National and English Review*, Lord Altrincham warned that when the Queen lost the bloom of youth, her reputation would have to depend on her personality, and he was not very optimistic – disliking her manner and her voice.

Aristocratic old gentlemen in the shires grew purple-cheeked over their port, enraged at the insult to their young monarch and their friends at court – horsewhipping, hanging and shooting were all recommended as soon as possible for the cheeky Altrincham. Joining in the anti-royal mood, John Osborne, the playwright, called monarchy a 'splendid triviality' and compared it to 'a gold filling in a mouth full of crumbling teeth'. Malcolm Muggeridge thought monarchy could best be explained as an 'ersatz religion' and was also extremely critical of the Queen's advisers. He argued that even the Queen's press officers must be top-drawer – making them 'quite exceptionally incompetent'.

The Queen, intuitively and coolly appraising the criticisms, did nothing dramatic but slowly introduced subtle changes. A young adviser from the Australian Civil Service, Bill Heseltine, now Sir William – 'I was just a brash young colonial really' – was drafted in. One of the things he did early on was to persuade the Queen to agree to a little gentle image-making, such as the 'Royal Family' film. It was first shown on Saturday, 21 June 1969 and was an extraordinary turning point.

The most remarkable thing about this film was the revelation in people's sitting-rooms that the Queen did not always talk in that squeaky, cold, high voice but was a super raconteuse with a great sense of humour which had never communicated itself before. The fear was that showing the Queen and her family in close-up could destroy the remoteness and the mystique – you could kill the goose that lays the golden egg. Royal dialogue, too, was a rich currency which in the wrong hands could easily be devalued.

Before the late 1960s all the public had seen was an occasional shot of the Queen with one of the children, the formal Christmas broadcast or the pictures taken at a distance for Gaumont British Newsreel March of Time, all rather formal and sickly. Press relations were handled by the stern, remote Commander Richard Colville, who, under duress, would receive the accredited Court Correspondents – in their striped trousers and black jackets – whom he summoned to give news of when the Queen would be going to the Chelsea Flower Show. He would shudder with distaste at impertinent questions about what she might be wearing or her taste in literature or food.

Now, out of the blue, Richard Cawston, the BBC Head of Documentaries, was approached by Lord Brabourne – the filmmaker husband of Lord Mountbatten's daughter, Patricia, and a great and close childhood friend of the Queen's. There was a lot of sitting round tables with Prince Philip in the chair as Cawston in his slightly academic, fussily urbane, way insisted that he should make the film his way – close-ups of the Queen at breakfast, at parties, with the family, talking to ambassadors, relaxing, joking with the children, at audiences with lots of spontaneous dialogue.

Prince Philip has said of photographers, 'All those chaps ever want is the moment when they catch you picking your nose.' But the decision had been taken to reveal more of the monarchy. Perhaps there was no harm in showing some of that 'fierce light which beats upon the throne'. And once the Queen and Prince Philip felt they could trust the film crew, it was fun. The Queen became professional about the lighting and would often make suggestions. 'Could we avoid shadow here?' or 'We can't have a backlit ambassador' and had a little smile when Cawston was tearing his hair out; she quite liked it when things went wrong! The exposed film was stored in a vault in Denham, stuffed away from the nosey and labelled 'Religious Programmes'. Only two people knew it was being made – one was Huw Wheldon, the other

David Attenborough, both producers at the BBC. Even they had misgivings about a royal family film. Attenborough – thinking anthropologically – felt it might chip off some of the magic of the monarchy. With a rueful shake of his head he would caution, 'Never let them inside the hut', as if a rare almost extinct tribe was about to be uncovered.

It took seventy-five days to shoot, and by the end of forty-three hours' filming, which was edited to 105 minutes, a bond had grown between the royal family and the crew; the more they were together the more relaxed the Queen became. But there were fraught moments. Nowadays we take it for granted to hear the Queen speak naturally and normally, forgetting the days when she sounded shrill and stilted. It was the sound recordist, Peter Edwards, who had the most delicate task of all. He had tremblingly to pin a microphone to the sovereign's bosom, watched keenly most days by the Household, whose noses were distinctly out of joint. Sometimes the Queen would invite Cawston to lunch, asking, 'Why won't you allow me to see the rushes, Mr Cawston?' And he would try to explain that it had always been a principle of his to refuse; it was fatal because it made people self-conscious; they started wondering which was their good side and their bad. This was accepted philosophically.

As they followed the Queen about the crew tried to merge into the background – not very easy as most of them were six foot tall and they had been issued with dark, formal suits for the purpose. But even so the Queen got to know the crew well and liked their attempts at tact. When the team went to Chile to film the royal tour, it was blisteringly hot and the sun was giving far too bright a light. The Queen had been talking to the members of the Government and a Chilean dignitary was walking her to her car, speaking earnestly about his country while the film crew, hidden behind some trees, were confident that they could not be seen. Cursing the heat and perspiring, the Cockney electrician, Dave Gorringe, was trampling in the bushes when he heard the unmistakably clear tones of the Queen – who had paused at the car – as she said loudly to him, 'You certainly won't need your lights today, Sparks!'

When the film came out, it was a national event. It was shown in 130 countries all over the world and the London water system nearly broke down because so many people had waited to go to the lavatory during the interval. It was a fabulous success, complemented by a lively script by Tony Jay, author of the *Yes, Minister* series poking fun at civil servants. The Consortium – Prince Philip again – did not want an oily commentary written on bended knee. In fact the film did not comment. But when it went to America, for some reason they wanted a voice-over by the actor Vincent Price. The royal family loved the film and laughed a lot – it was really home movies to them. It was such a success that there was an approach from the exiled Spanish royal family wondering if Cawston's team could do the same for them. But Cawston went back to his job as head of the department that produced such series as 'Sailor', 'The Fight Against Slavery' and 'Hospital' – which won the Italia Prize. The editor of 'Royal Family', Michael Bradsell, went on to edit Ken Russell's film *Women in Love*.

Early in December each year the same crew goes to Buckingham Palace to do the Christmas Broadcast. The cameraman now is Philip Bonham-Carter, who was assistant during the making of 'Royal Family'. The Queen much prefers their innovative approach to the Christmas Day broadcast to sitting behind a desk saying 'My husband and I'. She once gave Lady Longford a racy description of her first television appearance at Christmas 1957. Her face was painted yellow like a clown and she was made thoroughly uncomfortable with holes bored through walls for the television cables and icy draughts running in with them – even her family thought she was shivering with nerves.

None of the dignity and aloofness of office has been lost by a little gentle public relations. The Queen needed to meet a broader mix of people, so some informal entertaining would be done. The first lunch was on 11 May 1956 and invitations went out to a mixture of people – to politicians, writers, scientists, academics, entertainers and sportsmen. There was a series of cocktail parties in the Bow Room with a similar mix of people – the statutory footballer, the tiger of industry, winner of vast export orders and, perhaps, a tennis player and a musician. They may be thought of in royal circles as homely lunches but some of the guests feel almost shipwrecked in an unlikely situation, desperately trying to find something in common with one another and closeted together for two hours of polished conversation. Nerves make strong men ask for sherry when they would really prefer a Scotch or a gin and tonic. 'What a lot of sherry drinkers we have today', the Queen may remark with a sly smile. She puts down her pink aperitif or tonic with ice and lemon when the Palace steward announces, 'Luncheon is served, Your Majesty,' and leads her guests to lunch where they sit at an oval table. One guest remembers a terrified ballet dancer 'who looked rather like a plucked seagull'. He himself found it rather a strain to think of something to say and could not help overhearing royal snippets as he tried to keep his own conversation going. 'I'm amazed you manage to remember all the steps' – the Queen's inimitable voice – 'everyone must be absolutely puffed at the end of half an hour. I know I should be.' But most of the guests come away elated and stunned at having lunched with the Queen.

A trade union leader found his potato had slipped on to the floor, and all his efforts to curl his shoe around the escaping vegetable failed as it was squashed under the table. The Queen said with a twinkle, 'Life can be so difficult.' Some are disconcerted by the thought of watching the Queen eat. In the summer, she prepares her strawberries nursery style, mashing them together with sugar and cream. While some guests are overwhelmed by the occasion, others, such as David Gentleman, the graphic designer, find it a 'nice, imaginative, fairly informal thing to do'. Sportsmen usually feel at ease at the Palace. The Queen told Steve Ovett she had spotted the 800-metre Olympic gold medallist on his early-morning training runs in Hyde Park.

It did not need film cameras to show that if the royal family are with people who are themselves interesting, they respond. Once, escaping for a minute from a cluster of worthies, the Queen called the attention of the former German Ambassador, the silver-haired, courtly Dr Hans Reute, to a barefooted Franciscan monk in a group nearby. 'I am always fascinated by their toes, aren't you?' said the Queen, and anyone who had not heard her might have thought from her serious expression that she was talking about the mark against the pound in the Stock Exchange that day.

At an Investiture, the writer, Anthony Powell, was behind a man who was asked by the Queen, 'What do you do?' 'I kill mosquitoes,' he replied, and the Queen said with relief, 'Oh, good.' It is best to be brief, unless you have something really interesting or amusing to say. The Queen's skill at being surprisingly easy to talk to can lull people into the trap of talking too long or getting so excited they tell her ridiculous things. At another Investiture, a woman kept the Queen chatting for so long that she was making her late and monopolizing her, so, as the Queen said later, 'I gave her one of my chilly looks.'

When the Queen went to the annual party given by Hatchards of Piccadilly she met distinguished authors of the year such as Lady Longford and Margaret Drabble, all drinking champagne and with something to say. Carrying a tonic water, the Queen, who likes Dick Francis thrillers, met Hammond Innes and asked, 'Are you working on something now?' and Innes, a small, garrulous man, immediately said: 'Yes', and took the conversation on. 'You have someone staying with you at the moment I know rather well', meaning the Sultan of Oman, Sheikh Qaboos. Immediately the Queen was off about sailing through the Straits of Hormuz on her Gulf trip: 'They were called the Elphinstone Straits after an uncle of mine.' Sheridan Morley, son of the actor Robert Morley and never shy about coming forward, was told the monarch was enjoying his *Noel Coward Diaries*, which was at that time being serialized in the *Daily Mail*. Then he was asked, conversationally, 'Do you ever see Tony these days?' referring to Lord Snowdon, an old friend of Sheridan's. People like Hammond Innes and Wynford Vaughan Thomas, who are regulars at Buckingham Palace lunches, find the Queen very easy to talk to. 'Your corgi is moulting like my bitch,' Innes told the Queen, who gave the dog a reassuring pat, disliking any hint of criticism. Innes said that for some extraordinary reason they started talking about police helmets. 'How would you know about them, Ma'am?' she was asked, and replied, 'Of course I do, I knocked one off on VE Day.' Of course she was not using the Cockney alternative slang for pinching or nicking!

The elaborate courtesy and etiquette surrounding the Court never fail to impress Heads of State, monarchs and diplomats, and they give a feeling of stability to a country battling through the economic crises of the 1980s. What is not seen is the clever frugality of the Queen and the royal family. All the treasures of the royal ancestors are squirrelled away and never diminished by cavalier, self-indulgent use. After a State Banquet the treasure is all put away. The next night the Queen may well be having a boiled egg for supper.

While the guest of honour is putting on his cummerbund in the suite overlooking the gardens at the Palace, the staff in fine white wool breeches, black and gold braid livery and black pumps with buckles will be rushing about the Ballroom with controlled attentiveness. The footmen, who in royal circles are junior to the pages, are in scarlet livery with gold braid, scarlet plush knee breeches and, for them, pink instead of white stockings.

Once their wigs were whitened with a mixture of starch, flour and soap. But Prince Philip abhorred 'this ridiculous and unhygienic custom' and persuaded the Queen to abolish it. The Ballroom will be lit by six pink lustre chandeliers that pour soft light on the solid gold plate, the cut crystal fluted glasses with the hand-engraved cypher 'EIIR' and the nineteenth-century candelabra with their gambolling nymphs frolicking with Bacchus round silver tree trunks. The Queen always selects the menus and checks the banquet herself. The food is usually light. There will be soup, fish, and something very English, roast lamb, beef or duck, vegetables from Sandringham, a selection of fruit – strawberries, raspberries, blackcurrants, or the red Langley Gage, a sweet gooseberry very popular with George VI. At the banquet the Queen presides in fiery diamond tiara, necklace and earrings, kindling an insatiable romantic addiction to monarchy.

Even ambassadors can get nervous. 'How are you settling in?' the Queen asked with kindly concern as the new American ambassador was presented to her on 29 April 1969, ironically enough in the George III room. Normally a burly character not short of words, Walter Annenberg burbled on about 'refurbishing which disrupts rehabilitation'. The Queen nodded sympathetically, storing the word 'refurbished' in the back of her well-groomed head. Describing the meeting later she said, 'Oh, he's not bad', obviously preferring him to a lot of smoothiesticks with arrogant ways. She immediately spots any gaucherie, and then adeptly pretends it has not happened.

A classic example of this occurred on a royal tour of Australia in 1981. A guest at one of her parties on board the royal yacht was talking to the Queen when he dropped his glass of sherry at her feet on the flawless beige carpet. Burning with embarrassment, he stood before the Queen as if hypnotized but she talked gaily about changing times in Australia as if it was the most fascinating subject. Looking straight ahead, the unfortunate man watched a door open behind her and out came a matelot in sneakers with a bucket and spotless duster. He removed the offending spot while the Queen chatted on and, as noiselessly as he had arrived, retreated backwards with his bucket. The guest was immediately handed another glass of sherry on a silver tray. That night he was in a line-up with other photographers on a marble staircase waiting for the Queen to arrive for a Gala Banquet. As she drew level, coming slowly up the stairs in shimmering tiara at a regal pace, the same wretched soul dropped his camera at her feet. Purple with embarrassment, holding his breath in horror and thinking that the Queen would now take this as insolence and not clumsiness, he looked apprehensively at her only to find she was roaring with laughter (fortunately hair is threaded through a tiara to make it sit firmly). 'Oh, Mr ———, this really has not been your day,' said the Queen, making all the tension disappear in her amusement.

The Queen smiling, the Queen serious, the Queen walking – but not one photograph of her off guard. Yet in her own album there are pictures of her which capture brilliantly that double role of public image and private woman. Such a special photograph could only have been taken by one of the family – and this one was by a cousin, Patrick Lichfield, the bouffy-haired, fashionable photographer. It shows the Queen sitting on the stairs of the *Britannia* at the end of an evening when there had been a banquet on board. Her shoes have been kicked off, her tiara is on the stairs beside her and she is reading a letter from Prince Charles. This photograph will never be released for publication. The Queen likes it a lot and it is in her album blown up to twelve inches across. There are also lots of fun pictures showing her with Princess Margaret and the Queen Mother; in one of them they are looking mildly squiffy in wellingtons, headscarves and mackintoshes with their hoods awry, drinking something warming from paper cups under the sopping trees with the beaters in their deerstalkers standing respectfully some distance away. There is a famous photograph of the three clowning around with buckets, in tartan skirts, pretending they are expecting a royal visit.

Photographers all agree that the Queen is a professional – she knows the right angles and when to look at the camera. She knows about photography anyway, using a gold Rollei or Leica herself. Even Patrick Lichfield and Lord Snowdon become nervous before a royal photocall. Lord Snowdon gets particularly jumpy and the Queen is pleasant but brisk. Photographers are given a limited amount of time, so it is best to be decisive and know what one is about. But it never does to be pushy. Before the royal wedding, Norman Parkinson, who makes the most lacklustre women look beautiful, asked if he might do the pictures. But because he asked, he was told, no. Lichfield bided his time and got the summons, though he said being at the royal wedding made him feel like 'the bad fairy' disturbing the happy laughing time with his Olympus OM2.

He used a referee's whistle to gain everyone's attention, and he played a smart trick on his rivals. Everyone seemed to be taking identical shots – he wanted something different. So at the end of the time, he called out 'Have you finished?' 'Yes,' said the other photographers and, as they gathered up their tripods and bags he said to the royal group, 'You can relax now' and got that falling about wedding picture. Later he took a picture of the Queen and the bride trying to comfort a small bridesmaid on the point of weeping with exhaustion. A royal photocall 'hypes you up' Lichfield admits. He may take as many as ten thousand shots of the Queen, as he did on the royal yacht, but she will select only about twelve of these for general release. In some she may look grumpy. It is a pity we cannot see his pictures of her at Balmoral sitting on a rock with a dog on her knee.

Painters and sculptors catch more than the smile of the Queen. The distinguished sculptor, Franta Belsky, saw in the Queen strength with a tremendous natural dignity, poise and a deep humanity. He is an old favourite with the royal family; the Queen Mother often went to his parties, and once, when she heard his father had died, picked a sprig of rosemary and handed it to him as they walked along. Belsky works in a studio in Kensington and at dusk it is eerie to lean over the edge of the balcony and look down on the heads he has done – black ones, children, royals – all standing on plinths waiting for the last touches. Belsky complained about the light in the Yellow Drawing-Room at Buckingham Palace, shuddering at the brightness of it and fussed about, watched by an amused Queen, as he put up black paper to blot out the daylight. Prince Philip came in occasionally – the bronze head of the Queen is a companion to the one done by Belsky of the Duke of Edinburgh in 1979 – and sniffed approval.

It is always assumed that the Queen, Prince Philip and Prince Charles enjoy these sessions, or sitting for portraits which will hang in the Fishmongers Hall or the Royal Institute of Chartered Surveyors. They have about six sittings a year and often don't like the results.

In artists' eyes the Queen may not have a classic bone structure, but they see a contained figure with a hairstyle like Queen Beatrix, sometimes in a twinset and tweed skirt, sitting patiently without any saccharine qualities. They see a sensible, experienced, capable family woman who seems to welcome the quiet of being sculpted or painted. The Queen sees no reason why her ordinary face should not show.

CHAPTER 11

�֍ �֍ �֍

Don't You Look Lovely!

THE QUEEN PINCHED her cheeks and said with feeling, 'Look, I simply ache with smiling', and the friend who had suggested that she had looked a little withdrawn was outfaced and regretted the moment. From the time she was first in the public eye, the Queen has been plagued by pleas to 'smile more'. But she has not been blessed with a smiley face. It is a square face which in repose can look preoccupied and solemn. And the Queen will not smile inanely. The Queen Mother, on the other hand, has a sweet, round face which looks happy and contented. It makes the Queen cross and sometimes wretched when, after a day's engagement which she has enjoyed, she gets the 'Glum Queen' treatment. She once confessed to a woman friend, 'The trouble is that women are expected to be smiling all the time; it is terribly unfair. If a man looks solemn, it is automatically assumed he is a serious person, concentrating, with grave things on his mind.'

The Royal Walkabout was first tried out in Wellington, New Zealand, in 1970 and was a triumph. There was no loss of dignity, the Queen's ability to control the informal moment enhanced her, spelling out her royalty even more. Brought up in the tradition of royal stiffness – and often her own shyness still makes her appear a little remote – this was a brave step for her. The greatest walk-about, which still gives a tingle, was on the Queen's Silver Jubilee Day in 1977, when she walked through the City of London. The people roared and cheered as if saying their own 'thank you'. They had waited all night, beaming faces in funny hats, silver decorations, busty girls in T-shirts with Union Jacks, to see their Queen on this special day. Out of the cold and rain, a great roar went up when the Queen appeared, and suddenly she smiled. The gold State Coach which had brought her with Prince Philip was not needed; she began her walkabout carrying a bouquet of English-grown orchids and went towards a sea of outstretched hands. 'Don't you look lovely!' they said, quite forgetting themselves. It had been a miserable morning – and that was why the Queen wore pink.

'Oh dear, did you get awfully wet?' she asked solicitously, the pink bells on her hat bobbing furiously as she tried to talk to everyone. And she threw back her head and laughed when they replied, 'Yes, but it was well worth it to see you!' Prince Philip, in his Admiral of the Fleet uniform, was way behind, with lots of jokes for children with whistles who had waited from 5.30 am. 'Do they always make a noise like that or is it something special today?' he asked their mothers with that wry smile. And on they walked, through to St Mary le Bow where the Queen was given a silver replica of the Great Bell of Bow. All true Cockneys must be born within earshot of Bow Bells.

On that open-hearted occasion, when their Queen's walk seemed the expression of a private bond between her and her people and the ceremony and glitter of the pageantry of the Silver Jubilee for the tourists, she needed all her reserves of control and strength. There was such a surge of warmth and emotion from a people who pride themselves on being undemonstrative. The only sign that she was deeply affected was a little tremor in her neck; but otherwise it was, as always, that marvellously polished, measured walk.

Prince Philip and Prince Charles will lag behind the Queen, get involved with the people on the route with jokes, anecdotes, looking at budgies, dogs, babies – and banners; but all the time the Queen is ahead at a rhythmic pace.

The police are busy with their walkie-talkies; then there is a countdown and a vast, shining car glides soundlessly to a halt. The Queen looks rather tiny in this huge car and seems almost to walk about in it with her head down. Then the detective jumps out, lean, crisp and mouth firm. He will be ready later, with the rug to cover the Queen's knees for the journey home. At the moment of presentation the Queen smiles and those extraordinarily direct dark blue eyes seem to sum you up in a minute. After the bowing, the saluting and the curtseying, the Queen looks charmed by the

bouquet, as if it is one of the first she has ever been given. It helps
if the child presenting it is not too polished and forgets her lines; it
makes everyone laugh.

In the grounds of Leeds Castle in Kent in the spring, she wears
sensible black leather boots and a warm emerald wool coat, striding purposefully like a countrywoman to the Duckery set in a hol-
low in the woods. As the peacocks compete with the chiming of
the castle's medieval bell, the Queen says in that no-nonsense
way, as she spots some gawky Canadian geese waddling out of the
dark water, 'I've got a lot of those wretched birds in my own garden.' The conversation is much easier than expected; one almost
forgets that this is someone apart and that her back garden is the
fifty acres of the Buckingham Palace grounds.

She looks at the magnolias in bud and says wistfully, 'I always
have to go down to Windsor just when they are coming out at
Buckingham Palace.' The subtle blend of majesty and informality
makes one feel included but distanced. Then comes a strong reminder of the pressures of always being in the public eye. Leeds
Castle is looking at its prettiest but the Queen draws back, tensing
her shoulders, which are narrow. She seems to be thinking, 'Oh,
one more effort.' It is not one of her smiling days. The cameras go
up and there is the sound of the photographers' motor drives, a
remorselessly urgent gulping. Then on through the muddy grass
to a meeting with the disabled; the Queen's mood has changed
again from wary to kind, caring and interested. They have waited
in the cold for several hours and look a bit pale and pinched – sombre with illness; then suddenly the Queen approaches with a smile
and their faces flush and seem lit by her small, delicate figure
neatly picking its way round the group.

The guide dog standing docile by a wheelchair gets a royal pat.
Miss Sybil Collie presses a red feather brooch into the Queen's
hand, 'It is the emblem of the Cheshire Home.' Genuinely
pleased, the Queen says that of course she knows the Group Captain: she is Patron of the Leonard Cheshire Foundation. 'I saw him
only recently,' she says chattily, as if with friends she has not seen
for ages; then she looks at the brooch again. 'How sweet of you,
how kind,' and she moves on. There is another change of mood.
Away from the public, there is not the same need to talk and often
with the Queen there are silences; one feels in those quiet
moments how apart she is, but not in a cold, remote way. And

one is aware of the uniqueness about her as she is whisked away in the back of a large car to tea in the Fairfax Hall. Behind, the crocodile of people are becoming quite high-spirited – the visit has gone wonderfully well so far. They are chatting to the Household, who all seem to be fascinated by everything. 'Oh, how interesting, 800 revolutions per minute – really?' 'Do you all start work at six in the morning?' This in complete contrast to the mood around the Queen, the instant respect, and the silence which seems to give time to stare unashamedly as if transfixed at the enormous pendant sapphire which hangs delicately from a diamond bow on the lapel of her coat. The Queen stirs – there are children waving Union Jacks, held up by the grown-ups craning forward – and one senses a palpable aura of effort as the right hand gives a wave and then the famous smile.

The car swishes past and the children tell each other, 'I saw the Queen of England sitting on her throne in the back of her car,' and the mothers are saying, 'She smiled at us,' and there is a clamour of voices, 'No, at me,' 'At me,' 'At me.' In that split second the magic of monarchy has worked again. They waited for hours in the drizzle and it was worth every damp moment.

The Queen says that Leeds Castle has always held a tantalizing charm for her from childhood. She has often passed near to visit Lord Mountbatten's daughter, Patricia, and her family who live not far away in a pretty Kentish village of apple orchards and oast houses. But the real purpose of the Queen's visit today is to meet as many of the disabled as she can. Lord Geoffrey-Lloyd, one of the main trustees, who has done so much to make the castle the delight it is, understands this and has taken her to meet many more at the Fairfax Hall. This is an occasion when the Queen's wishes have been completely understood. There are times, though, when she wants to give more but officials close her up; perhaps they are worried in case she should become embarrassed. They need not be, for all they do is make her seem displaced, rather like a cat which has been turned off someone's lap.

Now everyone who has been escorting the Queen during the afternoon – Princess Alexandra's husband, the Hon. Angus Ogilvy, 'Oh are you a Trustee?' the Queen asked, surprised when she first saw him with John Money, the agent at Leeds Castle – stands back and admires a virtuoso performance which brings tears to the eyes. No apartness now, there is a word here or a smile there. The hall with its wooden rafters rings with a high, excited sound and one can watch the Queen 'giving'. Once, seeing how a number of blind people adapted to their disability, she remarked, 'What wonderful courage they have,' and, impressed, added, 'they were so gay. How they laughed at the mistakes they made.' This is really why she is at Leeds Castle on this cold March day.

Once that is over, she becomes different again, watched by a sea of rural Kentish faces behind the stone walls. She walks briskly across the croquet lawn to have a quick look at the moat. The Queen is withdrawn again – her work for the day is over and there is no sound except the clanging of the Catherine de Valois bell. It is as if she were an opera singer or a great actor – on stage with that magnetic quality and then afterwards, drained and exhausted. There is a tour of the castle, so lovingly restored, a quick glance at the tapestries, but the Queen is detached, interested only in the historical sense. If one lives in Buckingham Palace, Windsor Castle, Balmoral and Sandringham, fine china and furniture do not prompt the cries of admiration of the paying visitor.

There is a quick cup of tea in the drawing-room – the Trustees and their guests are waiting with cucumber sandwiches, sponge cakes, eclairs and anodyne conversation. But the Queen does not stay long; her Private Secretary, on the nod, says, 'I think we should be going.' A little relieved and with a half smile, the Queen puts her handbag firmly on her arm and says, 'Well, I can't keep everybody waiting!' The goodbyes are said in the hall beside the vast oak table with hats, walking sticks and the lead for Lord Geoffrey-Lloyd's great dane, Danny. The Queen gets into the car, its back window heaped with flowers. She waves at the cheering children and the car drives out of the great gates on to the Maidstone by-pass. She looks tired but settles back assured. In the drawing-room at Leeds the distinguished guests feel a bit flat. The Queen has hardly been there a minute, and suddenly she has gone. But over at the Fairfax Hall you would think they were drinking grand marque champagne instead of cups of tea – all the people the Queen really wanted to see are in soaringly good spirits.

Next day some of the children read the Court Circular for the first time in their lives:

> Buckingham Palace, 25th March 1981
> The Queen this afternoon visited Leeds Castle ...

Excitement and nerves can make people say amazing things. The

kooky film star Barbra Streisand asked at the 1975 screening of
Funny Lady in her New York nasal way, 'Why do women have to
wear gloves to meet you and the men don't?' Nonplussed, the
Queen stepped backwards as if hit by a missile. 'Really, I don't
know,' she said, smiling. 'It's a tradition, I suppose.' This
questioning of the royal family is quite out of order. They set the
pace of the conversation; they ask the questions. This is commonsense. But when meeting film stars – the Queen attended her first
Royal Film Performance in 1952 – she really does not object if
strict protocol is not observed. She was obviously touched by
Justin Henry, the eight-year-old star of *Kramer vs Kramer*, about a
child in the middle of a breaking marriage. 'Will it make me cry?'
asked the Queen, and the fair-haired boy looked up and said,
'Well, it might; it made my mum cry,' and looked round for his
mother, who was not in the line-up, and introduced her to the
Queen, who beamed at her.

Although the Queen may not put her arm round a child – or
give it a cuddle as the Princess of Wales might – children like this
slight distance because it is what they expect of the monarch. One
of the happiest days was at the famous Children's Party in Hyde
Park on 30 May 1979, when eighty thousand children danced on
the grass for the Queen to the tune of the 'Teddy Bears' Picnic',
hairslides and ribbons awry, chubby legs skipping – she could
hardly keep a straight face. It was the Year of the Child, and the
Queen, beaming, all in blue, was showered with posies, given
oranges, taken to see the longest sausage in the world and fed a
bun to a circus elephant which tried to eat her yellow roses.

'Can you see anything at all?' she asked fifteen-year-old Richard
Miller, who was in a wheelchair, but he nodded enthusiastically.
The Queen had said that she would appear at one big event associated with the International Year of the Child; but not a
fund-raising gala evening, she wanted to be with children. For
several hours she and the Duke were bumping into huge Kermit
Frogs and big yellow Buzby Birds. The children were superbly
well-behaved, almost too much so, an acute reminder that most of
them came from institutions. There was very little rubbish or litter, and the greatest noise was shouting 'Three cheers for the
Queen' as she rode by in her horse and carriage. 'We have had a
marvellous time,' said the Queen later.

Her diary is planned at least a year ahead and programme planning meetings are held twice a year at Buckingham Palace. An army of efficient Household staff help to sift engagements. As soon as an invitation comes in it is acknowledged and then raised at a programme meeting. But it is no use writing to Buckingham Palace and saying, 'Our hospital will be finished in three years' time. Could we invite the Queen now?' 'Sorry, but no,' is the firm reply. But also, 'Please do, by all means, write again in 1987.' The correspondence is all on cream writing paper with the royal crest in red at the top and on the envelope and signatures in blue-black ink. The planning meeting devotes mathematical attention to place, time and cause. Everyone sits around with diaries; Prince Philip asks people with colds to stay well away from him; and someone may say, 'Look, the Queen is visiting ten hospitals and no schools next spring, can we make an adjustment?' Or, if a part of the country seems to have been neglected, someone will argue, 'The West Country is getting several visits, but what about the north-east?' Flexibility is the keynote and everyone is surprisingly accommodating. If one member of the royal family cannot attend on a certain date the organizers might be encouraged to ask again or another popular member of the royal family might be free. The addition of the Princess of Wales, with her natural charm and ability to chat in a pleasantly amusing, non-controversial way, makes her an asset to the royal calendar.

In one week during the early summer of 1981 Princess Alexandra shook 455 hands, had 668 chats and met approximately 923 people. Her week included visits to a needlework exhibition in Twickenham, the opening of a leisure centre in Northern Ireland and a school in Colchester, a helicopter flight to meet a group of disabled people, an agricultural show and also the Derby.

The Queen sees through the ceremonial on visits, the flags the people dressed up and all the bunting hanging out. One of her advisers said, 'Make no mistake, she knows, too, what it is like to live in a high-rise flat.' This is an exaggeration, of course, but the Queen gets around much more than we imagine and surprised some housewives in Sheffield when she said, 'I find it difficult keeping my floors clean, too.' And she learns too from the estates at Sandringham and Balmoral, where the staff talk to her about what needs doing to their houses, and also because Princess Anne does not have an army of kitchen maids at Gatcombe. She has a minimal staff wearing jeans and everyone helps with the housework. At Sandringham a lot of the estate cottages have been prettily decorated with delicate Laura Ashley flower-sprigged wallpaper and one feels this may be the influence of the younger women in the royal family. She realizes also there are people who bitterly resent her. 'Did you say something, darling?' the Duke of Edinburgh said absently to the Queen sitting beside him in the back of the royal car in Norfolk. What she had said was, 'I quite agree with you, madam,' to a woman who had been splashed by the car. 'What did she say?' the Duke asked idly. '"Bastards!"' the Queen answered crisply, knowing there is nothing more annoying than being soaked with muddy water.

There is also the uncanny, intuitive royal knack of seeing what is, perhaps, not meant to be seen and a mischievous pleasure in the discovery. When the Queen came to the *Daily Telegraph* offices in Fleet Street, one or two of the more roistering reporters were asked if they would like the day off. They grumblingly agreed and said they would enjoy opening hours to the full. When the Queen arrived in the newsroom the goody goodies chosen to meet her were bowing and telling her about their stories on the day's news list. But out of the corner of her eye she had spotted one of the off duty men returning with flushed cheeks from a convivial lunch. To the horror of the news editor, the Queen turned and headed straight for this 'banished one'. They had a hilarious chat and he had her full attention, his tongue loosened by a few cheering 'snorts'. The Queen relished the meeting. 'Most interesting,' she commented. 'We talked about the cost of the royal train.'

CHAPTER 12

✽ ✽ ✽

Commanded by Her Majesty

'ROYAL TOURS MUST be marvellous.' They say. 'It must be wonderful going everywhere with the Queen.' Of course it is not a bit like that; they are fun, but terribly hard work. Before accompanying a royal tour, members of the press must be accredited. There is a security check, though nobody will admit it, and your photograph is put on a plastic card – with a chain to hang it round your neck.

For some trips as many as 150 journalists may apply, of whom only about fifty get accredited, a fruit-salad of correspondents from Tass, Agence France Presse, the *Daily Telegraph* and Asharq Al Aswat. Royal tours provoke a lot of jealousy, for the mistaken idea is that you are having a gracious time. Not even the Queen is having that; she and everyone involved are working incredibly hard, so tremendous stamina is needed. The remorseless organization means that early starts are inevitable. Suitcases are placed outside the bedroom doors at 5 am and that evening are at the next stop, sitting in the new hotel room with a distinctive red label saying Royal Tour Party. There was a time when the media travelled with the royal party, until a photographer, who is no longer working on tours, became rather happy on the flight and was down the aircraft steps and on to the red carpet before the royal couple. Nowadays reporters are occasionally invited to fly in the Queen's back-up plane and, more rarely, allowed to travel in the Queen's Andover, but not to see her dozing with her shoes off at the front of the aircraft.

Immediately on arrival the photographers set up dark rooms in their hotel bedrooms. Peter Kemp, who worked for Associated

Press and looks like a frenetic Shakespearean actor, remembers how in Casablanca, on the ill-fated tour of Morocco, the chambermaid walked in and found Les Lee standing in the bath drying off some negatives. Lee, a highly-respected photographer of many years on the *Daily Express*, is a tall, rangy man with spectacles who would never be taken as a likely candidate for bathtime frolics. Kemp was sitting on the lavatory with his back to the door and the whole place was draped with black cloth. Unless the Moroccan chambermaid was a keen sophisticated photographer, it must have been a baffling sight; what could she have made of the bidet which was being used as a tank for developer and the fixer which was in a bowl on the floor, with a long flex plugged into a power point? From such primitive conditions, glamorous, glossy pictures of the Queen flash all over the world. In equally small rooms the ITN crews fuss over the twenty-one boxes of new video equipment.

The Queen, who does not need a passport, has now made fifty tours and visited a hundred countries. The Foreign Office sees royal tours as 'frightfully cost-effective', their value incalculable, and invitations come in 'from all over the shop'. It used to be the job of Sir Roger du Boulay, a member of the royal Household also attached to the Foreign Office, to look at them first. He has now retired with honour and been replaced by the Hon. Eustace Gibbs. Sooner or later it is felt that the Queen may go to China and perhaps in time even invitations to Iron Curtain countries will not be refused. At the Foreign Office there is a long list of countries owed a visit, against which the Department of Trade and the Ministry of Defence put in their pleas. These invitations are discussed at the highest level; advice is submitted with the Prime Minister's knowledge and approval. The underlying feeling is that the Queen is a 'very big gun indeed – so be careful where you aim it!' Indeed the Foreign Office thinks of all the royal family as performing stars. Princess Margaret is, surprisingly, seen as something of a trouper. She gave value on a visit to Swaziland – was a great hit and endured gamely the heat, hours of tribal dancing 'and the air smelly with all those half-cured skins'.

Once a visit is established by the Foreign Office and the host country in principle, there is an exchange of talks and ideas. A complicated bureaucracy takes over as routes and costs are worked out. Occasionally, however, there is a late hiccough caused by political changes, or when, for example, the Queen's early summer visit to Sweden was planned for May/June 1982, before it was known that the Swedish Queen would be having her baby around the same time as the Princess of Wales.

A swing round Australasia for the Queen as the head of this multiple monarchy, seemed to make opening the Commonwealth Games in Brisbane a suitable engagement for late 1982, to be dovetailed into a sail in *Britannia* round the remaining bits of the Commonwealth – to places like Hohola in Papua-New Guinea.

Return invitations follow a State visit after a suitable three- or four-year lapse and are much valued by visiting Heads of State. The only tour ever cancelled was that of the President of Indonesia, who had flu. The King of Morocco will be on a future guest list and it is thought that he will respect the rules. A lot of headaches were expected when President Ceaucescu of Rumania visited; after all he had cut his visit to Norway short, flying home from Stavanger. There is a mischievous story that the visit by Ceaucescu to Britain happened by mistake, that it had been set up by Julian Amery without the Palace's wholehearted approval, but in the event it went surprisingly well.

When the Queen accepts in writing, her Private Secretary, Sir Philip Moore, takes over for the next stage. He sends a six-thousand-word letter to the hosts advising them that the Queen prefers not to start her engagements before 10 am and these days prefers hospitality in the sergeant's mess rather than the officers' on the grounds that more people can be met that way. Simple flowers, rather than wired bouquets, are preferred, not reddish-purple as fuchsia is a colour the Queen is not happy with and does not wear; gifts should be inexpensive: simple, sentimental even, but not commercial.

Long lunches and banquets are cut to a minimum; although Oeufs Drumkilbo, a shrimp dish, is a great favourite at the Palace, the Queen will not risk eating shellfish abroad. Just as dangerous as shellfish was the cuisine in Tonga, where they dug great deep trenches and filled them with warm stones surrounding chubby piglets for days and days of slow cooking. Eventually these were served to the Queen on a hot February day in 1977 as part of a traditional feast laid before her in a hut made of coconut and bamboo leaves. After grace the delicate muslin was lifted from the bamboo supports to reveal to the Queen her very own suckling pig with a rather desperate look in his eye and a curl in his tail. The Queen tried not to look too apprehensive as she was also given a turkey, two lobsters, water melon, yams, huge bananas and a coconut. Pretty girls in white with belts made from the bark of the traditional Taovala tree kept their guest cool with fans from the prickly-leaved pandanus. The Queen looked earnest and toyed with a bit of turkey and pineapple, doing her clever trick of concentrating on the King's conversation, and pushing her food about. But there was not a lot of conversation from the King of Tonga – Taufa 'hau Tupou IV – who likes to concentrate on his food. When he weighed over thirty stone he needed the airport scales to check it.

About six months before a tour a team from Buckingham Palace, led by the Queen's Deputy Private Secretary and including her detective, a press secretary and a royal baggage handler, set out on the reconnaissance. Every detail is worked out, down to the last minute. The press secretary works on accreditation and accommodation – then camera positions, press corners, transport and the 'Pool'. This is used where there is room for only a limited number of photographers, who are elected by the others to provide pictures for all.

Brigadier Stewart Cooper, who was given the temporary title of Queen's Canadian Secretary, is a meticulous man with a small moustache and clear blue eyes. His job was to smooth the plans for the royal visit to Canada in 1973. Before the royal visit to Ontario, Prince Edward Island, Regina, Saskatchewan and Calgary, he made eighty sorties altogether: 'Just to make sure everything was A1. There always has to be a delicate division of the Queen's time and, in Ontario, they wanted her to unveil a War Memorial. Well, it was pointed out by the team that this was an old one, which had been moved, so we suggested that the Queen would be pleased to "reconsecrate" it.' Brigadier Cooper remembers life being made much easier for him on the recce by the presence of Sir William Heseltine from Buckingham Palace. 'The people would accept things from him about wearing hats, gloves, etc. which they might not from me.'

Planning a royal visit does not mean that the co-ordinating team has *carte blanche* to commandeer any aircraft or transport in the host country it needs.

Early in January 1973 Brigadier Cooper put in his bid for

coaches for the royal train. 'I realized that, apart from the Governor General's two special carriages, we should need much more
rolling stock to accommodate the royals. Bedrooms, two room-
ettes for security, a dining-room, a State Room and a Royal Diner;
plus accommodation for the Household, a carriage for the media –
a party of between sixty and seventy, some dropping-off at different stops, an office carriage, a carriage for a post office and
another for dry cleaning where Miss MacDonald could press the
Queen's clothes.'

The recce team from the Palace sit round a table with detectives
and civil servants from the host country, planning, in almost
absurdly fussy detail, not every hour of the tour ahead but every
second. The co-ordinator always has to think the worst and there
are 'Jeremiah Sheets' in case anything goes wrong. They must
remember that the visit, though planned in the winter, will be taking place in summer and so there will be the benefit of more daylight. With air travel allowances must be made for the crossing of
time zones. Sometimes a last-minute discovery may mean that
forty minutes instead of twenty are needed for a journey by car
between two points and so a scheduled visit may have to be
dropped.

The Queen must get her State papers wherever she is, even
when she is looking at Eskimo sculpture in as remote a place as
Yellowknife. These 'red boxes' – secure containers covered in
scarlet leather and measuring 38 by 28cm (15 by 11 inches) – go by
Queen's Messenger in the diplomatic bag. He usually travels with
a spare seat beside him for the diplomatic bag and it helps to have
the bladder of a camel, restricting the number of visits to the lavatory, the nervous pastime of so many passengers on long-haul
flights. When the boxes reached Canada they were flown on by
the Air Force Mounted Police Carrier using Interceptor Fighter
Planes. Once the papers arrived from London, where they had
been dealt with by a Private Secretary, only the Queen or her
accompanying Private Secretary could unlock them. On tours
abroad, it is in the early morning or again between five and six,
when most of the Household are relaxing for the first time in the
day, that she works on her papers.

When the exploratory party returns to London, the Queen and
Prince Philip go over the schedule with the shrewdness of years of
travel. Prince Philip is sharp on logistics and will often point out:

'Look here, it is impossible to visit this school and still get to X on time.' The Queen, who has the last word on the programme, may say: 'Oh, but couldn't you lop half an hour off here?' Brigadier Cooper, who today lives in a cottage in Oxfordshire, where he is a churchwarden and chairman of an Army Benevolent Fund, was called to Windsor to an informal lunch with the Queen, Prince Philip, Princess Anne and Prince Charles; they almost played trains on the tablecloth as they planned that visit to Canada.

Each day's programme during a visit is likely to be very full, but there is usually a two-hour rest period from about 5 pm before changing for a dinner party or evening engagement. Eventually everything is set down in a royal booklet designed to help the Household, which may include the Queen's dresser, the maids, the ladies-in-waiting; the Queen's page, the travelling yeoman, the footmen, the equerries and the Page of the Presence; the royal chef, the sous-chef, the senior cook, the dining-room supervisor, his two assistants, a kitchen porter and an orderly – although such a grand entourage would only be needed in an emerging country where a Royal Banquet could be too much for local staff to handle. A second booklet is drawn up, with notes especially for the journalists.

Once the programme is planned, the protocol is checked; security is arranged – these days it plays a much larger role – transport and accommodation are booked. Good hotels with efficient switchboards and, if possible, international dialling from the bedrooms are essential; quaint hostelries with old-world charm only lead to frantic journalists arguing with distraught slow-moving hotel staff – and bad feelings all round.

A press room is laid on by the host Government with a constant supply of tea, coffee, beer and sandwiches until about four in the morning. There is desperate activity around five and six in the evening. Telex machines hop, often jealously watched for incoming messages. Television people get 'herograms' for surprisingly little effort: 'Your 2 minutes: 1 second decimated opposition. Greatest – best.' While high praise from a newspaper such as the *Daily Telegraph* might be a cautious, 'That didn't work out too badly, dear,' but much more appreciated for all its phlegmatic brevity.

There are interminable briefings the day before the Queen arrives and rows amongst the photographers and television

cameramen about positions and pools which are finally settled by
an almost military order and discipline that is recognized by the
Palace. 'It always amazes me to see you walking backwards,' the
Queen marvels at their precision as she approaches the photographers on a walkabout. There is a strange bond between the Queen
and these cameramen and if they have all been in a tricky skirmish,
manhandled by security, she may have a word with one of the
Household. The photographers can be used as security, too, creating a barrier around her at vulnerable moments. When the *Daily
Mirror* photographer Freddy Reed fell over a wall, he was asked by
the Queen later, 'Where did you disappear to?' This is called the
MP, the moving position. Tim Graham, neat, compact and nick-
named 'Squirrel', is the thinking photographer and snapped the
Queen putting her face on when a roof collapsed near her in Fiji.
Arthur Edwards, who follows the Prince and Princess of Wales
more, has a record of exclusives and a cheeky Cockney humour.
He can get away with remarks like the one in India, 'What we
want, Sir, is you with a stick-on turban and a polo stick, on top of
this elephant we've got outside.' Prince Charles grinned.

'You will not photograph the Queen eating or drinking. You
will not focus your lenses on her face for longer than a few
seconds. You will not photograph the Queen in a position of
hazard.' (This means when climbing up or down into something
like the Royal Barge.) 'The dignity of a formal ceremony must not
be impaired.' If a photographer breaks this unwritten code, or
goes too close to the Queen, he may get whacked with a rolled-up
umbrella by her press secretary. There is a lot of hysterical high
spirits on royal tours but, towards the end of the day, most of the
photographers are hanging around the telexes to see what kind of
'spread' they got just when the Far Eastern operators are trying to
get in a quiet prayer to the great god Shiva, do a bit of yoga or nod
off. There are arguments and rows with offices at first edition
time, elation or depression and then off to bed for another 6 am
start to get ahead of the Queen as she visits a liquefied petroleum
gas project or a sports centre. Briefings are usually at 7.30 am,
more for grouses and pleadings than information.

In addition to the usual inoculations against tetanus, polio and
yellow fever the Queen takes sophisticated anti-malaria pills and,
although the Press may be thought of as 'obligatory pests', they
are looked after by her Household in far-flung places. Mosquito

bites became a travelling entertainment, and one of the Queen's ladies-in-waiting – the jokey Mrs John Dugdale – used to crane over the rail as the royal yacht berthed to peer at the notorious legs of certain members of the female press; but the unsightly nibbles were covered by long cotton skirts.

The Queen's best parties on tour tend to be on board the *Britannia*. She always seems more relaxed and, apart from the Household, there are plenty of sun-tanned Naval officers only too pleased to pass a crisp and to enjoy acting as courtiers. The alternative is a reception in the British Embassy, usually more formal and lacking that sense of being entertained by the Queen at home. So for the press, amongst office cables, airline tickets, cameras, typewriters and heated hair rollers, there is a handsome cream envelope with the royal crest which is propped against the mirror; inside is an invitation with a gold E II R and crown at the top. It may mean an almighty last-minute scramble after a day following the Queen, changing in the middle of shouting to London or, worse, getting cut off in the middle of phoning copy. Make-up starts to run with the aggravation and one is likely to scurry off to meet the Queen still wearing walkabout flatties, with mascara on only one eye and in a white dress streaked with ink. For the photographers it is even worse. Just before 6 pm they are either chasing to the airport or developing films; but they get collars and ties on, change into suits and hide their cameras.

But no matter how sticky, how harassed, as soon as one lines up to meet the Queen and Prince Philip a calm takes over which has nothing to do with the silver trays or large gin and tonics, whiskies or sherries being offered. The drinks are curiously Establishment, old-fashioned; there is never white wine or vermouth. One is generally shepherded to the Queen by a member of the Household, having curtsied to her and shaken hands with the Duke in the reception line on the way in. She is always addressed as 'Your Majesty' when one is first announced; after that it's 'Ma'am' (pronounced 'Marm'). Prince Philip is 'Your Royal Highness' at first and then 'Sir'. The more dishevelled, hot and raggy you feel, the more welcome you are made. In Colombo, in the autumn of 1981, a group on the way to the Queen's reception got stuck in a taxi which ran into a bullock cart. In the desperate midday sun interminable arguments began, while both drivers, with their Eastern approach to eternity, stood on spindly legs in their wrap-around skirts amiably discussing the matter in high-pitched voices. Everyone jumped out in neat frocks and dark suits, several hundred rupees were exchanged and, drenched in perspiration, the group set out on foot for the party, already a few minutes late. Make-up running, hair ruined by the humidity, even the frangipani stuck, in desperation, behind the left ear, earned a 'You look somewhat bedraggled' comment from Sir William Heseltine. But from the Queen it was all consideration, amused smiles and chat about cool things: 'I heard from Balmoral that there is snow on the ground there and berries on the holly trees. A sign of a cold winter – that is if you believe the old wives' tales,' making everyone feel refreshed.

Nobody will give this advice but, at her own parties, the Queen actually likes you to keep the conversation going, so that the burden of finding something to talk about does not always rest with her. 'Oh come and listen to this, Philip,' the Queen said, laughing out loud as Chris Buckland, now Foreign Editor of the *Mirror*, embarked upon a story which he had rather panicked over initially, but somehow got away with, being an extremely amusing and rather audacious Yorkshireman. 'Oh do listen to this,' the Queen said with her head on one side. Chris was telling of their arrival once in the Bahamas at Nassau Airport. The reporters had just flown in from Canada and were too late to stand in their usual Pool on the tarmac, so where else to observe the arrival than the bar, helped by a cooling Cuba Libre? 'Heah come de Queen and de Duke down de ayahkraft steps lookin' quait smart and quait fit,' Buckland imitated the commentator on Nassau radio and that description of the Duke of Edinburgh, in the full-dress uniform of Admiral of the Fleet amused both the Queen and Prince Philip enormously. It had a special appeal for the Queen, who is an excellent mimic.

The Queen makes talking to her like this easy; the photographers and reporters, of course, are usually relieved to have got copy and pictures away before the reception, so they are jokey and unselfconscious. But although the Queen is as relaxed as the people she is talking to one never forgets that she is the sovereign. She generally wears a simple tailored dress in one of her favourite blues or apricots, with very little jewellery, a string of pearls which is not at all intimidating, a simple wrist watch and very few rings.

It is quite clear when the Queen wants to move on from a group

Glowing motherhood. This was the first picture of Princess Elizabeth and the Duke of Edinburgh with Prince Charles, released in April 1949. The portrait was by Baron, a photographer who was a friend of the Duke of Edinburgh.

Left This is the last time George VI saw his elder daughter. Although frail, he insisted on braving the harsh weather to be at London Airport to wave goodbye as Princess Elizabeth and the Duke of Edinburgh set off on a tour of the Commonwealth early in 1952.

Below Having succeeded to the throne at a game lodge in Kenya only the day before, Queen Elizabeth II arrives at London Airport with the Duke of Edinburgh on 7 February 1952. Earl Mountbatten is on the left.

Left Shortly before coming to the throne, Princess Elizabeth enjoyed some traditional square dancing in Ottawa during a royal tour of Canada in December 1951. The Princess's dresser Miss Margaret 'Bobo' MacDonald had to rush out to the shops and buy a skirt for the princess for the Barn Dance. Dancers noticed that the Duke of Edinburgh's jeans still had their price tag attached.

Above Relaxed days and no sign of a detective as the Queen drives her Daimler to a sporting event with Prince Charles, Princess Anne and a nanny.

Left The Coronation. The Queen returns to Buckingham Palace from Westminster Abbey.

Above The young Queen helps Princess Anne clamber up a wall while Prince Charles guards his sister's rear.

Above Sir Winston Churchill was always enchanted by the Queen. Here he is proudly holding open the door of the royal car as the Queen and the Duke of Edinburgh leave 10 Downing Street after a dinner party given by the Prime Minister and Lady Churchill. The Duke of Edinburgh enjoys the moment and Lady Churchill smiles.

Top Wearing fashionable long black gloves, the Queen shades her eyes as she watches the Comet bearing her mother and sister to Southern Rhodesia in June 1953 and waits until the plane has disappeared from view. The Queen Mother was opening the Rhodes Centenary Exhibition in Salisbury.

Above The Queen skilfully manages four corgis at Liverpool Street station on her return from her six-week holiday at Sandringham in February 1968. The four corgis are Heather, Buzz, Foxy and Tiny.

Top left The Queen visits Edinburgh in July 1952. In the entourage behind the Queen's lady-in-waiting, Lady Alice Egerton, is Captain the Viscount Althorp, an equerry to the Queen. He later became Earl Spencer and father of the Princess of Wales.

Left Racy and dashing, the Queen and the Duke of Edinburgh on a royal tour of Nigeria in 1956. The Queen is wearing a Hardy Amies blue and white embossed cotton dress.

The Queen always discusses forthcoming tours with her dress designers and they submit sketches and swatches of fabric. The sketches on these pages were by Hardy Amies. The white lace dress with fitted bodice, square neckline and straight skirt with fulness in the back was for the Queen's tour of Australia and New Zealand in 1953 and 1954. It made the most of the Queen's tiny waist and the photograph taken at a garden party in Sydney in February 1954 was a great favourite of Earl Mountbatten.

The Queen's visit to the Gulf proved one of the greatest challenges for her designers. Often the Queen had to wear long dresses in the daytime to conform with Arab etiquette, particularly in Saudi Arabia. This self-printed jade chiffon with a turban in the same material by milliner Frederick Fox was aimed at capturing the jewelled colours of the desert and the flowing robes of the sheiks.

The Queen's clothes for the State visit to France in May 1972 were planned with elaborate care. Mme Pompidou (opposite page), wife of the French President, looks admiringly at the Queen's evening dress as they walk to the state banquet at the Palace of Versailles.

Left The Queen arrives in Saudi Arabia in 1979 in stunning full-length blue. She is met by King Khaled at Riyadh Airport. Note that the Queen, always practical, refused to let her scarf flutter in the breeze in case it rudely landed on an Arab prince's beard.

Below The Queen had a smart new ensemble each day during the royal tour of Denmark in May 1979 and so too did the fashionable Danish Queen Margrethe.

Above The Queen's thrifty approach to her clothes is nicely illustrated in this and the adjacent photograph. The red and white polka dotted ensemble was specially designed for the Gulf. Long flowing scarf is securely on her arm.

Right The outfit designed for the Gulf is neatly shortened and is worn here during a visit to the Commonwealth Institute, Kensington, in July 1981 when the Queen opened the Festival of Sri Lanka. Here the Queen, who is not trammelled by the flowing scarf, and Prince Philip watch dancers with Prime Minister Premadasa of Sri Lanka.

at one of her parties – there will be a sort of finishing smile and a gentle half-step backwards. As she leaves the group it is immediately taken over by one of the Household. Groomed equerries pirouetting on gleaming black shoes, the ladies-in-waiting with neat hairdos, pale skins and tailored dresses; all skilled in the art of conversation. One of the reasons why the Princess of Wales was the right raw material for a future Queen of England was an early education at Riddlesworth Hall, her prep school near Diss, in Norfolk, where the art of conversation was taught: polite conversation means a neutral subject and should never go too far. The Household are so skilled in this that one wonders if, when they go home, these nice people go on with the same innocuous talk. 'Don't you think, Camilla, that this sixteenth-century architrave is frightfully decorative?'

As quickly as the Queen appears, she vanishes with an equal lack of fuss; leaving the ladies-in-waiting craning their necks. 'Her Majesty has gone,' and the party is over.

CHAPTER 13

❀ ❀ ❀

Abroad is not Awful

GEORGE V HAD a grumpy view of royal tours. 'Abroad is awful,' he said after visits to Europe. 'I know because I've been there.' His granddaughter may secretly share that view when dignitaries make long-winded boring speeches, the King of Morocco leaves her sitting at the foot of the Atlas Mountains without so much as a sandwich until four in the afternoon, or when she is being rocked from side to side by eager warriors carrying her on a wooden plat-form in the Pacific. But the Queen is proud to be the most travel-led monarch in Britain's history.

The cost of royal tours has never been published but it surely would be a false economy if the Queen never went abroad. The Foreign Office regards all tours the Queen does overseas as 'cast-iron boosts for trade and goodwill.'

Looking back on twelve royal tours: Finland in 1976, Luxem-bourg the same year, the South Pacific, Australia and New Zea-land in 1977; the Federal Republic of Germany and the Gulf in 1978; Denmark the following summer, and Africa later that year; Switzerland in April 1980, and in October the Vatican and the Maghreb; May 1981 Norway, and later in 1981 Australia, New Zealand and Sri Lanka, it is the silly, delightful things that one remembers. The Queen's diffident, 'I'm afraid this is rather small,' when she handed a modest gift to a sheikh's wife. Seeing Elizabeth the Second, by the Grace of God of the United Kingdom of Great Britain and Northern Ireland and of Her Other Realms and Terri-tories Queen, Head of the Commonwealth, Defender of the Faith, gliding through the tunnel of love in the Tivoli Gardens during the royal tour of Denmark; watching Her Majesty get on to a bus in Sri Lanka. Or in Zambia, when it was too dangerous for the Press to go on in their own chartered planes and they were given a lift with the Queen's luggage in a lumbering Hercules. The Press sat strapped in among crates of royal china and cases of excellent claret, which did not go untasted, while above them swayed one of the gifts to the Queen – a gloomy looking eland head. Or on the Gulf tour when a carrier bag full of Longines watches arrived in the coffee-shop of the hotel one morning, to be shared out among members of the Press corps. They are now worth well over £1,000. The journalists fared better than members of the royal Household, who were given much more elaborate jewelled watches covered with rubies and emeralds, but with a picture of the Arab ruler on the face, making them far too flash to wear.

Although Zambia, the Gulf and all the Commonwealth tours are of 'incalculable value', those one remembers are tinged with old-fashioned, 'Queen Empress' grandeur or with the sparkling elegance that characterized her 1980 visit to the Vatican; there was the naïve charm of the Silver Jubilee tour in 1977 and, more recently, Sri Lanka, with its caparisoned elephants with glitter on their decorated faces, bright lights and fire dancers.

The Queen has an unswerving confidence in her mission as Head of State, and when she went to Sri Lanka in 1981 they loved the old links with the Empire. Even though Sri Lanka is now a republic they remembered that it was as Queen of Ceylon too that she first visited this island some twenty-seven years before. The welcome was tinged with bygone splendour and thousands huddled for days and nights in monsoon rain under their black umbrellas to see her car as she drove through the forest up to Kandy, escorted by trumpeters in orange robes and musicians with conch shells.

The Duke of Edinburgh slipped away one day to see the old car he had bought when he was a Royal Navy Midshipman; there it was, gleaming like all the old Morris and Austins so lovingly cherished in India and Sri Lanka, though the horns do get overworked alerting the 'brake inspectors' as the bullocks are called. Buddhist monks clung precariously to the balconies to see the Head of the Church of England; schoolgirls in prim white blouses, gym slips and straw hats waved under parasols.

The Queen was taken to the sacred Bo tree; she had to remove her shoes and did a most unexpected commercial for Air New Zealand, which was stamped on her navy socks; they had been hastily found by a courtier for the muddy walk. At the dam being built with British money the father of the boy Marcus Sarjeant, who had fired a shot at the Queen during the Trooping the Colour ceremony in June 1981, was given the day off to avoid embarrassment.

It would be doing the royal family a grave disservice to imagine that they do not see through pompous bureaucracy. In the Caribbean in 1977 the Queen and Prince Philip were well aware of the economic problems and saw the poverty hidden behind a touching veneer of fresh paint. In India Prince Charles darted away from an official party to nip into a Harijan hut which was not jazzed up for the royal visit like the one he had just been shown, its smiling family an untypical picture of well being.

The royal baggage always includes China and Indian tea; fruit cake and shortbread biscuits; Malvern water, jam, barley sugar for energy, English mint sauce, sausages from Harrods. When Prince Charles was trekking in Nepal a message was sent from a remote Gurkha village to get sausages for the royal breakfast. Everything is loaded into chests marked with a cross and for each member of the royal family there is a different colour. These chests and cases either go ahead in the *Britannia* or are flown out in the Hercules or in a VC-10 – the RAF's 'Regal One' – supervised by the unflappable travelling yeoman Frank Holland, who patiently checks off the Queen's luggage – blue trunks simply marked 'The Queen' in gold letters.

Immediately the Queen arrives in a foreign country the maid puts out all her brushes, combs and mirrors, family photographs, a favourite feather pillow and a hot water bottle, and piles of white nylon gloves size 7. Silver brooches, silver pencils, cufflinks with the cypher, silver-framed photographs, cigarette lighters and powder compacts are taken as gifts. They are in excellent taste and represent timeless British workmanship, although they may sometimes appear trifling alongside an Arab stallion or a pound of diamonds, which is the sort of thing the Queen is given, or even a baby crocodile.

'No, I am here to see the people, not the scenery,' the Queen said firmly, turning down a visit to the Arctic Circle on a tour of Finland in 1976. Being a light eater, she also turned down Finnish breakfasts of rye porridge or pea soup. The Duke of Edinburgh had a sauna. The Queen, paying the first visit of a British monarch to Finland, tasted smoked reindeer and cloudberries and indulged a childhood fascination with fire engines. Over an hour was spent at Fire Brigade headquarters in Helsinki inspecting the bright crimson equipment. 'Royal Frenzy' the Finnish newspapers cried. The Queen had drawn the biggest crowd since Finland, formerly an autonomous grand duchy under the Tsar, declared itself independent in 1917. The tall, domed President Kekkonen was a punctilious host, towering above the Queen.

'Eee-liz-a-bet' thousands cheered in Bonn three years later at the start of the second State visit to West Germany. Security men of the Federal Frontier Guard – the force which provided the GSG-9 commandos which successfully stormed the Lufthansa airliner at Mogadishu – looked ill at ease pretending to be gardeners. Prince Philip chatted easily in fluent German. It was a warm day in West Berlin when the Queen made one of the most compelling and committed speeches of her reign. Her voice gathered strength as she spoke from the steps of the Blue Church – the divided City's war memorial. Thirteen years before, on a healing mission to West Germany after two world wars, the Queen had made a cautious low-key speech after an emotional stop at the Berlin wall. Now there was an eerie stillness. Old people had come across from East Berlin; some had paid £62.00 for seats; the balconies were crammed and young people climbed on to the branches of Linden trees to listen.

'My soldiers and men stationed in Berlin embody the British commitment to defend your freedom for as long as need be; till the division in Europe – and in your city – can be healed,' the Queen said firmly. Who says that she never makes political speeches? Matrons hugging poodles wept; street buskers in black and white stopped and waved bowler hats – hot chocolate, coffee and Black Forest cake were abandoned as the whole of the Kurfürstendamm thanked the Queen. 'I especially wished to return to Berlin where thirteen years ago you gave me such a heartwarming welcome,' the Queen said simply. She was wearing a large white hat trimmed with flowers, and her spectacles. It had been a tense day, with a rather macabre start in the Maifeld Stadium where Hitler had rallied the young people. The music was the Ride of the Valkyries and then there was the *feu-de-joie*. When the troops fired in unison it sounded like the ripping of silk across Berlin. Army helicopters sprayed the sky with red, blue

and white mist, forming a Union Jack which softened the gaunt-
ness of the stadium.

Bremen was all rather lighthearted after Berlin. The Queen
walked along the cobbled streets of the 'Doll Town' of Grimms'
fairytales. 'Have you been waiting long?' or 'Do you work here?'
were enough to produce a rapt 'Yes' from women standing behind
the barrier, who, when the Queen passed on to the next group,
couldn't speak, as if touched by a heavenly light.

At the start of the German visit, Helmut Schmidt had made it
plain that he found the whole thing rather a bore. He explained to
the Queen that he would not be able to accompany her on every
occasion. But it was quite remarkable how, as the visit proved an
obvious success, he kept turning up; quite often where he had not
been expected.

The Queen's finely-tuned sense of what is politically and diplomatically right was never better illustrated than on a desperately
muddy, depressing day towards the end of the tour. There was
something comical but also very nostalgic about the sight of the
Queen entertaining the German Navy on board her yacht. Much
of the morning had been spent bobbing about in the fog-bound
North Sea on manoeuvres. While many of the party felt decidedly
seasick, the Queen presided at the lunch table in excellent spirits,
surrounded by German Admirals. In a sense it was a final seal of
friendship with the Federal Republic of Germany – a rather emo-
tive and symbolic seal on the bond disturbed by events in 1914 and
1939.

In Bremerhaven – where the emigrants used to sail for the New
World – the *Britannia* was the next best thing to seeing the Queen
for the fishermen and their wives; a plump people whose familiar
talking point is the annual production target of eight million liver
dumplings, much in demand in Bavaria. 'Would you like to play
with these,' the Queen said jokingly to Prince Philip as they both
looked at some miniatures of the Kaiser's fleet, and for a moment
he stopped speaking German to his guide.

Glamour, excitement, style and flamboyance marked the
Queen's visit to America for the bicentennial celebrations in 1976.
The Queen's first words as she stepped on American soil were: 'I
speak to you as the direct descendant of George III ... he was the
last crowned sovereign to rule in this country.'

These opening words from the great, great, great, great granddaughter of George III in Philadelphia, the city where the Declaration of Independence was signed in 1776, set the seal on the proud rejoicing. The Americans were delighted that the Queen and Prince Philip should join them in celebrating freedom from the tyranny of one of her ancestors. For the first time since Watergate Americans were letting their hair down; the United States had relaxed, self-esteem was coming back. In six days the Queen and Prince Philip were whisked from Philadelphia to Washington, to New York and Boston, to parties, to Harlem, to Wall Street, to gala evenings and as the crowds stretched out their arms to her through the heat – hardly ever below 100 degrees Fahrenheit – they thought her 'really cool and ... well, yummy'. It was frantic, exhausting but dazzling – enjoyed as much by the Queen as by the American people.

The Queen and Prince Philip had flown by RAF VC-10 from Northolt to Bermuda with eight members of the royal Household and also the new Foreign Secretary, Anthony Crosland, and his American wife, Susan. The tour began on 6 July, but beforehand there were a few sedate days at sea on *Britannia*.

When *Britannia* sailed in to Philadelphia on 6 July there was an exuberant vitality about the city where the Quaker William Penn had landed a hundred years before independence and claimed the land. Massed bands played Sousa marches, and the Queen looked relaxed and cool in navy and white stripes at the head of a cavalcade, waving at the crowds from an open car. The Queen may have admitted afterwards that it was 'frightfully hot in Philadelphia' but you would never have guessed that she was being bothered by the heat.

Presenting the new six-ton Bicentennial Bell cast in the foundry at Whitechapel in London where the original Liberty Bell had been produced, the Queen said diplomatically, 'Britain should celebrate Independence Day as much as America and in sincere gratitude to the founding fathers of this great republic for teaching Britain a very valuable lesson. We lost the American colonies because we lacked the statesmanship to know the right time and the manner of yielding what was impossible to keep. In the following 150 years we learned to keep more closely to the principles of Magna Carta which have been the common heritage of both our countries. We learned to respect the right of others to govern themselves in their own way.'

After a speech like that the Americans took the Queen completely to their hearts. The carnival atmosphere took off with music by mounted hussars and a banquet in the Art Museum where the city's Mayor Rizzo – a dark-set Italian American – was so delighted with the occasion that he was in a constant dilemma as he sat beside the Queen that night; whether he should talk more to his royal guest or use the goodwill of the occasion to rush off to 'press the flesh'.

Leaving the city of Brotherly Love the Queen next went to Washington where she was welcomed on the White House lawns by President Ford, and military bands played 'Rule Britannia'. The Queen replied and spoke warmly about Anglo-American friendship which had 'brought benefits beyond measure to the people of both countries'. That night there was a gala banquet for the Queen and the 224 guests invited by President Ford included some of the Queen's favourite artists – Cary Grant, Telly Savalas, Alistair Cooke and Merle Oberon. There was a fanfare of fourteen silver trumpets, then after New England lobster, saddle of veal, ice cream with raspberries, President Ford led the dancing with the Queen. The President, fifteen stone and six foot two, waltzed with the Queen to the tune 'Getting to Know You' in the air-conditioned pavilion set up in the White House rose garden.

The Queen's next partner was Vice-President Nelson Rockefeller – rather a smooth dancer – so the Queen, in a citron organza dress embroidered with beads and a golden od motif, was whirled across the floor and seemed to be having more fun with this partner. Bob Hope – another royal favourite and newly created CBE – entertained and the Queen said she was reluctant to leave the party at 12.40 am.

Her banquet for President Ford was at the British Embassy. There was a reception in the gardens for 1,600 guests, who admired the Queen, the 5,000 blooms sent by American growers and speculated about what the Henry Moore statue might mean. The actress Elizabeth Taylor turned up in a low cut slinky sequined slip of a dress. The Queen was wearing a minty cool shade of green with bands of gold and a spectacular diamond and pearl tiara.

'It sounds very painful,' said the Queen solicitously to one of her guests, the heavyweight Muhammad Ali, who was recovering from a bout with a Japanese wrestler. For once Ali had been tongue-tied but afterwards he recovered enough to say: 'I've met all the Kings now I've met the Queen of England.'

At the banquet Mrs Crosland fainted during the soup course. 'When Her Majesty is unwell, Madam, she sometimes finds that Malvern water helps,' the Queen's footman had suggested. But it was too late, Mrs Crosland slipped, split her face and broke her jaw.

The Queen's doctor and the President's doctor left the banquet to look after her and she was whisked to the Bethesda Hospital worrying all the time about her niece, another Susan, aged fifteen who was due at the reception that night at 10 pm. But the Queen with typical thoughtfulness made a special fuss of the teenage girl and had a long talk with her about horses.

At a lunch in Washington given by the Vice-President and Mr Carl Albert, Speaker of the House of Representatives, the Queen recalled her previous State visit to Washington, in 1975, and said she thought that the world was now in some ways 'more troubled and uncertain than it had been then'.

In New York the royal yacht was glamorously anchored in the Hudson River right in the centre of Manhattan. The New Yorkers went wild and the security men had to link arms in a hopeless attempt to keep people back as the Queen laughingly was swept to the City Hall.

She shopped in Bloomingdales and insisted on going to Harlem. There was a hundred-yard walk down the ticker-taped street to Trinity Church where the Queen was made an honorary citizen. 'Let me see her,' the crowd yelled. Police used their fists, swung the odd karate chop and even hit each other on the head at times.

In Boston the 'Get Out of Ireland' protesters were few and in Massachusetts there was a man on stilts wrapped in a Union Jack cheering the royal guests.

Sailing into the city – the scene of the Boston Tea Party – the royal yacht was escorted by hundreds of ships as part of the naval welcome. The oldest American warship, the USS *Constitution*, 179 years old gave a twenty-one-gun salute from its elderly cannons. Boston was stimulating and everything went right.

Henry Kissinger, Secretary of State, went on board the royal yacht for dinner at Newport, Rhode Island, and summed up the feelings of a lot of Americans when he described the Queen as 'a very interesting lady with a lot of savvy'.

The Queen opened the Montreal Games and then settled down to fourteen-hour days meeting Redskin Chiefs, going to banquets and complimenting her host on the ability of the French and English Canadians to 'live happily together'.

The Queen visited several of the Canadian maritime provinces, while the rest of the royal family – Prince Andrew particularly – became entranced by Margaret, the racy wife of Pierre Trudeau, the Canadian Prime Minister, and spent hours talking to her. All the family gathered to watch Princess Anne take part in the Olympics – 'the ambition of her life' – and bit their lips when she fell and suffered bruises and mild concussion.

No stranger to Canada, the Queen's most delicate mission to that country was on 19 April 1982 when she proclaimed the new Canadian Constitution in an open-air ceremony on Ottawa's Parliament Hill.

Graceful in blue and wearing her major Canadian decorations the Queen signed 'Elizabeth R' on the proclamation scroll and, in the words of Pierre Trudeau, 'severed this last colonial link with Britain'.

Mr Trudeau spoke lyrically about this moment in Canada's political life. 'It was,' he said, 'the end of a long winter, the breaking up of the ice-jams and the beginning of a new spring.' As he spoke, the Queen and Prince Philip – he was in the uniform of a Colonel of the Royal Canadian Regiment – could see all around them subtle links with Britain which would hardly be changed because of the proclamation.

The traveller coming from the United States and crossing the border into Canada is immediately aware of the subtle attachment to monarchy – the crown on the royal mail and the mounted police.

This connection gives Canadians an identity distinct from that of the United States, their rather overwhelming neighbour. If anything, the proclamation made the links with Britain even stronger and the energetic young members of the royal family appeal to young Canadians. They like the Queen's two older sons who are not dilettante armchair soldiers and sailors and were particularly impressed by Prince Andrew's performance in the Falklands. When the Queen was in Canada for the new constitution, a 'hot line' was connected from her bedroom at the Governor-General's house to 10 Downing Street to keep her in close touch with the situation in the Falklands.

The less demanding the royal tour, the better the chance of a friendly word with some of the Queen's entourage. On one of the meanders in New Zealand – while the Queen inspected some special breed of sheep with chunky sideboards – one might hear that the Princess of Wales charms the Duke of Edinburgh and makes him laugh, that the only anxiety about her is that she has not enough interests. 'But she does; she loves music and ballet.' 'Exactly, that's what I mean,' replies the senior member of the Household, obviously feeling that the absence of interest in killing things is a worry. The words used about the young Princess are 'tough, resilient'.

'They don't even wear dinner jackets there,' the Queen said to a friend in dismay before going to Switzerland, where she spent most of the time on a train trundling through chocolate-box countryside, fields of buttercups and neat farms. It was in Switzerland, enjoying in the early summer of 1980 its first State visit this century by a reigning English monarch, that there was a great deal of uneasiness and riot police had to be called in to the two hundred IRA-inspired demonstrators shouting 'Queen Go Home'. However, it wasn't the tear gas which deterred them but doughty Swiss matrons turning on them with their handbags.

Irritated by the vigilance of the Swiss police, the Queen indicated 'Less security, more contact with the people,' and on the last day she went on board a Lake Lucerne paddle steamer. She spent the happiest day of the State visit walking up a valley with the Household puffing behind her, to make a speech at Rutli where Queen Victoria used to sketch and enjoy 'the bracing air'. Even so there had been very little contact with the people. 'Why is it that the first child I meet is English?' said the Queen astutely as Heather Watson presented her with flowers outside an eighteenth-century country house near Basle where the atmosphere was overpoweringly folksy.

'Don't bother to come to Switzerland,' she had advised a Royal Warrant holder, knowing that she wouldn't be anywhere for longer than a bit of yodelling, a hop round a maypole and the presentation of a posy would allow.

In Fiji in 1977 they danced their broad feet off in welcome, though there was some dismay at the inability of the powerful Waimaro tribe to bring about fine weather. This is done by asking for the opposite – please let it rain heavily for Her Majesty's visit!

The Chief then began his rigorous three days without food, wives or liquor. However, as it bucketed down with torrential rain, and tiny frogs, encouraged by the downpour, were trying to leap up the Chief's grass skirts, there was a feeling that he had not respected all three conditions.

A pilot boat took the Senior Chiefs out to the royal yacht. The Queen and Prince Philip came out on the verandah deck at ten o'clock and sat solemnly on two Hepplewhite chairs in front of the 150-year-old brass binnacle glinting in the sunlight against the white paint. The Queen looked pale and rather forbidding in her navy and white dress and hat trimmed with scarlet poppies. The Queen does not smile unless she wants to but sometimes this stern exterior is donned as a courtesy, to ensure she does not get a fit of giggles. Wearing their scanty costumes made from the bark of a mulberry tree, belts of shells and flowers, large Japanese bows and necklaces of whalebone, the Chiefs squatted on a white mat at the Queen Empress's feet. The royal Household stood reverently at the back of the two Hepplewhite chairs and the Queen looked as if she understood perfectly as the Chiefs clapped their hands and chanted 'Oi' and 'Aah'. Their leader, Ratu Jone Mataintini, trembled a little as he gave the Queen a whale's tooth and she, in turn, appeared earnestly impressed by the profundity of his words.

In New Zealand, Auckland with its bungalows and suburban English gardens filled with stocks, geraniums and antirrhinums, came as a shock after the lush greenery of the South Pacific. But curiously it was in New Zealand that the magic of the monarchy came alive. The Queen, in an evening dress by Norman Hartnell of white silk and bands of gold and a ruby tiara, shimmered into the Houses of Parliament for the State Opening in Wellington. Her two ladies-in-waiting, Mrs John Dugdale and Miss Mary Morrison, looked like vestal virgins, their long white dresses contrasting with the sombre suits of the politicians. Prince Philip was in white too – wearing the tropical uniform of Admiral of the Fleet. It was a very grand occasion, and the Queen had a tiny guide written on her white glove, cueing her when to say 'Pray be seated' and when to give the command 'Black Rod will summon the House of Representatives'.

The 1979 tour of Denmark got little coverage in the British Press, which was more interested in Copenhagen as a source of child pornography stories. But the visit was a meeting of old friends for the Queen. The lively Queen Margrethe II of Denmark, tall with stylish flair, teetered speedily along on high heels inspecting a Guard of Honour, unlike the Queen's normally much steadier pace.

The Danes like the link with Britain and are proud of their decorative Alexandra, who was Edward VII's wife. There seemed to be an appealing competitiveness as each day our Queen appeared in new pretty outfits beside the fashion-conscious Queen Margrethe in her pillbox hats.

Holding a bouquet of pink flowers, and looking carefree in her new Hardy Amies wild silk pink, grey and lavender outfit with matching hat, the Queen had obviously enjoyed lunch in the Tivoli Gardens. For a minute the royal foursome dithered before the Gardens' Tunnel of Love. 'Shall we? Should we?' as photographers slavered. The Queen and Prince Henrik got into the first boat. Behind them sat the Danish Queen and Prince Philip, laughing their heads off as the boats bobbed off through dark grottos, past spooky giant caterpillars and hobbit-like creatures peering out. And in the very first boat, cutting a most unromantic figure, was the head of Danish security, sitting uncomfortably and looking quite pink as his officers grinned back at him.

'You can't have had smoked salmon. Surely the Vikings never had that?' the Queen said when she came upon some of her party sitting in a forest in Jutland, all rather merry on mead at a 'Viking' feast. But a Danish historian said, 'Yes Madam, it was possible,' and the Queen, in apricot silk read the menu avidly, laughing as she came to: 'Ale brewed on malt and honey and flavoured with bog myrtle'.

If the Queen feels most at home anywhere abroad it is in Norway. 'Oh, it's so nice to be visiting you again,' she said to King Olaf of Norway, stepping ashore from the royal barge in Oslo on 4 May 1981. The courtly King, looking uncannily like his grandfather Edward VII, towered above the Queen. His pride in her visit could not be greater for, as the Queen herself said, 'Coming to Norway is a family occasion.' And instead of formal handshakes the Queen and Prince Philip exchanged kisses on both cheeks with the Norwegian royal family.

It was ironic then, that in this country of phlegmatic people, in a city where tea dances and white gloves survive there should be such an ugly demonstration. The Queen, looking good in

sealing-wax red, had stepped ashore to a quayside pink with
prawn shells, her small figure shadowed by two hundred of the
King's Guards, their horsehair plumes nodding. After a warm kiss
from 'King Oooh-laff' the Queen inspected the Guard of Honour
and narrowly missed being splattered with tomato ketchup thrown
by IRA supporters. Prince Philip cut short pleasantries with the
King's svelte daughter-in-law Sonja and looked distinctly ratty.
Impervious, the Queen carried on with good-mannered 'How nice
to be here's' and 'How kind's' to the line of diplomats and dignitaries.

Prince Philip nodded off at the State Banquet; and King Olaf
made chuckling, bearish sounds of appreciation as the Queen made
her speech. The Government's banquet was in the fortress
Akerhous – candlelit, panelled walls, the huge Russian ambassador
and his matching-sized wife amongst the guests. At a morning
spent at the Munch exhibition, the Queen didn't like 'The Shriek'
much and was told by the museum director that the artist was
gloomy because 'He was always preoccupied by death.' 'But everyone is,' the Duke replied.

'How fascinating,' the Queen said, as she looked up a horse's
nostril at the Norwegian Animal Hospital. And again, 'How fascinating,' peering at the largest construction hole in the world later
that same day.

At the British Embassy, hair shining, flowers held tightly, children sing after standing for up to two hours without a complaining
squeak. The Queen arrives 'How long … ?' 'How old … ?' 'Did you
have a long journey?' She smilingly asks the standard questions.
And then occurs one of those kindly and perceptive moments
which make you realize what a thoughtful man the Duke of Edinburgh is. The Queen had completely missed a group of children
who were bobbing about dementedly in a grassy dip. As she turned
to go inside the Duke spotted the crestfallen group and tipped off a
lady-in-waiting (Susan Hussey), who broke into a sedate trot and
lifted the cordon, releasing them to race up the slope, hair and ribbons flying, to the Queen, who loved the moment. 'How much did
you pay those children to come here?' Lord Carrington said to the
BBC cameraman; taking the lump out of our throats.

They threw roses and narcissi at the Queen as she left Oslo. Who
knows what the value of that tour was? But it was one of the
happiest.

CHAPTER 14

❋ ❋ ❋

The Captain General

THE MORNING OF her Birthday Parade in June is one of the rare occasions when the Queen shows any hint of nervousness. Her cup of Darjeeling tea is served much earlier than usual, between 7 and 7.30 am. Instead of her usual stroll admiring the azaleas, the purple and pink rhododendrons and the crescent border of red roses, there is a smart canter side-saddle round the Palace Gardens. The Queen, an expert horsewoman, who normally rides astride, does not do so on ceremonial occasions and likes to rehearse the art of riding side-saddle again and again in the week leading up to the Birthday Parade. Her horse is usually the biddable old Burmese – a present from the Royal Canadian Mounted Police twenty years ago.

This celebration of the Queen's Official Birthday is an unfailingly handsome display of royal precision, as hundreds of Guardsmen wheel and march in scarlet tunics and bearskins; they are the Queen's personal troops and the occasion gives the world a glimpse of high-class British ceremonial. Nothing is left to chance; there are two full rehearsals before the day, at which the only person who does not attend is the Queen. Prince Philip may take one salute, in full dress, and the Major-General commanding takes the other. The Queen's place is taken by Sylvia Stanier, an expert horsewoman and the niece of Sir John Miller, Crown Equerry in charge of the Royal Mews. At the rehearsals for the wedding of Prince Charles in 1981, on Sunday 26 July, Miller checked every hoof and fetlock, riding 'shotgun' on the empty carriages and landaus between Buckingham Palace and St Paul's. The ceremonial at the Trooping rehearsals is exactly the same as

on the Birthday, and afterwards Sylvia Stanier will report to the
Queen how Burmese has behaved.

The Queen is Colonel-in-Chief of the seven regiments of the
Household Division.. Many of her staff tend to be drawn from the
socially-acceptable Grenadier, Coldstream, Scots, Irish and Welsh
Guards and from the two Cavalry Regiments, the Lifeguards and
the Blues and Royals. There has always been an old-fashioned
military hierarchy at the Palace, with its merits of good grooming,
punctuality and deep loyalty. In the King's time, it tended to be
more naval with jolly Admirals and Commanders bellowing at
each other in the Palace corridors as if on board ship and not thinking to use the telephone, but also creating a 'remarkably nice and
unstuffy atmosphere'.

In the summer of 1981, on the Birthday Parade the month
before the royal wedding, Lady Diana Spencer and Prince Andrew
had just gone by in an open carriage as the Queen, dressed in the
uniform of the Welsh Guards, was turning out of the Mall, erect
on Burmese. Behind her were Prince Charles and Prince Philip,
trotting into the narrow approach to Horse Guards Parade as the
bands played military music and the crowds sat in tiers of silent
anticipation. What was not fully appreciated at the time was the
Queen's sudden realization that she was to be the target of an
assassination attempt, as she saw, ten feet away, a man raise a
black revolver and point it at her. There was nobody in front or
beside her who could protect her and she had never in her life
seemed so close to death. She told the royal family afterwards that
she had been aware of the gun coming up in the crowd long before
the shots were fired and her horse shied and threw its head about.
There were six shots, two spaced and the rest bunched. The
Queen, though pale, kept steady as they were fired; and her
thoughts were immediately for her husband, her son and the
escort, because, of course, at that time she assumed that real
bullets were being aimed at her.

'I didn't know what had happened to everyone behind.' As she
turned to look at them, Prince Charles and the Duke of Edinburgh
had already ridden up and closed in beside her. 'Are you all right?'
they muttered past the straps holding their bearskins. 'Fine,' said
the Queen, calming her horse in the smelly aftermath of gun-
smoke and against the fury of the crowd, who were shouting
'Hang the bastard' as a seventeen-year-old boy, Marcus Sarjeant,

was taken away by police. There was a reassuring smile from Prince Philip, a pat for Burmese as the Queen made it clear the parade was to go on and prepared to take the salute. Ironically, her crack soldiers had been hemmed in by ceremonial, unable to move a muscle to defend her.

When the Queen looked rather glum a little later at Ascot and foreigners thought she did not seem very happy at Prince Charles's wedding, some members of the royal family were at pains to explain this was due to delayed shock. On the day of the Trooping, the Queen Mother was so shaken, that she stumbled and hurt her leg badly on a step. This was to drag her down and there were doubts as to whether she would be well enough to attend the royal wedding. 'The spin-offs of an incident like that attempted shooting of the Queen affected the whole family.' Uppermost in the Queen's thoughts on the day of Prince Charles's wedding was, 'Please do not let anything go wrong today,' and it was not until he was back at the Palace with his bride that she could really relax and laugh.

But even though the likelihood of these assassination attempts is chillingly more possible now, the Queen is very reluctant to have more security and Prince Charles's attitude is much the same. The Queen is philosophical. She refuses to worry about the grim possibilities or to let them interfere with her job. After all, Queen Victoria survived six serious attacks. And, as the Queen says, 'If someone really wants to get me it is too easy.'

Marcus Sarjeant, sentenced to five years, was found guilty at the Old Bailey under the 1842 Treason Act of 'wilfully discharging at the person of Her Majesty the Queen, a blank cartridge pistol with intent to alarm her'. An appeal was refused.

The Queen has always resisted unsubtle security. At a private party she was talking of the outcry in America about the supposed presence of 'hit men' allegedly sent by Colonel Gadaffi. With a cool disdain for allowing such public fuss, she said she was greatly shocked by the President: 'Fancy him allowing such a thing to get about, I simply can't understand it.' This was typical. She would never fail to co-operate with security requirements, but her real peace of mind stems from the flying courage of the expert horse-woman.

A few days after the Trooping incident, the Queen was cheered heartily by the crowd waiting for her at Windsor at the ceremony of the Order of the Garter. She looked herself and walked about unconcerned in her robes and becoming huge white plumes. Her view was, 'I am keeping this public engagement and people must be able to see me,' and she firmly rejected extra protection.

The incident had been upsetting, but a deranged teenager with a toy pistol would not, in the Queen's eyes, be an excuse for a less than excellent Birthday Parade. Moments afterwards the Queen was smiling in reassurance at the crowds and the parade continued, finishing at the usual time, about ten past twelve. Those who criticize the Queen for not smiling enough, or not seeming to be outgoing, could see that day the reserves of strength and extraordinary self-control which did not allow the slightest hint of distress to show on her face. A price must surely be paid for this and would the critics prefer a giggly queen who laughed a lot but cried as easily when things went wrong?

Only war, the weather (1948) – or British Rail – could prevent a Birthday Parade. In 1955 it had to be cancelled because of a strike. Everyone remembers one of the most moving Birthdays – George VI's last – when he was so ill but insisted it should take place. He watched this most rigorously demanding royal occasion from an open carriage, and he took the salute. But in 1945, on 21 April, Princess Elizabeth had become Colonel of the Grenadier Guards, an appointment which she had accepted with great pride. For an heir to the throne who does not like horses, or is even frightened of them, the Trooping Ceremony would be almost unthinkable. But, say the Palace, this problem is academic. The date set for the Parade is usually early in June but varies each year, depending on Bank Holidays. It was always held on a Thursday in the days before London was snarled up with motorcars and wives did not go to work. In 1959 it was decided that a Saturday would be much better. About ten days beforehand the Queen will go and have tea with the regiment whose colours are to be trooped. Apart from the morale boost, it is also for the practical reason that it helps her to recognize the soldiers at the parade.

Each year she wears the uniform of the regiment whose colour is being trooped. It is always a scarlet tunic – made of a material like strong felt wool – but the grouping of shining buttons is the clue to the Regiment. In 1981, on 12 June, the Queen was in the uniform of the Coldstream Guards, with buttons in pairs and a red plume set dashingly in her tricorn – the three-cornered hat which has a rather fashionable look to it in these days of small pillboxes. In the Household Division offices there are vivid paintings of great Birthday Parades which convey all the feeling of the movement, the rhythm, the white and red plumes, the swords and splashes of scarlet and the shining horses surging and grouping. In glass cases there are the tall, gleaming black leather boots with their silvery spurs and the plumed helmets. In 1983 the 1st Battalion Grenadier Guards troop their colour (usually the flag is crimson). The uniform has single buttons, with a plain white plume on the tricorn hat. The Queen has five jackets, all waisted and specially tailored with the different insignia and button groupings. 'The Queen looks equally stunning whatever the uniform,' says one of the Household Division. Some remember 1951 with nostalgia; she wore a blue habit, a blue jacket and a peaked cap as it was not until the war was well over that tunics were restored.

So on the Saturday of the Trooping, instead of relaxing at Windsor the Queen is at Buckingham Palace, dressed and ready to leave by 10.30 am. Her horse will have been exercised strongly, 'to take the stuffing out of it'. She will leave the Palace at 10.45 am to arrive at Horseguards exactly as the clock strikes eleven. Rather enterprisingly, the clock was held back one year, but the Queen was furious and said this must never happen again. She would arrive exactly on time. It is a very long day for the Guardsmen, who will have been up soon after dawn eating hearty breakfasts, doing PT and attempting to improve the already perfect mirror gloss on their boots before going on parade. They march from Chelsea Barracks, leaving at 9.30 am for Horseguards. After the Parade the first two divisions of the Escort go into the forecourt of Buckingham Palace to mount a full guard.

The precision and timing of this ceremonial drill helps to create some of the best wartime soldiers. The Mall is marked with letters to indicate special sectors of the route – a cunning arrangement of letters which lets Guardsmen know that they should, at a certain moment, be between, say, the letters 'D' and 'E'. They run from the Palace with 'A' immediately outside the central gates. Three of the letters have been covered during road repairs over the years and have not been replaced.

If the weather is bad it is miserable for the Queen, the men and the horses. The horses may slip and slide and the men can have half a gallon of water slopping round their bearskins and rain splashing on their faces. For the Queen there is the same discomfort and also the danger that her horse might have an off-day. Occasionally a highly-strung animal starts bucking, throws its head or, even worse, its rider, and has to be removed from the parade in disgrace. But this rarely happens, and the Queen will want to know afterwards the reason for the slightest slip. 'She will let it be known that it was not quite up to standard, or was not particularly good – that sort of thing,' a member of the Household Division explained, his voice deep with respect. She will want to know such things as, 'Why was the dressing on Parade not quite right?' or 'Why did the Parade move half a yard?' but she will make no comment about an unfortunate Guardsman who faints on Parade. The media make much of the Guardsman who faints during the ceremony, but it does not incur royal displeasure although there is a thorough inquiry. A dim view is taken if 'the chap has been on the razzle the night before.' And, of course, there is a doctor's report.

David Hanlon, now a London taxi driver, has smarting memories of a visit by Princess Elizabeth to the King's Own Rifles in York in 1942, when he was twenty-four, and remembers 'she put two blokes on a charge for having dirty engines'. In his view the engines were like new pins; it was just their bad luck that the bonnets were up. As Colonel of the Grenadier Guards, the Princess always wanted to become more involved. Although only nineteen and not very experienced, 'I ought to do more,' she said – and did! At an inspection she gave a sharp rebuke to a young soldier which was deserved. But it had been embarrassing, and a tactful word to the perfectionist Princess suggested that, to be a really good officer she could be a little more gentle – a lesson taken to heart.

Much is made of the Queen's early training in the Auxiliary Territorial Service, when she, just like any young girl, was anxious to do her bit for Britain. However, she did not sleep in a hut with a mixture of other girls, some using swear words as often as the Princess said 'thank you'; nor did she have to eat powdered scrambled egg slopped out from a giant bucket, or have her hair checked for nits. But in fairness, hers was a genuine attempt to be part of the war effort; and even in those late war years girls of the 'right background' remained very innocent on the whole. Princess Elizabeth and Princess Margaret were even more protected, with very little contact with 'wild girls of their own age; or any who smoked, wore red nail varnish and drank gin', as the really flighty were described by Sergeant Pat Hayes, one of the young women who accompanied the Princess on her course.

The King and Queen felt it would be very useful for Princess Elizabeth to learn about driving and maintenance, with the ATS. It would be useful training, and would give her an insight into how the ATS girls lived. She did not go through the ranks, and eleven other girls of the 'right sort' were found to accompany her on the brief course. These girls, all sergeants and corporals, knew something was afoot and rumours flew at Camberley, though it was all highly secret. The news got out because one of their friends, Sergeant Brigid Bennett, was the driver of the Deputy Director of the ATS. 'London, Bennett,' snapped the Deputy Director, and the pretty sergeant drove the old Humber as far as Hyde Park Corner, still having no idea where they were going. 'Constitution Hill, Bennett,' and they turned into Buckingham Palace on a bleak November evening in 1944. Mary Baxter Ellis, summoned to Buckingham Palace, spent forty minutes alone with the Queen. It was solemnly agreed that the Princess, eighteen years old, had too much work on hand, learning to be Queen, to be able to spare two months in the ranks, but she might, her mother thought, find it a good thing to 'compete against other brains'. However, the two older women agreed that a 'ten-week recruits' course would be rather a waste of time, as HRH has a brain already trained to learn.' The King approved, and so did the War Cabinet. The Princess would learn how to be a mechanic, working on a utility vehicle and on a 15-cwt Bedford truck, jacked up, its chassis stripped to the bare bones.

All sorts of points had to be sorted out and letters went backwards and forwards to Buckingham Palace. 'Yes, the Princess would get clothing coupons.' 'No, she would not bother with lectures on camouflage, gas or domestic economy.' 'Yes, she would learn how to change plugs on a vehicle on blocks.' 'Yes, she would get her hands dirty and learn how to drive a heavy truck.'

There was then a hiccough which no one could have anticipated. The Princess got mumps – more official secret letters, and the course was postponed. Eventually, on 23 March 1945, a girl with hyacinth-blue eyes, dark-brown curly hair, a pretty complexion, with pudgy hands and figure, turned up. Ironically the girls chosen to sit in for the brief course were already instructors, but had to pretend, as they sat in class with HRH, an Honorary Second Subaltern, that they did not know anything about map reading, ignition, batteries, carburettors or fuel systems. 'We didn't want to make her look a fool,' Pat Hayes said, 'but we got ticked off after the first two or three lectures because we weren't asking questions. You felt a bit silly asking about plugs when you had been telling students these things for a couple of years.'

Classes started at 10.30 am and the Princess drove Commandant V.E.M. Wellesley – 'Aunty Violet' – from Windsor Castle, where she had learnt to drive in peace and quiet. The journey to Camberley was part of her instruction and once she drove to London and went round Hyde Park Corner three times before getting to the Palace.

Coffee break was in a small hut where tea, coffee and cocoa were swilled from a great urn. The other girls, in their early twenties, were poised and able to make small talk. Today most of them are still attractive, well-preserved and energetic, with fresh complexions and a way that certain Englishwomen have of wearing blouses and skirts with incredible neatness. 'We were all young,' they remembered, 'and after that first day Princess Elizabeth became relaxed once we'd said, "Would you like a cup of coffee, Ma'am?" Then somebody said, "It was written in the paper, Ma'am, that the King went to Church on Sunday." "Oh, I know," came the plaintive reply, "they put that he was in an Air Vice-Marshal's uniform but, in fact, he was in a tweed suit."'

The girls would sit on the grass and chat idly – even then the Princess's conversation was always very polite: 'How kind,' or, 'You liked Princess Margaret's dress? Oh, I am pleased,' though the view privately held by the rest of the group was that the younger Princess was a 'jealous, tiresome little girl, always needling her older sister.' They would ask each other what they were doing for the weekend: 'Oh, King Olaf is coming to stay at Windsor and it is going to be boring because he wants to watch a football match ...' Conversation was so relaxed that occasionally there would be a slip, 'Papa says ...' instead of 'the King', but very rarely. In class, if somebody was flippant, the Princess, in the front row, was always quick to turn round to see who it was, but never herself said anything frivolously out of turn. The rest of the class had slept in huts with twenty others; with 'tough nuts' who said 'bugger' and 'bluddy', had kept all their clothes on in bed to stay warm and got up at 6.30 in the morning to the tune 'Run, Rabbit, Run' on the wind-up gramophone. The 'biscuit', a rudimentary mattress, was filled with kapok and each girl had three blankets. There was conscription for women in 1942 and Princess Elizabeth registered when she was sixteen. All the girls doing the course with the Princess had volunteered.

The Princess had mixed with so few outsiders that she cannot really have been part of the mixed atmosphere at Camberley as she learnt to bleed the brakes on a utility which is now in the Museum there, alongside her uniform with its narrow waist. Nor was she roughing it, though the girls with her thought it was pretty hard having to eat with the 'Old Dragons' in the Officers' Mess each day. On Thursdays there was always horsemeat and soggy greens and nearly every day there were pilchards in tomato sauce. For the Princess there was a small jug of condensed milk – a treat nobody else got. She was always touchingly delighted with her chocolate ration, a 2 oz bar, hardly enough for a sweet tooth which later could not resist her children's fudge, peppermint creams or chocolate cake. Today there is a plaque on the wall at the slightly bleak and windy No. 1 Mechanical Transport Training Centre at Camberley, which simply records that they had a royal recruit in 1945.

Each evening the Princess would drive back to Windsor for more work with her tutor on Constitutional Law and politics. The King and Queen were amused by the constant talk about 'D and M' ('driving and maintenance') at dinner. Her aunt, the Princess Royal, had been instrumental in setting up the course for her niece. Everyone remembers how, when she arrived for what became known as 'Aunty Mary's day', Princess Elizabeth avoided kissing her aunt, who had inclined her beaky head forward; instead she saluted the Princess Royal briskly and correctly. The royal family were almost as proud of Princess Elizabeth in the ATS as they were nearly forty years later of Prince Andrew in the Task Force in the Falklands.

The day everyone remembers is when the King came to inspect the Training Centre. 'Parents' Day', they joked, but they were frantically scrubbing and tidying, giving the Princess a minuscule insight into the passionate preparation which goes on for a royal visit. On 9 April 1945, the King enjoyed the sight of his elder daughter scuttling about in dungarees, not terribly flattering to the hips in those days. 'What are you doing, or don't you know?' he asked quizzically. The Queen, in soft, frivolous clothes, was frankly 'not awfully interested' in the work going on under the bonnet, but talked as if she was having a fascinating afternoon. Princess Margaret was very bored.

At the end of the course they all took tests and parted friends. The course finished on Tuesday, 16 April 1945. Five days later the Princess celebrated her nineteenth birthday, and less than three weeks after that the war in Europe was over.

At a small reunion in the spring of 1981, in between shrieks of horror at how fat they looked in photographs taken with the Princess, with their permed hair and plumpness from wartime starch, the group agreed, 'Really we would have done anything for her.' 'She was delightful and so pretty ...' She had been terribly easy. They called her 'Ma'am' – that was no trouble as all the officers were called 'Ma'am' anyway. They said they even forgave her their unnecessary half-hour on the square to fill in time every morning before her arrival.

Sergeant Pat Hayes was one of the fizzier personalities of that group. One day she went to the Princess when they were having a break. 'We knew we shouldn't pester, but I clicked my heels, saluted and asked, "Would you be kind enough to sign my little book, Ma'am?"' Ten minutes later, with 'Elizabeth' written in the autograph book, Pat Hayes was summoned to the Duty Commandant's office and, clamping her brown shoes together again, was asked 'Why did you leave the Princess to make her own way unattended back to class?' Many years later, Pat Hayes, now Mrs Blake, was at the Royal Tournament and got a message, 'You are wanted in the Royal Box.' At first she thought it was a joke; but one of the Queen's ladies-in-waiting, Mrs Jean Elphinstone, assured her that the Queen did want to see her. In the Royal Box, side-stepping banks of flowers, the Queen asked wistfully, 'Do you ever see any of the others? I saw Smithie the other day,' and there was an appealing imaginary picture of the Queen standing at a number 11 bus-stop and running into Subaltern Smithie who used to queue up with her for sweets and soap coupons. The Queen was reminded again of ATS days when she went to a sixtieth reunion of the WRAC Association in Guildford on 26 May 1979. She stood in front of the yellow chassis of the old utility she had worked on, and remembered that 'Assorted Eleven' who had been with her in 1945.

Now the head of the Royal Navy, the Army and the Royal Air Force, the Queen has a soft spot for her personal troops. The appointment of high-ranking officers has royal approval and once or twice there has been a royal 'No' to the Major-Generals' suggestions. For a less conscientious woman the involvement in military matters might be onerous, but she said once, 'I take great pride in my Army' – at the Army Council Dinner at the Royal Hospital in Chelsea on 27 November 1976. Prince Philip holds the three top ranks in all three Services. He is a Field Marshal, an Admiral of the Fleet and a Marshal of the Royal Air Force. But a typical example of the Queen's thoroughness was the way in which her husband had to cut his teeth first on the Welsh Guards. There was no question of his lightly taking over the Grenadiers. But now that Prince Philip is their Colonel, the Queen is delighted. He takes an acutely informed interest and any briefing laid on for him had better be sharp and sophisticated. At a recent meeting on tactics, other Field Marshals were impressed by his grasp of information which was not all that familiar to some of them!

By a neat bit of logical progression, Prince Charles then became Colonel of the Welsh Guards and there was more good salty humour for the men. 'Any children yet?' he asked a young soldier standing with his pretty young wife. 'Not yet; we are keeping our fingers crossed, sir,' the guardsman answered, as honestly as he could. But his young Colonel retorted, 'You certainly won't get one that way!' Prince Charles likes his equerries to be chosen from the Welsh Guards if possible. He is also Colonel-in-Chief of the Royal Regiment of Wales and, exactly like the Queen and Prince Philip, will make perceptive enquiries. They are couched in courtly language, 'Prince Charles would like to know,' but, as a member of this regiment remarked, 'You jolly well make sure you get it right.' In time, the Princess of Wales may become Colonel-in-Chief to a less senior Cavalry Regiment to initiate her gently in military ceremonial – the 16/5 Lancers or the Royal Hussars, commonly thought to be 'full of nice people, rather dishy chaps', have been suggested as ideal.

The Duke of Kent is regarded in military circles as the royal family's finest soldier. He is a Lieutenant-Colonel in the Royal Scots Dragoon Guards, Colonel of the Scots Guards and Colonel-in-Chief of the Royal Regiment of Fusiliers, but was bitterly disappointed that he could not serve in Northern Ireland. The Duchess of Kent takes her duties seriously as Controller Commandant Women's Royal Army Corps and Colonel-in-Chief 4th/7th Royal Dragoon Guards. But her health is not good and often arrangements have to be made to ensure that she does not stand too long.

A special Army occasion for the Queen is when she dines at Woolwich approximately every decade with the Royal Regiment of Artillery, including her father's beloved King's Troop, whose title she was happy to leave unchanged on her Accession in 1952 as a mark of her respect to her father and to the Royal Regiment whose battle honours over two and a half centuries took them from Waterloo to Lucknow, true to their motto *Ubique* – 'Everywhere'. She is their Captain General, a now defunct Army rank dating back to a Danish mercenary called Borgard in the early 1700s. It was used first in 1951 by the monarch in the context as head of the Royal Regiment of Artillery.

The band plays 'The Roast Beef of Old England' as the Queen walks into the Mess to sit at the top table.

The superb regimental silver is brought out, including the William IV silver candelabrum of which, when it was presented, the monarch is believed to have said, 'Splendid, but no royal lion,' and the unfortunate silversmith had to squeeze one in. Diamonds glitter in the fourth-century Abyssinian Cross taken from a Greek Church in 1868. The Queen knows that a 'stuffy Anglican padre' once complained about its being on the table, but if she looks half right, she can see it on a splendid corner bracket. It has been argued that trophies like this and the ram's head covered in gold brought back from the Ashanti War in 1865 should be returned. But the suggestion was rebutted when Haile Selassie came to dine in 1938. When the Lion of Judah was told that there had been pressure on the Royal Artillery to return their trophies he immediately called for the Cross, held it close to his black beard and exclaimed emotionally, 'I bequeath it in perpetuity ...'

When the Queen dines at Woolwich, stewards in eighteenth-century wigs, red kneebreeches with white hose, white cravats, tailcoats in ivory with red cuffs and red waistcoats trimmed with gold serve the meal. The atmosphere must be exactly as it was when Queen Victoria visited. At the end of dinner there is the Loyal Toast, the National Anthem and then the Posthorn Gallop.

The Gunners also honour the Queen on her Official Birthday. The King's Troop fire a forty-one-gun salute from Hyde Park when she has led her Guards back down the Mall.

The Queen is Lord High Admiral of the Navy. It is close to her heart – her husband and two of her sons are sailors. Her sea-faring father was a sub-lieutenant in HMS *Collingwood* at the Battle of Jutland in 1916, but poor health prevented him from staying in the Navy so he qualified as a pilot with the newly-formed Royal Air Force in 1918. There is perhaps a tendency to underrate the Queen's involvement with the Navy because it is more difficult to capture the occasion. If the Queen is giving new colours to the First Battalion of the Grenadier Guards which has six hundred men stationed at Chelsea, they just march up to Buckingham Palace. But it is not so easy with the Navy. The two remaining aircraft carriers can hardly be brought to anchor up the Thames. The great recent naval occasion for the Queen was the Silver Jubilee Review in 1977, when every ship in the Fleet lined up at Portsmouth. The Queen loves the *Britannia*, and the flag of the Lord High Admiral is flown when she is on board.

They get rather annoyed at the Palace if you suggest that the Queen perhaps has less contact with the Royal Air Force than with the other two Services. 'The trouble is,' they say, 'that royal visits to Cranwell only get publicity if the goat runs amok on Parade!' Or if, as happened during the Jubilee, the Minister of Defence, Mr Fred Mulley, falls asleep beside her as the Red Devils fly over-head. '"Poor little Mulley" is all people remember!' groused one member of the Household.

The Queen is Air-Commodore-in-Chief of the Royal Auxiliary Air Force, the Royal Air Force Regiment and the Royal Observer Corps. She became Commandant-in-Chief of RAF Cranwell in Silver Jubilee year. In April 1960 she became the Honorary Air Commodore RAF Marham – which is the local base where so many of the men in her family take off from and land. The Queen is surrounded by a family of highly-competent pilots: Prince Philip, who was asked recently to test a sophisticated Boeing 757; Prince Charles, who takes the controls on long-haul flights; and Prince Andrew, who is a helicopter pilot. They can all fly helicopters but the Queen is not allowed by Parliament to travel in one as they are considered dangerous. The only time was during the Silver Jubilee tour to Northern Ireland, when it was believed

to be the only secure way to get her from the royal yacht to Hills-
borough Castle. It is said that the Queen does not like helicopters.
In 1967 her Captain of the Queen's Flight, Air Commodore John
Blount, aged forty-eight, was killed flying as a passenger in a helicopter of the Queen's Flight which proved to have a hairline frac-
ture. It is said too that she does not like escalators, but it is not
likely that she comes across many of those. Even when she shops
at Harrods at Christmas, the escalators are stopped and the lifts are
waiting.

The Queen is dependent on the RAF for some of her
long-distance travel. The 32 Squadron of the RAF supplements
the work of the Queen's Flight. It is an act of mercy as the three
Andovers of the Queen's Flight are nearly eighteen years old,
slow, and have limited range. In the late sixties it took the Duke of
Edinburgh a week to get to Australia in one of the Andovers,
which are lovingly maintained and have a sentimental value now.
The Duke might have been overtaken constantly on the journey,
but there will hardly have been a more gleaming, trusty old silver
flying bird on that journey down under. It is often embarrassing
on royal tours when the Queen's host has a personal Jumbo jet – as
in Morocco and Saudi Arabia – and then the Queen arrives in a
little Andover which looks extraordinarily old-fashioned beside
the 747s, as if Britain were still in the Biggles age of discovery!
There has been pressure over the years to replace these propeller-
driven Andovers. But often the Queen does the major part of her
overseas journey in a British Airways or other domestic jet and
then, if possible, changes to the Andover for the tour, as if it were
a flagship Britain wants the world to see! The Government has
never responded to pressure to take the Queen into the jet age –
the BAC 1-11 was seen as ideal, but the production line is now
closed.

CHAPTER 15

❋ ❋ ❋

Courage and the Commonwealth

THE QUEEN HATES fuss about her safety. And it is no secret that she was extremely irritated when Mrs Thatcher felt that she should not go to Lusaka in July 1979 for the Commonwealth Conference. The visit to Zambia was a high-risk operation, but the Queen, who cherishes her role as Head of the Commonwealth, was not going to be put off and certainly not by 'that woman'. The Queen, as always, listened to the arguments, then made up her own mind.

The anxiety had increased that summer with the acceleration of guerrilla tactics on the Rhodesian border, and a serious row blew up between Buckingham Palace and Number Ten. The Palace made it clear, in no uncertain terms, that it was not for the Prime Minister but for the Head of the Commonwealth to decide whether she was going or not. Although the pinstriped courtiers were outwardly as civil as ever, the atmosphere was tense, for the newly elected Prime Minister had overlooked one of the most sensitive issues, where even *premier cru* diplomats tread with extreme care at Buckingham Palace. Anything to do with the Commonwealth is jealously guarded by the Queen and she protects her rights with the determination of a tigress. On the other hand, the British Prime Minister has a duty to protect the Queen; but to overlook her relationship with the Commonwealth Heads and their wishes was unacceptable. Anyway the royal view was that it was not a British decision alone. Here was a genuine need to fulfil Sir Walter Bagehot's view of the monarch's role – 'the right to be consulted, the right to encourage, the right to warn'. The Queen is too politically astute to have been unable to assess the atmosphere in Lusaka. She knew better than anyone that her role in the

Commonwealth was not seen as that of the old-fashioned Queen Empress, but more as a high-powered influential friend who understood their affection for the Club, even if it had become temporarily unfashionable. Her role as healer, comforter, consoler and counsellor at every Commonwealth Conference since Ottawa, in 1973, was not going to be swept away because of a few terrorists. She knew the risk and was fully prepared to face any danger.

So, the tour was on. The Queen would go first to Tanzania, because Julius Nyerere was avid that he should not be left out, and then to Malawi. The Foreign Office thought it was important to visit Malawi to make the people there realize that they were still very much part of the Commonwealth; and to make up for any feeling of alienation since Dr Hastings Banda severed his relationship with South Africa.

When the visit was first discussed there was a Labour Government and Dr David Owen was Foreign Secretary. He admires the Queen: 'I am a great devotee. I respect her enormously; she handles herself well in every situation; a lady of quality,' but he remembers many a good-humoured brush with her over the visit to Africa. One of these was about Botswana, which Owen thought should not be excluded, although there were problems. 'It did not fit into the planning,' and it was so poor as a country, could it even cope with a royal visit?

The Queen never openly says she disapproves, although there is a subtle way by which Ministers and civil servants are left in no doubt about her wishes. Her thinking is flexible and she is a sensible creature. Owen insisted on the Botswana visit. 'I was anxious the Queen should go there because it seemed that this was the one democratic country in Africa and it was too easy to forget it ...' When, later, he met the Queen at a reception he said, 'I'm awfully sorry to be such a pest about Botswana,' and recalls receiving a sympathetic smile which implied, 'I think you were right.'

When the story of Zimbabwe is written the Queen may not get the full credit due to her. During the talks, the rows, the changes of heart about Zimbabwe she stayed steady – unswervingly detached. This could not have been easy. Some of her close family had, perhaps predictably, taken up right-wing positions. Her husband came down firmly on the side of the whites of Southern Africa in 1965 at the time of Ian Smith's unlawful Unilateral Declaration of Independence. And the Queen Mother, who had been Chancellor of the University College of Rhodesia and Nyasaland and had a former Rhodesian farmer on her staff, also felt for the white man about to be upstaged in the seventies by a Marxist, Jesuit-trained black African called Robert Mugabe. But curiously the Queen was put in the position of persuading her British Prime Minister to make a 180-degree turn that was not at first reassuring to the white farmers clinging on to their hard-won chunks of Rhodesia. It seems that, as Britain's world role diminishes, the ability of the Queen as Head of the Commonwealth to influence its leaders has increased.

In those early days of planning and talking about the problem of Bishop Muzorewa, Owen felt that: 'It would have been awfully easy for the Queen to come down on the side of those right-wing critics of Rhodesia, who were calling me a terrorist for getting involved with Nkomo and Mugabe.' But she remained impartial and inscrutable, so that Owen, like other Foreign Secretaries and Prime Ministers before him, felt he was being supported and given special understanding.

If the Queen was not scared about the visit to Zambia, many others were. The Editor of the *Daily Telegraph*, William Deedes, lunching with Rhodesian friends at the Hyde Park Hotel, was advised by a black diplomat that there was a very real danger about the visit. 'A deep anxiety about the Queen's safety,' was spelt out over the lamb cutlets, he said. A personal letter was sent by the Editor to the Queen's Private Secretary and to Number Ten. He was to be reassured later, on a golf course by William Whitelaw, that a dozen extra security men would accompany the Queen, but without her knowledge.

At Buckingham Palace for the pre-tour briefing, the Press were told baldly by the men from the Foreign Office that this was the Zimbabwe-Rhodesia battlefront. There would be the constant threat of 'activity' during the royal visit. Lusaka and the surrounding countryside was the major base for the Nationalist guerrilla campaign. The camps near Lusaka had been razed by the Salisbury forces, and the guerrilla leader Joshua Nkomo had pronounced a halt, but there was a real fear that the guerrillas might still identify the Queen with the Salisbury administration.

While the Queen was approving last-minute arrangements such as her white silk dress by Hartnell and her Simone Mirman cloche hat with red frills, and her maid was packing the Thawpit cleaner and iron for the plane, her Private Secretary, Sir Philip Moore, was talking to Number Ten, for nothing could demonstrate the Queen's commitment to the Commonwealth more convincingly than her willingness to allow Prince Andrew, then only seventeen, to go with her. And Air Commodore Archie Winskill, Captain of the Queen's Flight, had rather more to worry about than usual, for recently two Zambian Air Force jets had been shot down by mistake.

In Dar-es-Salaam roses were flown in from Kilimanjaro and special banana and spinach dishes prepared in honour of the 'Great Malkia's' arrival. Easy-going labourers took a desultory swish at the grass around the harbour with their pangas, fearsomely long knives which one can imagine being put to use on something less supple than feathery fronds.

When the Queen's press secretary in the same hotel got to his hotel room late one evening, he found that a black rat was joining him for the night. He spoke to the manager, and wondered amiably how the rat had got up to the sixth floor. 'Oh no, sir, he is not climbing up de stairs, he is coming down from de top floor where de restaurant is.' Shea had been offered Dar-es-Salaam as a posting before he joined Buckingham Palace but turned it down saying: 'My wife faints in the heat.'

The Queen, Prince Philip and Prince Andrew had rested for the night in a peaceful hill town called Arusha under the white shadow of Kilimanjaro. When their British Airways 707 landed on the newly-swept runway at Dar-es-Salaam the crowds shouted 'Uhuru' (freedom), and the Polisi – women police in special yellow T shirts – had their hair done in arches, twirls and beehives. President Nyerere, graduate of Edinburgh University and known as 'Father of Our Struggle' by the people, met the Queen.

'How nice to see you again,' the Queen smiled up at silver-haired Nyerere in his grey Mao suit. Six teenagers of the Militant Party Youth did a black goosestep on the red carpet and gave the Queen some frangipani, and she, more widely travelled than any Government servant alive in the Commonwealth, presented her Household as some Ngoma dancers energetically pounded out their welcome on the hot tarmac. Yet faced by a modest acacia tree planted by Princess Margaret in 1956, even the Queen was at a loss for a suitable word. How long? How old? Nothing seemed appropriate and it had hardly been worth the unedifying scramble up a muddy hillock. 'There is not a lot you can say about a tree,' one of the royal party sniffed. Of course, skill with a shovel is practically essential for a royal, but it can be embarrassing for them to see the fruits of their labours at a later date. Prince Charles has a theory that wherever he goes he finds that the trees planted by the Queen flourish, while his father's often remain pathetic and stunted. The spin-off for the locals of a royal visit is that the bureaucrats get things done. In Dar-es-Salaam pot-holes were filled in for the Queen's visit and in Lusaka tons of lavatory paper were flown in. Though despising the capitalist trappings, the Tanzanians had imported a fleet of Mercedes and a Rolls for the Queen.

The Queen, in diamonds and green chiffon, chose the State banquet to stress deep concern about the freedom of the individual in oppressive regimes. Nyerere spoke about liberating Africa from 'colonialism and racialism' and looked at the Queen, whose face had such an expression of polite interest he could have been praising the ladies' homemade sponge fingers at the Sandringham Women's Institute. But these exchanges brought the equivalent of nudges in the ribs from members of the Household, as if watching two of the family enjoying a favourite argument again. The Queen enjoys dining with Nyerere, Banda or Kaunda, finding them more fun for an evening than her own, clear-headed Prime Minister.

Malawi seemed luxurious after Tanzania. His Excellency the Life President, Dr Hastings Banda, that North London GP with his sinister dark glasses and unsmiling face, is different again from the statutory young law graduate from the London School of Economics leading his people along an enlightened path. He is, indeed, of a different generation. 'You are almost the same age as my mother and there's no stopping you,' the Queen once teased him. He has excellent taste in furnishings, wine and food, and the Queen was beautifully looked after in the Sankia Palace which, with its designer-chic from Europe and stilted grandeur, seemed opulent. On the evening of the State banquet there was a stunning blue and white marquee – that designer at work again – with a platform built over the swimming pool. The women's high heels sank into the soft turf round the pool as they were waiting to curtsey to the Queen.

The Queen disapproves of elbows on the table and once ticked off a member of the Household for this lapse. 'Are you tired? Are you certain you are not unwell?' But Banda is yet another of those African potentates whom the Queen has known from her teens, and for most of the State banquet her own elbows were on the table as she became wholly absorbed in Banda's serious political chat. Occasionally using her hands to emphasize a point she seemed completely unaware of her surroundings, the dignitaries unacknowledged in their imported finery, her Amontillado Victoria ignored, her Château de la Rivière 1967 untouched and her Rack of Mikolongwe lamb merely toyed with as the string orchestra sawed away at such extraordinarily British tunes as 'Berkshire Hills' and 'Hearts of Oak'.

Laughing women in special national dress, their leader's face imprinted on their rippling red calico bosoms, went by the lorry load each morning to be in position for 'spontaneous cheering' hours later when the Queen arrived. 'And where do they come from?' the Queen piped solemnly to the 'Lion of Malawi', seeing a horde of warriors swooping towards her in Lilongwe, the capital. Either the question was one of the safe old standbys dredged up from an apparently limited repertoire to cope with the unfamiliar, or it slyly acknowledged that the Queen knew many of the warriors were really bank managers and businessmen wearing nothing much more than ankle-bells, furry tails and disarming grins. She looked extraordinarily pale beside them.

The Queen and Prince Philip then met veterans of campaigns in Burma, India, Germany, East Africa and Ethiopia. Few of them had more than two or three teeth, but they threw their shoulders back, stood to attention and, when the Queen asked their names, just shouted their regimental numbers: 'Number 2723, sah', but had no idea about their ages. The cheering housewives were packed back on to their lorries again – although others walked fifty or sixty miles home – and the Queen drove off in a red Rolls to plant a tree brought from Windsor. A lot of care had been taken to make sure it would flourish but, even so, an English rose seemed slightly out of place in that atmosphere of lion-masks and leopard skins.

If Malawi had been comfortable – though the Press never got a chance to see under the costly façade of the tough regime: French wine and Rolls Royces can hardly have painted a true picture – Botswana was touching in its honesty. Formerly Bechuanaland and independent only since 1966, it had an unsophisticated, earthy welcome for the Queen. Her host was Sir Seretse Khama and his English-born wife, Ruth. On the way from Malawi the Queen's VC 10 skirted the sensitive area near Victoria Falls; the leaping spray was about as much of Rhodesia as she was likely to see, and at Francistown she changed to a trusty Andover because of the small inadequate runway at Gaberone. But there was room enough for small children, like elves in beaded skirts and Davy Crockett caps, who made the Queen laugh out loud as they danced their welcome. Bare-breasted nymphets swayed gracefully to the music, showing Prince Andrew more than a smile. But he was learning fast. He studiously talked to a couple of Government officials, knowing the lenses were trained on him, longing to catch his eye wandering. Members of the Household were keeping a careful eye on him, but he was acquitting himself well on this first major tour. Prince Philip could get away with a salty grin at the topless Welcoming Committee.

At the State Banquet tall, scholarly Sir Seretse Khama praised the Queen's 'great personal courage and commitment' in her determination to visit Southern Africa at 'the most difficult period in the history of the area'. There was a certain quiet satisfaction at the top table.

'*Pula*,' the Queen said with that clear diction, and this limited knowledge of the local dialect was enough to bring excited shrieks from the women, sounding like seagulls hovering over a haul of fish. *Pula* means 'rain' and of course in that dry red earth the word also means 'with blessing'. The market fair in Gaborone had never been so grandly launched. Security men with truncheons and grim looks were unnecessarily stern with the crowds. The nearer the Queen got to Zambia the greater the security. Even the royal detectives were pushed around, but were amused when they asked the names of their burly black chauffeurs. One said he was called 'Adolf' and another muscular fellow answered to 'Phyllis'. Sleek Brahman bulls and snooty camels with that look of 'you'll never catch me at a thing like that again' were shown to the Queen, and at the agricultural fair every sort of vegetable had been coaxed out of that arid earth. 'They must be well travelled,' the Queen said wryly when she saw gaudy reproductions of her crown jewels.

A village chief in Botswana, hearing the Queen was coming, asked conversationally, 'Oh, is that Queen Victoria?' 'Oh no,' he was told by a member of the royal reconnaissance party, 'I am afraid she is dead.' 'Well then,' he said huffily, 'why weren't we invited to the funeral?'

Friday, 27 July, and the flight to Zambia with all its uncertainties for the Queen. Ahead of her, in Lusaka, British High Commission officials were caring, but a bit taut. Zambian officials were tetchy. The Information Officer at the British High Commission, Richard Wilkins, allowed the Press to sit under the shade of trees for their briefing as, for security reasons, the airport buildings were closed and they faced a wait of nearly two hours in the sun. The atmosphere was tense as the Press moved to their pen near the end of the runway for the Queen's arrival. Crowds held up banners saying 'The South does not drink tea or coffee but Zambian Blood', and there was another, more direct, message: 'Britain should not remain impotent'. Richard Wilkins had not long recovered from hepatitis but he bore up with predictable Foreign Office grit, his wide mouth no barometer of his true feelings.

The tanks and guns lined up. Kenneth Kaunda, clutching his invariable white hanky, watched the Queen's plane come out of the clouds at 3.38 pm with a proud authority. As the pilot taxied along the runway everyone held their breath, tautly silent, dreading the sound of any gunfire. Some held their stomachs – already stricken by a virulent bug which made it impossible to stand even for the National Anthem. Cool, no hint of a worrying journey over terrorist country, the Queen came down the aircraft steps.

Banners saying 'Queenie Welcome' competed with the angry messages. Kaunda introduced his ample wife. The Queen met the British High Commissioner, Sir Leonard Allinson, KCVO, an ideal, pragmatic diplomat for these sensitive Anglo-Zambian relations, and with a nice sense of humour too. Then the Queen, Prince Philip and Prince Andrew were driven to Kaunda's country retreat, the State Lodge. It gave the Queen a chance to see a Lusaka sunset over a cluster of small hills: pink-gold skies, with scrubby trees and whirling vultures. Kaunda's two-storey house, built by a Swedish architect, gave the Queen simple comfort. There was a large reception room, enough bedrooms for the ladies-in-waiting and a fair-sized swimming pool.

Never an emotional lot, at Lusaka the Press were glad to see even the royal Household. On tours abroad, even though there can be testiness between the Palace and the Press, it only takes an implied discourtesy to the Queen, hustling security bullying and manhandling the photographers or a dangerous journey like the one just undertaken to produce a closer bond. Even so, conditions there were overcrowded and uncomfortable. Tummy troubles were rife; so were burglars and cockroaches. The best hotels had been taken over by the Household, the Foreign Office and the Number Ten staff. As the Press suffered in a fairly primitive university hostel it would have been nice at the time to know that even the Thatchers had discomfort. 'No hot water, Denis,' Mrs Thatcher said briskly to her husband on the first morning. Before he had time to work out how he would shave for the midday reception the ceiling suddenly fell in on the bed.

The delicate role played by the Queen at Commonwealth Conferences is a conundrum. Why, as Head of the Commonwealth, does she not officially open the meeting? This is always done by the host country. Nor does she take part in the Conference sessions. Yet in Lusaka, sitting in a simple room, she became privy to most of the secrets, aims and ploys of the countries taking part. These meetings took place in the Mulungushi village, where an office had been set up for the Queen in a compound bungalow like a small stone suburban cottage. There, with the minimum furniture and a bleak view of a grey enclosed courtyard, she received a vital piece of paper from Sir Philip Moore before each audience. All the Prime Ministers and Presidents will tell you, 'She is a marvellous listener', and that brief always helped by pinpointing the difficulties and traumas of each country.

Her programme during those days read like some frenzied tour arranged by a mad travel agent:

11.00 am	Malawi
11.20 am	Australia
11.40 am	etc.

Audiences went on all day until five. The Queen, simply dressed, became a sort of superior civil servant, never lecturing, but occasionally saying: 'Yes, well, I remember that was a plan which was talked about in the fifties.' Guiding and calming but, as a member of her Household pointed out, 'It was never a bland chat.' These were talks between the Queen and Heads of State in which she played the role of a detached and problem-solving umpire.

She was a stabilizing influence at Lusaka, and the feeling is that she persuaded Mrs Thatcher to take her time: 'Steady on, we must avoid the Commonwealth breaking up.' There are those who believe that it was she who persuaded Mrs Thatcher to change her mind about recognizing the Muzorewa regime and to go for a settlement. The Australian Prime Minister, Malcolm Fraser, was a more open influence but tangentially it was the Queen. She would never openly say, 'Look, I am very worried,' but found ways, with a skill both feminine and diplomatic, to steer people towards what she believed was right. It is said that when Queen Juliana of the Netherlands once asked the Queen 'What do you do when your husband wants something and you don't want him to have it?' Queen Elizabeth replied: 'Oh, I just tell him he shall have it and make sure he doesn't get it.' An unlikely answer but reflecting a woman's way of sidestepping without the loss of much fur or too many feathers.

In every sense of the word it was a potentially explosive Commonwealth Conference that summer of 1979. Now it is seen as a triumph, and it might be easy to forget the Queen's skill, spending day after day in her bungalow while some of her Household sat by the swimming pool. The Commonwealth Secretary-General, Shridath Ramphal – known as 'Sonny', an old Empire abbreviation – said afterwards that the Queen was among the best informed of all Commonwealth watchers. Lyrically he described how 'the Queen brought to Lusaka a healing touch of rather special significance.' Kenneth Kaunda, who can turn unnervingly glacial if he is displeased, felt that she had been a 'tonic for race relations everywhere', and indeed this Conference was to give a new perception of the Queen. Like the horsewoman she is, she wanted to be the leader, to be up with the hounds, to assess the challenge and to be the first to skim the fences. The fact that she was in Lusaka reminded everyone of her ability as Commonwealth Head to soar above the transient threats and the tension. She may in one sense symbolize the old-fashioned Queen Empress but the Conference is no longer an old-fashioned get-together of her devoted black chiefs. And the Queen knew most of the leaders better than they knew each other. For her, talking to Banda, a member of the Household said, 'was like talking to Uncle Dickie' – the late Earl Mountbatten.

One irreverent opinion is that the Queen gets on so well with the African Presidents because, to her, they are like butlers – slightly bumptious butlers. But she is a success precisely because she does not see them like that or patronize them. These extraordinarily strong men value the personal contact and they queue up to see her.

On one occasion when the Queen did venture out from Number 3 Mulungushi Village she got a verbal buffeting. Wearing a rather becoming apricot silk dress and matching pillbox, she was to be given a civic welcome in Lusaka. But the Mayor of Lusaka, Mr Simon Mweme, in ermine-trimmed robes and wearing a copper chain of office, harangued her, going on about the 'war of liberation' and pausing occasionally to invite the Queen to reply. Deadpan and calm, the Queen replied lightly, 'No, thank you very much.' There was then some 'traditional, spontaneous dancing' but it was soon apparent that the dancers were wearing white 'settler' shorts, bush jackets and hats and were laying about them with swagger sticks – a crude message conveying resentment of the days before independence. The Queen is at her best in a crisis. She may not laugh a lot on relaxed, easy going occasions, but she is a model of cool appraisal in moments of gaucherie. This was the first ugly incident in Lusaka. The Mayor, known locally as 'Baby Elephant', claimed later 'I did not offend the Queen.'

After such a high key intense week Lusaka Agricultural Fair was just what everybody needed. Looking completely relaxed in the shade of a feathery jacaranda tree, the Queen chatted to the farmers about familiar breeds. 'Of course, I'm a farmer myself,' she said, watching a massive prize-winning bull called Karl Marx, with thick curly jowls, disgrace himself by having a run at the Supreme Champion's rosette. Twelve Zambian Lancers on greys cantered on the grass in front of the stands where the Queen was now sitting. Women in the crowd in sugar-candy colours – limes, yellows and pinks – craned forward. It was a bit like a fair in Norfolk, a lot of white faces well tanned. Later, inspecting blue and white chickens, the Queen commented: 'I can't think of a better way to mark the last afternoon of my stay.' 'We can tell our children that once upon a time we saw a most gracious and beautiful lady, the Queen,' said an emotional commentator to great cheers.

In seventeen days, the Queen had covered 15,000 miles. The cost to the Foreign Office of the visit of the Queen to Kenya, Tanzania, Malawi, Botswana and Zambia for the Commonwealth Heads of Government Meeting 19 July–4 August was £61,665.59. The figure covers advance visits by reconnaissance parties, gifts and gratuities, outfit and luggage allowances, freight and insurance, hotel accommodation, subsistence and cost of State dinners, extra communications equipment and miscellaneous expenditure. Not included is the cost of transport to and from Africa and within Africa. The visit was more complex than most for many reasons, of which security was the most important.

The Palace is not shy about submitting meticulous bills to the Foreign Office for the unexpected 'extras' of a royal tour. In Lusaka every stick of furniture was pressed into service for the Conference so that even tables and chairs had to be flown in for the royal banquet.

The visit had been a triumph. Once the Queen had arrived in Lusaka all suspicion and hostility evaporated. Its success made everyone high spirited on the royal flight home. The Queen would never boast. 'It is not in the Queen's nature to,' a member of the Household said with some pride. Instead, sitting at the front of the VC 10, she sent for her Household and complimented them on the way the visit had gone. For Sir Peter Ashmore, Head of the Household and a man of quiet modesty with a look of Sir Alec Guinness, there were special thanks. He had the greatest headaches of the tour, organizing the banquet to the smallest detail, making sure that there was ice for the drinks but also that the water had been boiled beforehand.

Saturday, 4 August 1979. It was one of the most moving farewells the Queen has known in all her years of travel. As the plane took off she could see Kenneth Kaunda still waving his white handkerchief and the crowds kept chanting 'Bye bye, Queenie'. She looked down and then quickly had to look away. Those near her know that her 'glum' face is often a visor pulled down as a shield against any show of emotion. But even years of relentless self control can sometimes give way to a sudden tear or glittering of the eyes. She settled back in her seat and was glad to be reminded of the moment on the tour which she savoured most: overhearing one astonished African chief saying to another a minute after meeting her, 'My God, the Queen is a woman.'

CHAPTER 16

❇ ❇ ❇

Ho-ho, Mr Wilson?

WHATEVER THE QUEEN is doing, each Tuesday evening at Buckingham Palace will find her, just before 5 pm, walking along the corridor to her sitting-room/study with her handbag over her arm. This is when the weekly audience takes place with the Prime Minister, when both are in London. The atmosphere is intimate, in winter there is an open fire, and the Queen and the Prime Minister sit rather cosily in armchairs. Working with the Prime Minister's Private Secretary at Number Ten, Sir Philip Moore will have prepared a brief with a number of topics to be raised, but woe betide the Prime Minister who goes along ill-prepared, assuming the conversation will stay on these fixed lines. 'I was so interested to see that point raised at a Cabinet sub-committee,' the Queen might say ... and the poor Prime Minister might just have missed it. The wise ones always confess. 'I would tell her if I did not know and go back to my secretary and give him hell,' one said, with a chuckle.

The Queen is now dealing with her eighth Prime Minister and talking to Sir Harold Wilson one has the feeling that she got on best of all with him. There is no doubt that Sir Harold's style did entertain the Queen at those weekly audiences. As someone at the Palace remarked, 'It is funny really; the royals will often get on with a bit of a rum cove – suppose it is the attraction of opposites.' And it would be quite wrong to imagine that the Tory Prime Ministers were always the favourites.

Churchill was her first Prime Minister and he was a bit in love with her – 'she's a pet' he told his physician Lord Moran and said he prayed that she would not be overworked in that first year as

Queen in 1952: 'She's doing so well.' In fact, Churchill had been almost embarrassingly besotted by her since her days as Princess Elizabeth. At a dinner party given by the Speaker of the House of Commons at which the Princess was guest of honour, he became, according to another guest, 'very noisy and all over the place'. The Princess watched him, her father's closest adviser and a man of seventy-four, with a deeply affectionate, almost maternal look, her head on one side. 'What extraordinary wisdom on that young woman's face. Sitting there in full fig, with the Garter, Churchill clearly regarded her as magical,' a Privy Councillor who was present said.

Edward Heath was terribly shy and hesitant at the audiences and, of course, very often, it is the person the Queen is talking to who sets the pace: if he or she is easy and unselfconscious then she herself unbends. Sir Alec Douglas Home – now Lord Home – was only Prime Minister for a year. Sir Harold Wilson had an easy relationship. There was a terrific rapport with Callaghan, and lots of fun. With her first woman Prime Minister, Mrs Thatcher, it is always formal, very correct and concerned, certainly no giggling. In a way the two women are perhaps too alike: meticulous, well-groomed, controlled, informed and in the same age group. When Mrs Thatcher suggested that the Queen should not go to Lusaka there was a burst of irritation at the Palace. The advice might have been better taken from chunky Jim Callaghan, but never from another woman. It is the Labour Prime Ministers who are lyrical in retirement about the Queen, some of them almost surprised to find that she really is Britain's best-informed person. Jim Callaghan, that extremely experienced politician, said that he always left the Palace after his weekly meetings feeling marvellously refreshed.

When Prime Ministers arrive, they are given a cup of tea and then taken by lift to the Queen's study. If the meeting is taking place at Balmoral, they will be offered 'the wine of the country'. The Queen will never lecture or say brusquely, 'I never heard of such an idea.' If a Prime Minister should suggest some crazy notion she might say gently, 'I think you'll find that idea was tried out in 1951 and was rejected.'

Prime Ministers all find that a great commonsense shines out; there is the reassuring feeling that the Queen knows what she is talking about and cares. She is always 'anxious to know what is going on, and loves good constituency stories,' or so she would have her Prime Minister believe. But any civil servants who may have been a bit slack over a briefing policy document are soon caught out.

The regard Prime Ministers have for the Queen is partly because she is a skilled counsellor but has no itch to interfere in public affairs. After all, if you are Queen, why should you want to be a politician? Unlike Queen Victoria there is no high-handedness either: her great-great-grandmama would ask queru-lously, 'Why is my Navy not being put to better use in India?' in her idiosyncratic way. The Queen's role is as a wise, dispassionate stateswoman. On the other hand, if she feels that Government has done something of which she disapproves, a Minister will be firmly ticked off.

The Hilton Hotel in Park Lane overlooks the sensitive north corner of the Palace where the royal family lives. At the time per-mission was given for its building there was a direct rebuke. Geof-frey Rippon was the Minister of Public Buildings and Works and the blood drained from his face as the Queen unexpectedly chiv-vied him before lunch at the Palace. How could he have given per-mission for such a building? The Queen and her family were furious at the thought of being overlooked by this skyscraper hotel. Poor Geoffrey Rippon went into lunch chilled by that cer-tain coldness in her voice. If the Queen is cross, she will ask, 'Why are we doing this?' and then move on to the next point.

Another thing Prime Ministers appreciate is that she is not taken by surprise. She has had a lifetime's hard training, is equal to any-thing and extremely adept at thinking quickly. They find she never makes a frivolous or fatuous remark. This is more than can be said for her uncle, Edward VIII, who would often offer a slightly inane aside which would leave even the silkiest politician open-mouthed and only able to mutter, 'Well, Your Majesty ...' And the Queen, again unlike her uncle, assiduously reads her State papers, spending up to three hours a day on them. Sometimes Prince Charles is invited to study them with her, but never Prince Philip, who is not in line of succession. However, his advice and modern flair have helped the Queen grow in confidence and politi-cal understanding. In Edward VIII's day these boxes, in bright or battered red morocco leather with a brass handle, were often left lying around Fort Belvedere, the papers coffee-stained or flipped through by bright young things with excellent martinis in thin, jewelled hands. In contrast the Queen does her homework and expects her Ministers to have done theirs. In the same way, if she is going on an awkward State visit, she feels that the Foreign Secretary should go too.

There is a curious and charmingly old-fashioned custom by which a member of the Lord Chamberlain's office goes to Parliament each day and takes a handwritten note of the proceedings. He takes his place at 2.30 pm and, with a fountain pen filled with blue-black ink, writes his notes. Then they are delivered by hand direct to the Queen before dinner. This enables her to be as well informed as any of her guests that evening. There is a rather feminine touch about this, because very often the Queen will pin the note to a bracket on her dressing-table mirror and, between dabs with a powder puff, bring herself up to date on the day in Parliament. She keeps her eye on that piece of paper except for a quick glance to see that lipstick is going on straight; but tiara, diamond earrings and bracelets all go on in abstracted seconds with scarcely a look.

When the Queen goes to Parliament, she is, as one politician put it, 'the third wheel of the invalid carriage; the other two being the Lords and Commons!' Unlike her predecessors, she no longer appoints a Lords Commissioner to signify Royal Assent to Bills in the presence of both Houses, except on the last day before prorogation of Parliament. The change was made because the Commons objected to the flummery interrupting their deliberations when they were summoned to the Upper House. Her formal relations with the two houses are now reduced to one personal appearance at the beginning of each session – normally a late October or early November day. This is the only time the Queen wears the Imperial Crown of State: just for that brief half hour at the State Opening of Parliament, which is part social and part constitutional and, of course, a full-dress affair. The State Crown is brought under guard in a horse-drawn brougham to the Palace of Westminster. It is then carried reverently up the stairs to the Queen's Robing Room. This is a splendid Chamber and is not used for any other purpose, although the final hearing of the case against 'Lord Haw-Haw' – William Joyce – took place there in 1946 when he had brought an appeal to the House of Lords.

The robing of the Queen is not a public affair, and indeed when she appears in her Crown, dazzling with jewels and with her procession behind her to go to the Lords, it is a miracle that the regalia and robes are in place, because there is no full-length mirror. There is only an ugly Georgian dressing-table laid out with a brush, a comb and a hand mirror – typically masculine thinking. Kings probably never wanted to look in a mirror even to see if the Crown was on straight. As soon as the Queen emerges from the Robing Room, and glasses of champagne are put down hurriedly in the wings, one of the Women of the Bedchamber tidies away the things on the dressing-table in case anyone nips in and tries to collect them as souvenirs. It is a long walk to the Lords. The procession has formed up in the Royal Gallery, headed by heralds dressed rather like mobile playing cards in tabards and long hose. They are followed by two great officers of State, the senior is the hereditary but apparently unsalaried Lord Great Chamberlain, Keeper of the Palace of Westminster and not to be confused with the other Lord Chamberlain, Lord 'everyone calls me Oyster Eyes' Maclean. He sends out invitations to garden parties at Buckingham Palace and is also in charge of ceremonial at royal weddings and all grand royal occasions. These leaders of the procession walk backwards, the tradition being that they are guarding the Sovereign. But probably they are just keeping an eye on the country's other main asset – the State Crown with its Koh-i-Noor diamond and the Black Prince's ruby. After all, a nineteenth-century Indian prince, the deposed heir to the Punjab, referred to Queen Victoria as 'Mrs Fagin' after the receiver of stolen goods in *Oliver Twist* and claimed that she had no more right to the great diamond than he had to Windsor Castle!

When Richard Crossman was Lord President of the Council in 1967, he thought in his blustering way that he could not be bothered to hire morning dress for the State Opening of Parliament and sent a letter to the Duke of Norfolk, the Earl Marshal, Hereditary Marshal and Chief Butler of England, saying he had a phobia about such occasions. He received a stiffly outraged reply suggesting he was not attending the State Opening because of anti-monarchical sentiments and that only the Queen could relieve him of such an obligation.

The whole affair escalated, and the Prime Minister, Harold Wilson, who enjoyed such a favoured relationship with the Queen, became rather embarrassed. Then an adroit pulling of strings at the Palace totally disarmed Crossman. He tells of meeting the Queen's Private Secretary, Sir Michael Adeane, to explain why he would not attend the State Opening the following week. 'When we had driven into Buckingham Palace it was pitch dark and I found some difficulty in discovering the door to his little office,' he remembered. Adeane, clear, cool and respected, said in a frank way, 'You mucked things up terribly by writing to the Duke of Norfolk,' adding that if only he had been approached, he could have cleared it with the Queen straight away. 'In fact, I can clear it now if you really do not want to go.'

Suddenly faced with the choice, Crossman, like a mulish child, began to think again and Adeane took the opportunity to let him know that the Queen did not relish these public ceremonies either. Thinking out loud, he said, 'It will certainly occur to her to wonder why you should be excused when she has to go, since you're both officials.' Game, set and match to the Queen and her team!

That night Crossman wrote to Sir Michael and said he would be there; as a politician he relished the masterly way he had been manipulated. And when he went, sulky still about the formal clothes, he slipped into the Palace of Westminster still in his ordinary suit. But surrounded by robes and splendour and the festive atmosphere, he sheepishly put on a morning suit and 'actually found it perfectly comfortable'. The Queen enjoys this sort of skirmish – much more fun than dealing with an obsequious Lord President.

Like his father before him, George V had the eyes of a falcon where dress was concerned and could spot the tiniest slovenly mistake. He was insistent to the point of being pernickety on correct dress for his Ministers. Harold Nicolson, in his *Life* of the King, highlights his difficulties when faced by his new Labour Government's relaxed attitude to clothes. The King was sympathetic about the cost of evening clothes. 'In no case do I expect anyone to get more than the levee coat, full dress is not necessary on account of the expense.' But when his Private Secretary, Lord Stamfordham, made enquiries he found that a full coat of levee dress would amount to £73. 2. 6d, an enormous sum which the Labour Ministers would not dream of spending on clothes. Further enquiries were made and there was the delightful discovery that a well-known, dependable firm, 'Messrs Moss Bros', had in stock a 'few suits of Household, Second Class, Levee Dress from £30 complete – a coat, a cocked-hat, trousers and sword being the regulation dress and the figure £30 being most accommodating for the Labour MPs ...'

Crossman wrote afterwards, 'The only grand things I saw were the Crown ... and the Queen herself with the royal princes and princesses.' He added, waspishly, that Lord Snowdon's top hat had fallen off before he even got out of his car and concluded that really the older royals were best. Like a true Socialist, he appreciated the true aristocracy; admiring the elegance of the Dowager Duchess of Kent 'but not the goofy Duke of Gloucester, looking terrible with his very dull wife.'

The measured procession reaches the Chamber of the Upper House, the Law Lords like a pride of lions, the Bishops and the diplomats, the peers and peeresses, jewels twinkling in the arc lights. The Queen – nowadays with her spectacles: a moment of anguish, has she forgotten them! – reaches the throne. There is rustling of silks and satins as the Queen invites the audience, 'Be seated!' Black Rod now summons the Commons to attend Her Majesty immediately in the House of Lords. They slam the door in his face, then relent and open it. This is an annual reminder that the Queen must wait for the Commons, and it is not lost on her.

When the Commons eventually arrive, the Lord Chancellor, Lord Hailsham, in his long black gown, offers the Speech from the Throne and everyone holds their breath as he does the long walk backwards from the steps of the Throne. Lord Hailsham, though thoroughly dependable in nearly every way, is always expected to take a flier, for he usually has to have the support of at least one walking stick as he reverses on his hazardous journey from the Queen, waiting with a sympathetic twinkle. (A royal concession spared him this ordeal in 1982.)

The spectacles are on and the reading of the Speech begins. Those who have heard this speech over the years say that the diction is better now, with much more expression in the voice. There is always a slight frisson and change of tempo when the Queen says directly to the House of Commons: 'Estimates for the public service will be laid before you.' This is the tactful way of asking for money to cover her official expenses as well as those of the Government.

Although she is expert at ceremonial, the Queen does understand that, for portly gentlemen of uncertain years, walking

backwards can be an awful hazard. A typical example of this is the
ceremony at Buckingham Palace for the creation of Privy Councillors. These appointments date back to the days of absolute
monarchy, when the Privy Council, a group of handpicked advisers, really ran the country. At a solemn ceremony before the
Queen, members of the cabinet of each new government are
sworn in as Privy Councillors, an honour lasting a lifetime and
entitling them to be known as 'The Right Honourable'. For nearly
an hour the new Ministers have a rehearsal: learning how to kneel
on one knee on a cushion, how to raise the right hand with the
Bible in it, how to advance ten paces towards the Queen, take her
hand and kiss it. However accomplished in their own fields, it can
be awesome for the Ministers, and even the Queen is uneasy as
they make their obeisance in the great drawing-room. One of
them remembered her as 'this little woman with a beautiful waist',
standing with her hand on the table for forty minutes. At the end,
when they had all been sworn in, the Queen laughed as they
breathed a sigh of relief. 'You all moved backwards very nicely,'
she said with a gracious smile, then pressed a bell and the senior
politicians left as high-spirited as schoolboys.

Generally only the Privy Councillors in the Cabinet attend meetings with the Queen; there are about twelve each year and very
formal, but they can be hilarious. If the meetings are in Balmoral
the Privy Councillors usually catch the overnight sleeper or fly to
Aberdeen early in the morning. They drive along the Dee Valley
into the Grampians and then to Balmoral, finding themselves at an
imposing Scottish baronial house with a rose garden and a golf
course. Some of them manage a quick game before the meeting.
Often the Queen will have been out riding and her Privy Councillors see her galloping back into the yard. They change into formal
clothes and stand round the Queen as the Lord President drones a
list of fifty or sixty items, to which the Queen, sitting down, must
say, 'Agreed'. It is very solemn, 'Seychelles Legislature' – 'Agreed'.
But the real test for the Privy Council is to stand firm through the
often persistent snuffling at their ankles by the corgis.

Once, late by half an hour for a Privy Council meeting, the
Queen, who hates unpunctuality, later explained over drinks. 'My
horse got a stone in his foot when we were farthest from the
house. One always carries one of those penknives, doesn't one, as
an instrument for taking out stones, but today was the one day I

didn't have it.' With a deadpan expression she added that the horse she was riding that day was Russian, a present from Bulganin, but obviously it had a rebellious streak. 'Margaret took it out once and had gone over six bridges but at the seventh it refused: it wouldn't budge, though the bridge was exactly like all the others. Hours later we all found Margaret standing by the bridge and the horse as mutinous as ever.' The thought of Princess Margaret standing with a wry expression and a stubborn horse was quite ticklish.

When Roy Mason, then Secretary of State for Northern Ireland, was unexpectedly called to Balmoral for a Privy Council meeting, he said, while walking with the Queen, a bit uneasily, 'I see, Ma'am, that all your Ministers are in their tweeds.' The Queen smiled and tapped her finger on his chest. 'How useful a string vest is, Mr Mason,' neatly making him feel at home in his light-weight suit and transparent shirt.

Sir Godfrey Agnew, who was Clerk to the Privy Council Office from 1953 to 1974, once had to keep the peace when it seemed the Queen would be unable to give the Privy Councillors lunch in Balmoral because of a private engagement. Crossman said sulkily, 'We shall have to have it in the servants' quarters.' But the Queen altered her private engagement and was able to entertain them to lunch. Once there were scathingly sharp words for a Labour Privy Councillor who grumbled about one of the Titles of Orders, saying, 'This is the first I've heard about this.' The Queen swung round and said, 'How could you? You have not attended the last two Privy Council meetings,' and he went rather quiet and white. But most of the Privy Council meetings are very short and as happy as the one approving the Prince of Wales's marriage. Afterwards, when they all went into the dining-room at Buckingham Palace, Lady Diana Spencer was sitting demurely at the lunch table smiling shyly under her fringe at them, pretending she did not know whether they had said yes or no.

Every September the Prime Minister, with wife or husband, goes to Balmoral for the weekend. Late on Sunday, as after any good house party, they take their leave, often with a present of game from the Queen. Sir Harold Wilson cherishes the memory of one particular Balmoral weekend. They had been to church in the morning, had lunch – 'often a Scottish relative would be invited' – and then changed into something comfortable; for the

Queen that meant a headscarf, wellingtons – nowadays rather trendy ones by Lady Northampton – one of those distinctive quilted jackets known as a husky and a tweed skirt. Sir Harold always eschewed wellingtons and wore his golfing shoes. The Queen said airily, 'Let's go and see Philip's house.' Quite often she might say, 'Let's go and see my mother.' This may sound very informal and spontaneous, but is actually a carefully calculated way of keeping guests entertained – the royal family shares the load. If there is a State visit to London, on the day of arrival the King of Nepal – or whoever – will have lunch at the Palace, go to Westminster Abbey and nearly always have tea with the Queen Mother at Clarence House at about five.

The Queen said she had built the house for Prince Philip in the woods down by the river. Sir Harold got into the car – 'Just Mary and me, there were no detectives, and we drove for quite a long way on winding roads through the estate past those tiny, well-built houses including the famous one used by John Brown in Queen Victoria's day. There were lots of barbecue spots, too, where the Queen and Prince Philip cook steaks and sausages outside.'

Once they got to the house they wandered round and then the Queen made some tea. It was 'completely informal'. Sir Harold puffed his pipe while his wife and the Queen dealt with the dishes, one with a tea towel in her hands the other washing up the cups: just the sort of thing that was going on in those back-to-back houses in Sir Harold's birthplace, Huddersfield.

Weekends at Windsor were different, and much grander, Sir Harold recalled. Once, when Hubert Humphrey, the American Vice-President, was in Britain on an official visit he was invited to Windsor Castle for dinner, 'a black tie affair, of course'. There was a sparkling dinner party and at the end of the evening the Prime Minister thought he'd like a nightcap with his old friend, Hubert. Their rooms were near each other in a long corridor so he went to say goodnight and suggested a noggin. 'I pressed a button and a chap came in, he had taken his hair off – his wig – and I don't think he was too pleased; anyway, I asked him for a couple of drinks. He disappeared and came back with a bottle ... Hubert was terribly moved by all this and was quite emotional ... He kept saying: "Just think, a lad from a Milwaukee drugstore sitting here drinking the Queen's whisky."'

The Queen does not make fine distinctions between politicians of different parties. In her view they all belong to roughly the same category. Three times she has had to play her constitutional role and send for someone who, with the succession unclear, would command a majority in Parliament. The first time the Queen exercised this political prerogative was in 1957, when Sir Anthony Eden – later Lord Avon – was forced to resign because of ill health. His successor, Harold Macmillan, got on famously with the Queen, and he was impressed by her grasp of political events, how she enjoyed the fun and games of political fencing, loved watching the professional antics of politicians and was intrigued by the personalities. Macmillan remarked to a member of the royal family that it was a pity the Queen's sparkle and humour were so often hidden under a solemn face. The answer came back from the Queen herself that as Sovereign she should look serious; people expected it.

The second time the Queen invoked her prerogative was in 1963, with the fall of the Conservative Government under Macmillan as a result of the Profumo scandal. Harold Macmillan was visited by the Queen in his hospital bed. It was an emotional moment. 'She came in alone with a firm step and those brightly shining eyes which are her chief beauty. She seemed moved, so was I.' Macmillan took a number of soundings on his successor and the vote reported to the Queen was: 10 for Home; 4 for Maudling; 3 for Butler; 2 for Hailsham.

Sir Alec Douglas-Home was witty, a friend of the Bowes-Lyons and Elphinstones in Scotland and often a guest at Balmoral at shooting parties – almost one of the family. He believes that the Queen would never hesitate to use her prerogative. 'If someone was contesting the leadership and was known to get drunk three times a week, the Queen would put her foot down!' Like other Prime Ministers, he found her 'marvellous' and left weekly audiences feeling encouraged and cheered. His view of Elizabeth II is that if she were not the Queen she might be Head of Chatham House or the Jockey Club.

The third occasion was in 1974, at the uneasy time when Edward Heath was forced to resign. Their relationship had been stilted and he often appeared cold and distant. One of his contemporaries said, 'Ted was rather shy and reserved, but the Queen brought him out of his shell, you know.' And of course the Queen is now more experienced than any of her senior Ministers. 'You find that you are talking to somebody much more experienced than anyone round the Cabinet table because they would have their heads down, while she rises above it all.'

There are ten things the Queen could do with the royal prerogative: dismiss the government; declare war; disband the army; sell all the ships in the navy; dismiss the civil service; give territory away to a foreign power; make everyone a peer; declare a state of emergency (as she had to do on 31 May 1955 because of the railway strike); pardon all offenders; establish a university in any parish. It is only the selection of Prime Minister and the granting or withholding of a request for the dissolution of Parliament that she does without the advice of Ministers.

In the same way that other people prize royal anecdotes, the royal family love to come up with a good dinner party story about some political intrigue. Once Sir Harold (at that time, Mr) Wilson was caught on the hop at one of the weekly audiences at Buckingham Palace, not on some constitutional point but on the question of Lieutenant-Colonel John Brooks, famous in November 1974 as the Spanking Colonel in honour of his unashamed fondness for spanking nubile young women on his boat on the Thames. There is often some rivalry between the Queen and her Prime Ministers about the latest news. The Queen wanted to know all about that rather racy case and her Private Secretary received a mock stern query, 'Why didn't I have a later edition?' The following week Sir Harold turned up and said, 'Have you seen the latest editions of the *Evening Standard* today, Ma'am?' The evening papers were full of a story about Giscard d'Estaing driving all over France with some ladies of doubtful virtue in his car. Sir Harold told the Queen about this as she always loved stories about the French: 'Ho-ho, Mr Wilson!' she said with relish.

Mr Wilson then had to go to France and Prime Ministers always have to ask the Queen's permission to leave the country. 'It is my humble duty to beg Your Majesty's leave to go to Paris, Ma'am.' The Queen chuckled and was obviously very amused, 'thinking I'd be taking Giscard's car all over Paris, etc.' He went to France, had a private dinner with the French President; reported to the Foreign Office officials travelling with him that he did not feel too well, and had an early night.

As always, with that slightly mischievous interest in political gossip, the Queen could hardly wait to ask the Prime Minister the following week how he had got on. 'Well, how did it go?' she asked immediately, and Mr Wilson, gravely sitting on the other side of the fireplace, reported in detail about the meeting and the points raised until the Queen leant forward and, with a solemn look, inquired, 'Ho-ho, Mr Wilson?'

'Ma'am,' he replied with a saintly expression. 'There was no ho-ho; everyone went to bed early.'

The prospect of the Queen's weekly audiences with her first woman Prime Minister filled everyone with gleeful anticipation but they were to be disappointed, although there is just a hint of the distaste felt by Queen Victoria for the patronizing attitude of one of her least favourite Prime Ministers. 'Mr Gladstone speaks to me as if I were a public meeting,' she confided to her diary.

Mrs Thatcher treats the weekly audiences with great respect and discretion. But there is a feeling among the Household that the first woman Prime Minister may not, perhaps, be quite as much fun as the avuncular Callaghan or, indeed, any of the men invited to stroll round the Palace gardens or have a de-briefing Scotch with the Private Secretary afterwards. There was delight on board the royal yacht in discovering that Mrs Thatcher called her husband, Denis, 'DT'. They noticed her curtsey was one of the lowest and the most correct, and Mrs Thatcher loved being taken over *Britannia* and admired the chintzy furnishings, which are very much in her own, Peter Jones, taste. Mrs Thatcher is always immaculately groomed; in this the Queen and she have much in common; even their hairstyles have the same imperviousness to wind. Before the Prime Minister's visit to the Gulf in April 1981 the weekly audience ended with a womanly chat as the Queen suggested what she should wear and when she should wear long clothes, 'all the time in Saudi Arabia'. At one point, Mrs Thatcher was very nearly being shown the Queen's wardrobe. At one of the Buckingham Palace garden parties, soon after the Conservative victory when she freshly enjoyed being Prime Minister, Mrs Thatcher saw people waving, thought it was for her, and gave a warm wave back. The Queen, watching this, gave her a frosty look and went into the Palace with her corgis.

Once the Prime Minister felt she had made a *faux pas* when both she and the Queen wore blue to the same banquet. Her Private Office discreetly tried to enquire at the Palace if there was any way her staff could check on what the Queen might be wearing on a certain date ahead so that she did not make the same mistake again. There was an extremely brisk reply from Buckingham Palace to Number Ten Downing Street which advised Mrs Thatcher not to fret: 'The Queen does not notice what other people are wearing!'

CHAPTER 17

✾ ✾ ✾

Down Under

QUEEN VICTORIA ONCE got so cross about things in Europe that she seriously thought of going to Australia. 'I am sick of all this horrid business of politics and Europe in general and think you will hear of me going with the children to live in Australia.' That was in 1859, and the voyage would have taken her about five months. The visit to Melbourne for the 1981 Commonwealth Conference, which earned the ugly, unwieldly name CHOGM (Commonwealth Heads of Government Meetings) was the Queen's eighth to Australia. And that perhaps is one reason why that tour of Australia and New Zealand, 'always loyal', was low key. It was rather like a favourite aunt coming to see them even though she had been staying only the previous weekend: an assured welcome but no need to fuss.

The New Zealanders claimed that they were emotionally exhausted by the Springbok rugby football tour – which split several families and gave rise to discussions on such fundamental subjects as the role of monarchy. Only highchairs and wheelchairs seemed to have turned out to see the Queen and Prince Philip. The royal wedding had whetted the appetite for a sight of the Prince and Princess of Wales. A lesser woman than the Queen might have even felt a tinge of jealousy at such fickleness. 'Sex and glamour, that's what they want,' Jim Biddulph, Hong Kong correspondent for the BBC laconically summed up the mob's eagerness for the newly-weds. But the Queen seemed sometimes blissfully unaware – waving, smiling, being kind, sometimes wearing blue, which the writer Patrick White cynically saw as 'her pale-blue-specially-for-the-Colonies dress', when he was invited to lunch on the *Britannia* in Sydney in 1963. He remembered, too, in his self-portrait *Flaws in the Glass* (Jonathan Cape, 1981) how, as soon as he set foot on deck, an 'amiable Anglicized equerry' assured him he had read *Voss*, one of White's most challenging books, and that indeed a copy was lying on Her Majesty's bedside commode!

On the Queen's first visit to Australia in 1954, nine months after the Coronation, a crowd of 300,000 went mad when they caught a glimpse of the twenty-seven-year-old monarch. She was a glamorous figure then – but also the mother of two young children. In 1981 she returned as a grandmother, aged fifty-five. There was no television in 1954 so it was thought well worthwhile to line the streets for hours. Today, thousands – and this applies in Britain too – might fail to turn out for a royal visit to their home town but can still enjoy the ceremonial later on television. Yet republican rumblings in Australia did not dull the regard for a hard-working Queen. Her courage at the recent Trooping the Colour had impressed them Down Under more than any royal patronage could.

These days, too, security men insist on secrecy. Advance notice on where the Queen is going is never given, so that demonstrators – Black Power, Lesbians, Maori Unemployed, IRA and Anti-Monarchists – will have very little time to prepare their banners, stale eggs and free-flowing tomato ketchup. A member of the royal Household says they are not dismayed. 'In a changing world the Queen feels she is the last link between our island and certainly the two former great dominions – Australia and Canada. But this is nothing to do with imperialism. And it is perhaps a more attractive notion that the Queen should jet into Sydney or Melbourne and not have a huge fuss made; less expense for a start and a genuine appreciation.'

'It's so nice to be here again,' the Queen says, looking very perky after a punishing flight and wearing a much prettier and more frivolous hat than usual. (There are whisperings amongst the women – 'Diana's influence.') 'Yes,' a member of the Household confirms through clenched lips, 'the Queen got the ritual spraying of all passengers arriving in Australia, but her luggage was *not* sniffed for heroin by police with tracker dogs.' Over the weekend she sparkles and seems to enjoy being 'solo' – the Duke of Edinburgh is arriving later. She has lots of new clothes – rather smart ones, too – and is superbly relaxed in spite of bomb scares.

Sunday is a drab morning, but the Queen's sapphire blue wool gaberdine by Ian Thomas, in fact the thrifty re-use of an outfit worn previously in Switzerland, cheers up the handful of people waiting outside the Scots Church Shrine of Remembrance. The IRA have threatened this visit to Melbourne, but fortunately they get the wrong church and the Queen is able to continue serenely with her prayers. In a less spiritual mood, the choir and vicar of the evacuated Unity Church of Australia stand dolefully in the street, avoiding the trams and clutching their Bibles. Unperturbed by the police sirens, the Queen smiles a lot, as she often does in moments of stress to ease the nervous concern of the people around her.

That evening she is in high spirits at the reception for the Press on the royal yacht. Chris Buckland of the *Daily Mirror* was asked to tell his hostess how he'd got himself into Albania. 'I'm not sure I should tell you, Ma'am, because as a British subject I defaced your passport.' Encouraged by the royal interest, he went on to explain his nickname 'the Albanian waiter'. 'My passport says "Profession: Writer", and I just altered the R to A!' The Queen smiled mischievously; he hadn't gone too far.

At the ballet, *Eugene Onegin*, the Queen notices minutiae of the performance. Rita Traynor, a member of the corps de ballet, limps off with a sprained ankle and, 'I saw you disappear in the first act; how very sad,' the Queen commiserates backstage. Malcolm Fraser gives a party for the media at the august Melbourne cricket ground at which the Opposition Leader, Bob Hawke, says, 'The Queen is a decent hardworking lady doing a useful job but by the end of the century the monarchy will be phased out, not to mention the expense of the tour.' David Adamson, diplomatic correspondent for the *Daily Telegraph*, writes a strong piece to this effect and, surprisingly, it goes untouched on to the leader page. Apoplexy sets in on the royal yacht; Michael Shea telephones to say, 'Sir Philip Moore is displeased. He wants you to stress the good the Queen is doing just by being here,' and follows up with a letter to the *Daily Telegraph* in London. Needless to say, the executives in Fleet Street are not pleased. Editorial independence is prized, no matter how loyal the paper is to monarchy. There is a tendency among the Household to think that certain newspapers are just convenient chroniclers of royal doings, scribbling away eagerly without raising their heads from the parchment to analyse what is going on around them.

After Prince Philip arrives, on 30 September, the Queen now takes a back seat for a while as Heads of State arrive in Melbourne and attract all the headlines, but she puts in a request to see round the village built specially for the Conference. It always seems odd that she has to ask, but that is the deliberate style of her role as intangible Head of the Commonwealth. She obviously prefers Malcolm Fraser, with his handsome pushed-in face and great paws at the end of expensively tailored jackets, to dumpy Muldoon. Indeed she is often at her best with broad-shouldered men in the old-fashioned movie style of Gregory Peck and John Wayne. There are banks of flowers at the formal opening of CHOGM and good speeches – but the Queen, of course, is not there as she never attends any of the sessions. Another person with a difficult role is Denis Thatcher. He sits inside between Mrs Fraser and a heavily turbanned black lady watching his wife with his chin in his hands rather like a St Bernard patiently hoping for a walk. Mrs Thatcher is neat in black; Denis surreptitiously looks at his watch. The Prime Minister calls for her husband: 'Come along now, DT.'

The Queen receives the Governor-General, Sir Henry and Lady Winneke, on board the royal yacht. There are loyal toasts, a stately tradition maintained in sharp contrast to the problems of the Third World which are exercising the politicians ashore. During this time, the Queen plays a delicate, misty role behind the scenes. In fact audiences are held every twenty minutes on board *Britannia* in a day cabin only ten foot long. Visitors thought it surprisingly frugal and modest.

In that small functional space, playing her godlike role as fount of all knowledge, wisdom and goodness, the Queen absorbs the confidences and worries of forty-two nations. 'A fifty-five-year-old grandmother cooling the family squabbles,' was how one down-to-earth Australian paid tribute to her skill.

10.00 am	Gambia
10.20 am	Grenada
10.40 am	Western Samoa
11.00 am	Swaziland
11.40 am	New Zealand
12.00 noon	Mauritius
12.20 pm	Tonga

and then a break for lunch with a stimulating mix from Canada, India and Guyana.

The Duke of Edinburgh, shooting off before lunch, bumps into Mrs Gandhi coming up the gangplank and, like many a husband, is rather taken aback to be caught leaving so blatantly. He blusters on about getting to the airport in time for his flight to Singapore, perfectly true of course. He is escaping to a board meeting of the International Equestrian Federation and gets a bit testy at the airport when a fuel leak delays his take-off for ninety minutes. After all, if the Head of the Commonwealth has to remain off-stage on these occasions, her Consort's role is even more equivocal.

In the absence of anything more stimulating to write, stories filter out about the royal yacht. 'Disgraced sailor sent home' screams one headline. A rating had become tired and emotional after a night in Melbourne, that rather sober city. You are never given a second chance on *Britannia* and the hungover matelot was flown home to general duties the next day. The honour of serving on the royal yacht applies to all 276 on board. 'If their behaviour falls below the very high standard we require, their continuing service may be reviewed.' This unwelcome publicity was marginally hotter than the scandal aboard earlier in the year, when there were homosexual high jinks at sea which led to a play on the television commercial for paper tissues, 'Whoops, Yachties!' But most of them were red-blooded enough to enjoy ogling the Princess of Wales in her bikini during the royal honeymoon voyage. Another bonus for the crew then was the sight of the heir to the throne being drenched with a bucket of water when, committed to a cocktail party on his own, as he reboarded the yacht a blond head popped up from the deck. 'You're late,' the Princess said, emptying the contents of a large bucket over his head. When the Queen is on board there is a less frivolous atmosphere.

Setting sail from Melbourne late on a cold Saturday night the Household is in a lighthearted mood. At a place called Wineglass Bay the royal yacht makes a stop. The Queen busily barbecues steak and sausages and then asks 'Who is coming for a walk?' Who can refuse? Untroubled by late nights, rich food, cigars or unwinding brandies, the Queen sets nimbly off in sturdy shoes for a seven-mile walk. 'She is very fit,' pants one of the Household. *Britannia* then sailed up the Derwent estuary past high, green cliffs where convict settlers in ferry boats used to haggle over whale meat. The royal yacht berths at Hobart's Macquarie Wharf. The Duke of Edinburgh has just flown in from Singapore, a bit tired and drawn.

A well-washed wholesome crowd watch the Queen and the Duke come ashore. By the time she gets to her car both she and her lady-in-waiting are laden with sticky bunches of wild flowers and daffodils in jam jars. The Queen's Page, Christopher Bray, his own arms filled with flowers, is asked: 'Hey – what are you going to do with those?' 'I shall arrange them in the Queen's room,' he replies primly.

In the evening there is a State Reception at the Laetare Gardens. It is all high-necked crimplene, satin long frocks over ample fronts and hair freshly permed, rather like the Queen's own. The men, with their healthy bright skin, are a tribute to hard work in the open air. This reception begins at 9.45 pm and represents a new ruse by the royal visitor. Instead of long, wearying formal dinners, the Queen was going to late receptions and meeting more people that way. An evening on your feet in a hot room is taxing for most people, but particularly so for Frank Carter, who worked for the Premier as Head of Office in Tasmania during the Queen's first visit. Frail now, he leans on two walking sticks and remembers her diffidence in those early days. 'I hate honouring people wearing glasses,' the Queen, then only twenty-eight years old, had confided. A few days later at Government House Carter removed his spectacles before his bow. 'Oh, you've remembered,' the young monarch said gratefully.

On the flight to Launceston next day the Queen picks up a magazine – the Australian *Women's Weekly* – which speculates about her abdication. 'She is tired, not well.' In fact she has rarely looked better and, even more important, is giving a lot, in sparkling good form. There has not been a glum day so far and this is the twelfth out. So much so that on the RAF BAC 1-11 the roses on her jade straw hat seem almost to fall off in enjoyment as she reads from the magazine in that unmistakable voice. 'Are they trying to put me in my grave now?' the Queen asks. On the ground at Launceston there are simple messages. 'Dear Queen, keep our country good' is propped up outside white weatherboard houses with wrought-iron balconies and gardens of pink and rose camellias. We go on to the Elphin Showgrounds for the National Agricultural and Pastoral Society Show. It is a rural occasion with a marvellous blue sky dotted with meringue peaks of still white cloud and a hugely enthusiastic crowd. 'Are these full size?' the Queen asks, gazing impassively at a parade of special brown sheep. A few more minutes are spent watching a big Australian champion demonstrating his skill as Chief Sheaf Thrower.

You could hardly say that Western Australia lived up to its boast of being 'A State of Excitement' the week the Queen was in Perth. It was all a bit prim. Yet Roy Galvin, the Royal Baggage Officer appointed for Australia, who looked after the three hundred cases of the forty-six members of the royal party, says that for him the Queen is 'magic. When I met her I tingled all over.' Chunky, big-shouldered, he is not the sort of man who would tell you a lie. There is a jolly lunch for the Queen at which the retired Governor of Western Australia, Sir Charles Gairdner, harks back to the old days. An engaging character, he describes his house with its camellias and a view of the Swan River as 'Squalor Hall', and remembers her first visit, in 1954, when a special lavatory had to be installed for her use at Government House.

In an attempt to liven things up there is a nudge from Sir Philip Moore outside the Perth Concert Hall, where he spots a little girl apparently giving the Queen a kiss. But the warm human story is not at all what it seems. Little Joanna Bjelanovic told how she had asked if she could give the Queen a kiss after she had presented the flowers, and according to a bewildered Joanna the reply was, 'No dear. I'm sorry'. It seemed to be an exact account except for the word 'dear', which is not one the Queen would use. Back to the Household, who now find that they have steered the Press to a story they would prefer not to see in the papers. It was now a question of 'Did the Queen say "yes" or "no" to the eleven-year-old?' It would have to be checked, and only the Queen herself could say. 'In the cause of accuracy,' the Press, and Sir Philip, hoist by his own petard, has to grab a moment during a reception by the Lord Mayor; normally the Press never gets this sort of instant help. Eventually word comes filtering down; the Queen refused the schoolgirl's request. End of sweet, human story, but the photographers remain reluctant to give up the chance of a good picture on a dull day.

The Queen never encourages children to hang on to her hand, give sticky kisses or sit on her lap, no matter how adorable or appealing. The rule is a wise one and will probably be learnt eventually by the Princess of Wales, who thinks nothing of getting down on her knees and hugging a small child. The Queen knows that her appearance to children, and indeed adults, is all part of the royal aura. If she warmly cuddled a child it might cry, be sick on her dress or, worse, embarrass the parents and ruin an otherwise innocently happy afternoon. The other danger of being too tactile is that people get over-enthusiastic. If they are a bit elderly, or a bit potty, they can hang on to a royal hand for far too long. This has already happened to the Princess of Wales, when an old man in a wheelchair was so overcome by emotion that he clung to her hand and wept. As the Sovereign the Queen feels she must stand apart, which sometimes makes her appear unbending.

The doctor from the royal yacht, Norman Blacklock, strolls along the flower beds at Government House in Perth talking amiably and knowledgeably to delighted guests about the qualities of the Sturt pea. In his soft Scottish voice he recalls seeing a rare eucalyptus on a previous visit to Australia; but all the time behind his back on this day of perfect sunshine he carries a black plastic mac. This is Surgeon Captain Blacklock's garden party accessory and conceals vital medical equipment and a supply of blood. Normally he is never without his black case, but it might look odd at a party. Meanwhile everyone who is anyone in the State of Excitement clusters around the Queen on the lawns as the garden dips down winding paths like a cultivated crater. The Queen, in harebell-blue silk with an orange splash design – new and by Hardy Amies – is watched by solidly muscled plain-clothed detectives, looking very obvious as they try to toy with the teacups and collapsing Pavlova cake.

The final stop is Adelaide, which seems almost Viennese, with its cloak of snow-covered mountains, bright sunny days and fondness for music and the theatre. The first royal visitor to South Australia was Alfred, Duke of Edinburgh, one of Queen Victoria's sons, who stepped off the ship *Galatea* in 1868 to a very simple welcome. By contrast half a million people were in the streets in 1954 for the Queen and Prince Philip. The pleasure given by their first visit to South Australia was conveyed with a gift to the Queen of the largest fine quality opal ever found in those parts and a necklace made of 180 diamonds. Although the atmosphere was different in 1981, with demonstrators against the Queen shouting 'Troops out of Northern Ireland', there is still affection and certainly no grudging regrets about the gifts.

On the Saturday afternoon the Duke relaxes among some hairy-nosed wombats and the Queen goes racing at Morphetville, which couldn't have been prettier. But it is in Adelaide that the Duke of Edinburgh shows strain most. Outside St Peter's Cathedral, before an Ecumenical Service for the Order of Australia Association, more demonstrators chant 'Royalty ponces on the poor.' 'Open the door,' the Duke snaps, as he is forced to sit for half a second too long inside the car, a helpless verbal target. After the service the children are allowed to rush forward from behind the usual demarcation line to surround the Queen and give her flowers – an astute way of protecting her and also distracting the crowd's attention. One of the Duke's staff says that since the assassination of Earl Mountbatten Prince Philip and Prince Charles have almost to grit their teeth whenever they see a demonstration by IRA supporters. For Prince Philip it was the death of a favourite uncle and for Prince Charles, 'Well, after all – they killed his best friend.'

The first stop in New Zealand is Christchurch, as English as Winchester with a touch of Oxford thrown in. This is the Queen's seventh visit to a traditionally loyal member of the Commonwealth, whose people, this time, seem rather uninterested. On the first evening there is an excellent reception on board the royal yacht in Lyttelton Harbour. Everyone, including the Queen, remembers joking about the Russian ship moored intimately close to *Britannia* here on the Silver Jubilee trip in 1977. Laurie Skerten, District Officer of Internal Affairs, who was allowed to rest his broken leg on a chintz sofa with its pattern of green leaves and rust birds, said, 'Isn't the Queen in wonderful spirits? I always think she feels very much at home here.' There is no doubt that the Queen is happy among New Zealanders, whose style and values are close to those of Britain in the fifties. After the abrasiveness of Australia, New Zealand is more like a big loyal suburb filled with wholesome mums from TV commercials in mail-order, sleeveless frocks and white sandals. The men have two forms of dress: at home shirt and shorts and at work shirt, shorts and briefcase.

But the Duke of Edinburgh is sometimes impatient with the slow-moving ways. Skerten recalls how, one evening years before, he was asked to get part of a speech retyped. 'I'm sorry. I can't do that', Skerten apologized. 'Why not?' the Duke snapped, and Skerten replied, 'I'll never be able to get a typist at this hour.' The Duke shrugged. 'Oh, all right, we'll leave it.' It was coming up to midnight.

'Can you find it?' the Queen asked the Duke as he fumbled about looking for the Lesson he was about to read at a service in the cathedral at Christchurch. Just in time his Secretary, Lord Rupert Neville, nipped across to the royal pew and handed over a Bible. In an unusual sermon the Queen was reminded by the Dean, the Very Rev. M. Underhill, that other visitors to the cathedral had included 'Gert and Daisy, those famous entertainers ... Sir Ernest Shackleton, Sir Vivian Fuchs and Ronnie Corbett,' all of whom had read the Lesson too.

At drab Dunedin – all bleak Scottish granite, but smelling of chocolate – the only bright spot is the Wizard, who manages to turn up in his black cloak and pointed hat on all big occasions. His name is Wayne Eveson. 'I was presented to the Prince of Wales,' he tells the Queen. 'You do seem to get around,' is the royal reply; rather a change from the standard response. But it is soon back to the stereotyped 'How long have you waited?' 'How old are your children?' and then, untypically, to a beaming English granny, 'Oh, we do meet in the strangest places.' The Queen is happy and industrious, and her smile is not in the least diminished by the lacklustre crowds.

But in Dunedin there is an ugly demonstration outside the Otago Museum, and foolish security men allow the Queen to walk head-on into it. Maoris' rights, Black Panthers, the Homeless, the Aged, the Infuriated – all shouting on either side of a narrow footpath. The Queen has never been closer to the tonsils of the indignant. 'Jobs not Tours!' and 'Royal State Bludgers!' scream the Committee opposed to the Royal Tour. 'These people have a right to free speech,' was the view taken by Police Commander Bob Walton.

Inside the museum, the Queen, ever the unflustered professional, manages to look fascinated and asks fourteen-year-old Louise Young, 'Do they like running around?' as she watches some mice in a wheel. Sir Philip Moore makes an emphatic phone call that certainly gets the security men running round. 'Oh, it's nothing,' one of the Household says. 'He's checking a speech!' Later that night in Wellington there was an explosion under the Petone bridge at 10.16 pm. The Queen was due over the bridge in a black Rolls at 10.15, but was alerted and left forty-five minutes later than planned. For a less-experienced member of the royal family these incidents could be unnerving, but they seemed to

Above The Queen, wearing a Maori cloak of kiwi feathers, meets Maori warriors at Rugby Park, Gisborne, during the 1977 Silver Jubilee tour of Australia, New Zealand, Fiji, Tonga and Western Samoa.

Right In the Tunnel of Love in the Tivoli Gardens, Copenhagen, during the royal visit to Denmark. Showing the Queen round the Tunnel is Prince Henrik, husband of Queen Margrethe.

Left The weather is no respecter of
royalty. Here the Queen struggles
to hold on to her hat as she stands
on the lawn in front of the Sultan of
Oman's Palace in Muscat for the
welcoming ceremonies. Sultan
Qaboos is standing to attention and
so too are the Queen's
ladies-in-waiting who rush forward
as soon as the formalities are over to
offer hatpins.

Below The stalwart, enduring figure
in the Queen's life – Miss Margaret
MacDonald, the nurserymaid
employed by the Duchess of York
to look after her first baby, Princess
Elizabeth. Miss MacDonald later
became the Queen's dresser. Now
in her seventies, age prevents her
from going on royal tours but she
would strongly disapprove of hats
being worn with an insufficient
number of pins.

Left The Queen and Prince Philip
presenting Pope John Paul II with
their gifts at the end of their visit to
the Vatican in the autumn of 1980.
Looking on over Prince Philip's
shoulder is the Queen's Private
Secretary, Sir Philip Moore.

Right One of the happiest moments in the Queen's reign was when she walked amongst her people after the service of thanksgiving for her Silver Jubilee in June 1977. Here she is in vivid pink and wears a hat with bells on it which danced every time she laughed.

Below The Queen as Captain General of the Combined Cadet Force visits the Cadet Training Centre, Frimley Park, Surrey, in July 1978. After a display on the obstacle course and assault boat training she shares a joke with a couple of cadets.

It would take more than mud and rain to deter the Queen from enjoying a horseshow. In the background in a belted raincoat is the Queen's former detective, Commander Michael Trestrail.

Right At Sandringham just before Prince Charles announced his engagement to Lady Diana Spencer in 1981, the Queen raises her voice in anger at waiting journalists who hope for news of an engagement. Commander Trestrail is on her left.

Below The Queen with one of her trainers out in the early morning mists on the Berkshire Downs. This moment, with the Queen in check wool coat standing alongside Ian Balding, was captured by BBC cameraman Peter Bartlett and recorded by Peter Edwards for the "Royal Family" film shown on both BBC and ITV in 1969.

Left The Queen is a
keen photographer
and uses a Rollei or a
Leica. She also likes
to film events like
Prince Andrew's
homecoming from
the Falklands with
her cine camera.

Below A rare, relaxed
moment during the
hectic 1977 Silver
Jubilee tour of the
West Indies. Here on
Mustique Princess
Margaret welcomes
the Queen and Prince
Philip during a break
in their tour. Mr
Colin Tennant, who
formerly owned the
island, and his wife
Ann are standing
beside the Princess.

Left The Queen visits her first grandchild at St Mary's Hospital, Paddington, where Princess Anne has given birth to her first baby, Peter Phillips, on 15 November 1977.

Above The Queen in relaxed, happy mood at the 1982 Braemar Games in Scotland, with the Princess of Wales in a fetching tam-o'-shanter and tartan outfit.

Left Prince Andrew comes home from the Falklands on board HMS *Invincible* and the Queen does not hide her pride and pleasure in his safe return.

make the Queen more determined that the tour should go on and go well.

On the flight to Wellington, New Zealand civil servants reminisce about an informal dinner party with the Duke and Duchess of Kent earlier that year: 'He might look a bit glum but he is a great guy.' One of them took up the story, 'On that autumn tour the phone rang in a God-forsaken hole and I was asked "What are you doing tonight?" What could you do in a place like that? "Well, would you like to have dinner with Kathy and Ted?" Eight sat down to dinner. We talked about everything. Her lady-in-waiting, Carola Godman Irvine, was teasing the Duchess, saying she behaved like Queen Victoria at Rotarua, that celebrated place which smells awful and is famous for its springs. As the lady-in-waiting went on teasing the Duchess, Kathy was toying with a chocolate mint. Well, the teasing went on so she picked up a handful of mints from a silver dish and threw them down the table at her.'

Windy Wellington is a city where the gales blow you from one ugly block to another, where Katherine Mansfield lived in a leafy suburb and where the Duke of Edinburgh could not stop laughing at a State lunch. Normally during pompous lunches and dinners he keeps interested with that keen, scrubbed, flinty look – the penetrating blue eyes boring into the guest next to him. During the speeches he might smile lightly. But on this occasion he caught the eye of Lord Rupert Nevill during one of the speeches and was convulsed. The no-nonsense, firm-set mouth was hidden behind his hand and he doubled up with laughter like a schoolboy. The Queen could not see him and it was a delicious moment, like catching him in a sports jacket with his Admiral of the Fleet uniform. Lord Rupert Nevill said that evening, 'You will never know what we were laughing about,' and chuckled.

Thursday, 15 October; fanfares and flowers welcome the Queen to the Beehive, the circular building where the bureaucrats drone. Wearing lilac linen and a paler dress picked out in white with a frilled tie and pearls, the Queen looks chic. The outfit is very becoming and upstages the elaborate garments of some of the Wellington wives. Poor Mrs Muldoon, who always dresses neatly, has drawn the Duke of Edinburgh on her left again. He can barely bring himself to address a word to her. The Queen has the Speaker on her left, Sir Richard Harrison, who in his anxiety keeps offering her bread rolls. The Queen tucks the pussybow of her dress into her coat before eating her soup, crumbles a lot of bread and drinks her Malvern water. The Duke is on Perrier and Muldoon's plans for winning the election. As the lunch is nearly over, the Queen surreptitiously whips out her compact. Has a look up and down the table and round the room to see if she is being watched, and then quickly dabs her make-up with a powder puff in a crimson hanky. She also deliberately puts her mouth on a lot: three fresh layers of strong red lipstick. This is for television and the photographers. She stands up to speak. It is a curious thing that whenever she speaks indoors it is a reminder of Christmas Day: that smell of mace and cloves in the bread sauce, sweet sherry and grandfather drowsing on the sofa. 'As we are gathered here today ... ' The voice and the poise never falter. Nor does she ever flap beforehand. Only once in thirty years has she asked: 'Have you got the speech?' She rightly assumes it will have been put into her handbag, or that a courtier will be standing beside her chair at the right moment with the text, typed in large letters. There is no scrabbling about in the bottom of her bag for a few smudgy, scribbled points. The Duke never actually watches her speaking.

The morning had started with an Investiture in the Town Hall at Wellington: Palm Court music, ferns and flowers and an intimate atmosphere. The relatives sit in the dress circle, smiling, nudging each other and leaning over. The Queen's Equerry, Adam Wise, in his RAF uniform holds the honours like chocolates on a cushion for the Queen to pick off. She wears red and white crêpe-de-Chine and there is a word for everyone. It is a grand occasion but it is not the splendid uniforms of the worthy workers who catch the eye but the humbling dignity of a very old Maori woman, handsome face, white hair and Kiwi feathered cloak, who comes forward on sticks supported by her son.

In Auckland the Queen looks fairly glum at a Variety Performance, claps with her white gloves off, left hand down, the merest acknowledgement only; not really amused.

On the eighth and last day in New Zealand the Queen has a heavy cold. She had spent the day before sailing round the Northland Peninsula seeing Maori villages. She looks pale but manages a bright interest in a typical royal engagement, a swimming complex in Hamilton.

The last call of the day is a visit to a stud farm, Middlepark, and naturally everyone expects it to be fairly dull. But as it happens, it provides one of those rare moments that give a glimpse of the private Queen. Oblivious to a ladder in her stocking, she laughs with delight when a skittish chestnut filly is led out on to the perfectly even, green grass surrounded by a white wooden railing. Totally absorbed, she walks around this yearling bred from one of her mares covered by Balmerino, one of New Zealand's best racehorses. The Queen takes photographs and looks with a completely professional eye at the filly, shortly to be returned to her racing stables in England. 'She is well grown, walks very well and has the family chestnut colour,' the Queen says, engrossed. No doubt her clover tweed suit and pleated skirt would willingly have been swopped for wellingtons, a quilted husky and headscarf. 'It looks just like any other horse to me,' the Duke of Edinburgh says, slightly embarrassed by the Queen's absorption in this four-legged, finely bred creature called Annie. It is amusing to watch some of the less horsy members of the royal Household pawing the turf with bored, highly-polished black shoes as the Queen laughs with delight.

In squelchy mud and jet-spray rain the Queen and the Duke of Edinburgh, in their own Kiwi cloaks, hear thousands of Polynesian voices soar over the Auckland domain. The cry is 'Te Kotuku Rarenga Tahi,' which the Queen well knows in Maori means 'Welcome Rare White Heron of Singular Flight.' She smiles at the exceptional compliment, or is it at the use in the native costumes of plastic garlands and anklets made of bottle tops instead of shells? Away from the royal canopy the Household get very wet, longing for an end-of-the-week gin and tonic in a warm hotel. But they have to endure watching the Queen being presented with three baskets of knowledge by an eighty-seven-year-old Maori woman, Dane Cooper, who said she was offering wisdom, understanding and perseverance. The Queen and the Duke roar with laughter and look quickly at each other in the middle of the Maori address. Graham Latimer, President of the Maori Council, suggests that Prince Charles is about to make them grandparents – not bad information for Saturday, 17 October 1981, two and a half weeks before the pregnancy is announced.

CHAPTER 18

An Honorary Gentleman

'I AM AFRAID this is rather small,' the Queen apologized to a sheikh's wife, as she handed her a small silver salver and a framed photograph of herself with the Duke of Edinburgh. At this point in the Gulf Tour of 1979 the *Britannia* was practically sinking under the weight of goodies from the desert princes. There were gold handbags; gold palm trees eighteen inches high with pearls and rubies standing in for fruit; necklaces so heavy with gold they reached almost to Sir Philip Moore's sturdy knees when he tried one on, the pink amethysts and sapphires twinkling against his dark suit; exotic carpets in pinks, blues and beiges woven with fables of the desert; and lapis lazuli fruitstands with prancing gold horses encrusted with diamonds. And for Prince Philip, gold and platinum watches and a gold sword with a mother-of-pearl inlaid handle and a scabbard covered with rubies and diamonds. The Foreign Secretary, Dr David Owen, had to return his sword. As a Member of Parliament he could not accept a gift worth more than £50. For each journalist there was a Longines watch, in perfect taste. News of these soon reached the Queen, who is not so absorbed in her red boxes that she doesn't enjoy a bit of gossip. Entertaining guests at a royal banquet on the yacht, she said, 'I was talking to Mummy last night and she says that the Customs strike is still on. Good news for some, I thought, with their nice presents ...'

During that tour gifts to the Queen amounted to more than a million pounds' worth. Each would be labelled, some put on show in the royal homes, and all meticulously listed by the household filing system and brought out as the emirs, sheikhs and princes made their inevitable return visits to London, to see the Queen and talk over the price of oil. 'Don't you think my pearls are lovely?' the Queen asked, running between her index finger and thumb the three-strand choker given to her by the Emir of Kuwait. He, too, got a salver – probably costing no more than £150 or £200 and epitomizing the royal family's lack of ostentation. Royal gifts are usually limited to a royal photograph in a silver frame, a salver or a book. For the tour, a pleasant work on Bedouin jewellery was hunted out by the royal advisers in London as another suitable gift. Today that visit to the Gulf is looked back on as one of the most successful the Queen has made.

Before the tour there was unease about the Queen's visiting Saudi Arabia, because of that country's attitude to women. However, the Saudis very much wanted her to visit them, and ingeniously decided that the Queen would be treated as a man; no ordinary man, but an exceedingly 'honorary gentleman'. In addition the ladies-in-waiting, Lady Susan Hussey and the Duchess of Grafton, would be allowed to attend the Queen in this totally masculine province; another gesture from the House of Saud's 5,000 princes. But long dresses would be worn, and necks, elbows and ankles would be covered, too. For the women journalists, the same rules applied. There had been some doubt whether they would even be allowed to Riyadh. In the end they were treated civilly, but rather like pets one lets into the house but doesn't like sitting on the furniture. The women on the trip knew that, in many parts of the Gulf, their place was in the wrong. 'Will he be coming in the first or second car?' asked the protocol chief in his cream silk robe, referring to the Duchess of Grafton.

This 'most important' tour, as described by the Foreign Office, began flamboyantly with the Queen's arrival in Kuwait. Her Concorde had made a silky landing, arriving so silently that it did not disturb those kneeling barefoot on their prayermats near the end of the runway. 'I am delighted to be setting foot on Arab soil for the first time,' said the Queen to the Emir. She was delicately regal in peach sorbet silk with a matching pillbox, subtly cool against the Emir's gold and brown robes.

That night there was a banquet of lamb done in rich spices at the Salem Palace, which was draped lavishly in eau-de-nil silk shaped like a Bedouin tent. In return, the Queen brought out the silverware from the old royal yacht, the *Victoria and Albert*, the crystal

engraved E II R, the Minton and Spode, and gave the Emir fillet of
beef. Some of the Household found that a bit hard to take without
a glass of claret, having to pretend that the orange juice was full-
bodied. In the centre of the table there was a silver model of a
dhow, a gift to the Queen from the Emir on an earlier visit to
England and a credit to that royal filing system.

The Emir of Bahrain, Sheikh Isa bin Salman Al Khalifa, who
likes to be known as 'Jack', took the Queen to one of his old
palaces, with bleached eggshell shutters and white crenellated tur-
rets like the top of a paper hat. Now a museum, its gardens were
filled with French marigolds and oleanders. There was citronella,
jasmine and rose oil in small silver caskets set into the walls, and
much rich Arab jewellery, amethysts, great amber prayer beads
and old brass coffee pots.

The Queen and the Duke of Edinburgh were driven along the
corniche into town. She was tickled to see a colour painting of
herself at one of the roundabouts which gave her a tanned,
full-lipped, Arab look. Trees had been hurriedly planted, and the
tiny shops, selling gaudy gold jewellery and spices such as corian-
der and saffron, were smartened up for the occasion.

There was a gargantuan picnic out in the desert. Dr Norman
Blacklock looked askance at the flies settling on the whole lambs
oozing on beds of Basmati rice. In a smaller tent, perspiring servants were dipping their arms into huge pots of aubergine and
cucumber, lifting out great dollops by hand. Packets of Kleenex
tissues were proudly put in front of the Queen. The women turned out in their best dresses and burkas, those yashmaks in plastic
which seemed to give the softest face the angry look of a black,
beaky bird.

At the races at Suwayfirah, the armed guards stood silhouetted
behind the dunes; rugs had been thrown on the sand to give it a bit
of formality. The Queen studied the horses, their coats glossy
from eating lots of dates. Before every race the crown of her hat, a
deep pink straw, could be seen alongside the Emir's white head-
dress as they studied form. Sipping orange juice and switching
between her binoculars and gold Rolleiflex, the Queen studied the
greys, blacks and blue-roan runners of legendary beauty and distinction. Clouds of sand billowed up behind the horses and their
diminutive, goggled jockeys as they came into the straight at the
end of their seven furlongs. Betting is not allowed, but the media

set up an informal book by the rails, well out of sight. The photographer on the royal yacht, Tom Suddes, known as 'Snaps', joined the Press and there was a lot of hilarity for they were a long way from the royal box. Later, the Queen said sternly to Snaps, 'I saw you enjoyed the racing,' letting him know that she had spotted the betting. 'How did you do?' she asked in her dry, serious way. Snaps, thinking he was going to get the imperial rocket of all time, offered, 'Well, Ma'am, I won a lot of money from the journalists.' 'Oh, that's all right then', said the Queen, her eyes sparkling.

The Queen left, laden with gifts. She had seen a lot of hennaed feet, ankle bracelets and toes with rings on them whirling in welcoming ritual dance, heard the bagpipes again and been astonished by the British family who had galloped out on horseback to see her when she visited the large prehistoric burial ground at Delmun. It had looked like a hundred thousand rounded sand dunes, so remote one could taste the salt of the desert and so quiet one could almost hear a cascading grain of sand. The Queen could hardly ask, 'Have you been here long?' of the perspiring family group delighted by their own initiative, and they stayed discreetly out of the way as she enjoyed the seals and designs of the sun and the moon. The heat was terrific, in the eighties, but the Queen stayed cool. Face-firmer by Cyclax and rosewater toner defy even the desert wind and dry heat.

Apart from the diplomacy of a royal tour, it can also include old-fashioned royal pardons. The Saudis made their goodwill gesture even before the Queen arrived, and she heard 'with considerable pleasure' that twenty-eight of her subjects, arrested on charges that included drinking alcohol, embezzlement and theft, were to be released. But they were not seen at the welcoming ceremonies; thankful to have escaped prison or a humiliating flogging, they left for London without delay. The stern rules of Riyadh mean that bikinis can be impounded, and one can spend two or three hours in jail for driving through a red light.

At Riyadh airport, the military guards prostrated themselves on rugs at the prayer hour, laying their guns beside them. Old King Khaled sat impassively in the front of his Rolls; watching with hooded eyes. The Queen's arrival was one of the great moments in royal tours. She stepped out of the plane dressed from head to toe in sapphire blue, with her desert scarf wound round her neck; the element of surprise took the breath away and stunned the

Saudis. Only her small patent handbag was curiously at odds with the free-flowing fabric. The ailing King moved forward, leaning on a heavy walking stick with a black rubber ferrule, a green leather copy of the Koran peeping out of his robe, and bowed. He was watched by the proud Saudi princes, smelling of rosewater, a certain arrogance about their movements as they flicked back sleek headdresses, their patent leather shoes – often with gold insets and trims – give-away signs of shopping in Paris and Rome. Sophisticated and travelled, they knew that the Queen's grave acknowledgement of the rules of Islam was a sensitive gesture to their King, who had never entertained a woman ruler before. There was a great scattering of incense from silver filigree holders in halls of shiny green marble studded with gold palm trees, the royal emblem. Then the Queen was whisked to the Nasiriye guest palace, past goats foraging in rubbish bins, their small, feathery tails quivering with excitement.

That night there was dinner with the King at his palace; preceded by the swish of cars bringing guests to the courtyard, which was filled with the scent of yellow and pink roses. Palace guards, seated on greys in green cloaks threaded with gold and with ornamental sabres, looked on impassively. The important guests embraced, and tall men in military uniform arrived hand-in-hand. Before dinner the Queen was given a silver falcon and a gold pitcher. On her hair, freshly set by Charles Martyn, sat the diamond tiara given to her by King Faisal when he came to London on a State Visit in 1967.

The next morning the Queen surprised everyone by turning out for her first engagement in a short rose-pink and green Liberty-printed dress. It was most unlike her flagrantly to go against the rules of Islam. But it was a subtle, queenly gesture, since 'Long skirts only have to be worn when the King is present,' one of the ladies-in-waiting confided. But later that afternoon, for the camel racing, the Queen was in a long coral outfit, which was later worn cut short on lots of royal tours.

All day long, on 18 February, refrigerated vans sped up and down the dusty highway to prepare a picnic on the road to Khurais. It was just an ordinary royal picnic in the desert – sea bass, great silver dishes of lobster, roast turkey and beef, fifty lambs roasted over a spit, mangoes and pineapples and orchids from Holland. On the way to the picnic one could see a bit of bargaining going on, under the few trees, over luxuries such as a Lipton teabag or a few gallons of sweet water. To make sure the picnic was grand enough, the enterprising manager of a local hotel in Riyadh sent to London for a copy of *Treasures of Great Britain*. He studied this and asked his chef to sculpt a unicorn in butter. The elaborate creature, all whorls and horns, stayed intact in the evening chill of the desert. Wearing her white boots, the Queen went to this picnic up the Mecca road, past the Pepsi roundabout and, incongruously, Cardin and Dior boutiques, and then out on to the arid flat stretch. As always on this tour, flowers were presented to her by a man: an acute reminder of the absence of women in public life.

'Why couldn't I sit on the floor like everyone else?' the Queen asked wistfully afterwards. And, 'Really I didn't need those white boots; there were carpets everywhere.' Yet though the Queen had struck a blow for women, when she went to the University of Petroleum Minerals she was rather surprised to see the wives of visiting British academics segregated from their husbands, and sitting demurely on the far side of a white paper cordon. 'The Queen is here, but we live in Dhahran. If we do not conform we could have acid thrown in our faces by the religious fanatics, who would think we were insulting Islam,' one of the British wives whispered. But sophisticated Saudi girls in their Estée Lauder make-up and silky separates – and not from boutiques in town either – claimed, 'Life for us is everything we want; we feel sorry for western women.'

At the White Palace in Doha, Qatar, the Queen took tea with the Emir's senior wife, Sheikha Roda, a stilted affair of cucumber sandwiches and teabags rather than the traditional sticky nutty cakes and bitter cardamom coffee. All these tea parties with Arab wives were rather stiff; no one really dared to express an opinion. The Queen learnt a lot about oil, gas, the finer points of camel racing and Arab cookery, but not much about the women's lives although she was told how the wives are rotated in the order in which they were married, stemming jealousy by ingenious protocol. The seventeen-year-old fourth and newest wife, Sheikha Mooza – 'My name means "banana"' – stayed in the background with her two babies, both under two, while the Queen took tea with Sheikha Roda. She giggled with excitement at the prospect of meeting the Queen later at the banquet on the royal yacht and sent for a young hairdresser to go to the palace. One female journalist sneaked in as her assistant and was sprayed with scent chosen from a gold tray littered with almost every French perfume, including Joy. As her hair was set Sheikha Mooza sipped mango juice and a huge box of French chocolates was produced, all gold wrappings and tarty frills. The photograph album was sent for, and it was a minute or two before one could adjust to the idea of seeing several children of the same age, with their mothers, all in one family.

A kindly man, the ruler had showered this latest wife with Cartier watches and diamonds; but she was still a prisoner despite the Dior nail polish. She was frightened that something might be done to her hair which would displease the Sheikh and said, rather touchingly, 'I hope that if I am good I may be allowed to go back to my studies in Cairo.' As the royal chauffeur drove the Press out of the palace grounds, its gardens filled with lovebirds, gazelles and Arab horses to please the royal children, the English hairdresser opened the envelope she had been given and found a tip of £80.

The best tea party, but the hardest work for the Queen, was in Abu Dhabi. The women journalists were allowed inside, and it was rather enjoyable seeing male members of the Household forced, with British Embassy officials, to wait outside. This tea party was with the favourite wife of Sheikh Zaid, the comely Fatima whose face is believed to have been seen by only three men in her life, her father, her brother and her husband.

The Queen is at her best during their 'short, private conversation', handbag sitting on her lap in a most homely way. It is not difficult to eavesdrop. 'Do you live in the city? We had a very smooth journey here,' as if the Queen were a housewife who had driven through the traffic to have coffee with a friend. Her English voice is clear and distinct, the Sheikha's a gentle mutter through soft lips. To a softly worded question: the Queen replies, 'Well, yes, they go to boarding school,' and, with a little shrug and regretful smile, 'I haven't seen them since Christmas.' To another question, this one obviously about Princess Anne, 'She lives in the country and has her house to look after,' like any country mum. Then it is the Queen's turn. 'You enjoy London? I can't understand why you go there in the winter, so cold, but I suppose it is a change from all the heat here.' Then, 'Do you go to London quite often?' 'Yes,' replies the Sheikha, and clearly, despite her burka, she has recognized a good address. 'We have a house in the Boltons,' she tells her royal guest. There are several long pauses but, in the Gulf, with its outlook of 'insha Allah' – if Allah wills – they did not seem embarrassing.

Hearing that one of the sons, Sheikh Sultane, was at Sandhurst, the Queen asked whether his mother would go and see a parade. 'No.' 'Mmmh,' the Queen muses. 'It is always a rather proud moment when one sees one's children ...' The Sheikha's eight children had, apparently, become quite used to living in England, 'really rather like a second home.' There is a desultory chat about the work of women in the United Arab Emirates. 'There is a great deal of work ladies can do,' and a fleeting reference to the 'women's movement', but it is not a subject either wants to dwell on. The Queen fiddles with her handbag and makes another heroic run at getting the conversation going. 'I've never been to the Gulf before; the progress is very remarkable,' she says, and, on that suitably flattering note, it is time to exchange gifts. This is the occasion when the Queen said: 'I am afraid this is rather small,' as she handed over a photograph of herself in a silver frame and a modest salver. In return the Sheikha gave the Queen a gorgeous necklace. 'Too kind,' she says, handing it to the lady-in-waiting nearest to her and preparing to leave. She looks rather fashionable against the black robes in her silk print dress in unusually sophisticated navy and mustard, a nice change from primary blues and yellows.

There was a moment of lightning enchantment in the United Arab Emirates when the Queen landed in the desert on a makeshift strip with only a ramshackle wire fence to keep out the wild camels. Her trusty Andover had flown the hundred miles from Abu Dhabi to Jabal Dhana, where there isn't a lot except rolling hillocks of ribbed sand changing from caramel to rose. As she came down the steps from the Andover, the young Sheikh Rashid greeted her and then, suddenly, had to leave her side to join in the dancing; a whirling figure in brown, gold-trimmed robes, he swayed to the music of the drums. The shepherds, bearded and turbanned, beat their camel sticks and joined their ruler, who was trying to entice the Queen to join in the dance. Captivated she was, but dancing? With a vigorous shake of the head she laughed and said, 'No.' She was wearing a crisp dress the colour of watercress dotted with white, and she hugely enjoyed the spontaneous moment; and that's all it was.

'Please, can you ask the drivers to slow down to fifty miles an hour?' the Queen asked on the way to the Buraimi oasis on the border with Oman. There she admired the Sheikh's dedication to trees and oleanders, shrubs and frangipani, growing in the most unlikely beds. Slowing down was a delicate point because, for the driver, speed and one hand on the wheel of her American limousine were matters of pride and deference. Several times the Queen's chauffeur came to a halt in order to prostrate himself on the sand, praying to Allah and leaving the Anglican Defender of the Faith sitting in her car for fifteen minutes at a time on the dusty edge of the road.

Oman, and the security men were at their worst in the medieval region of Nizwa, which was colourful and marvellous for pictures. There were old warriors with Union Jacks on their spears and girls in deep purples and reds, with jewelled noses, hid in whitewashed winding streets to peek out at the Queen. 'Baaa, baaa,' the photographers wailed in a pen in the square, and the Duke of Edinburgh roared with laughter, appreciating the problem but, at the same time, enjoying seeing them in what he secretly believed to be their proper place. Eventually they were let out, while the People of the Palm hid behind the bars in the windows of their mud houses and set up a howl like an African war cry.

In Firq, with temperatures in the nineties, clouds of dust, shrieking crowds, squashed mangoes and dates underfoot, the Queen realized too late that this was not the place for a walk amongst the people. Up and down the hilly streets the excitement of seeing her with their Sultan drove them wild. There was a crescendo of excitement, and the Queen, bewildered and unable to reach her car, looked vulnerable. Her plight was spotted and a quick change of cars organized; the royal standard was switched, and she sank thankfully into the cool of the substitute car and sped off with the Sultan to a picnic. But Prince Philip, who had lost sight of the Queen for nearly ten minutes in the mêlée, was testy and perspiring as he stood amongst the mob in his shirtsleeves saying, 'Where is the Queen?' He might have been asking directions to The Oval cricket ground; English hasn't made much headway in Firq. Clutching a gold camera no bigger than a Dunhill lighter, he looked irritably around the mob; then, infuriated and obviously worried, he could not stand a moment longer the sound of the police cars with their American sirens, new toys imported for the royal visit. He banged his fist on one of the bonnets. 'Why don't you shut that f____g thing off?' and, putting his hands to his ears, was driven off.

That night the use of the expletive, which had been denied by the Duke's detective, Chief-Inspector Brian Jeffery, provided a God-given line for ITN's Anthony Carthew, who told the story in his inimitable way and ended with, 'This is Anthony Carthew, News at Ten – F-F-F-Firq.' 'But you find everything amusing, Mr Carthew,' the Queen told him afterwards when they were chatting about the tour.

CHAPTER 19

A Bloody Trip

THE TROUBLE WITH the King of Morocco is that, unlike the Queen, he never had a British nanny to say 'No'. This is the quite serious Palace view of the awful royal tour to Morocco in the autumn of 1980, when the Queen was treated with a rudeness she had never experienced in twenty-seven years.

At the time the visit was announced, nobody quite knew why she was going to Morocco. There seemed to be no more substantial reason than that King Hassan, one of the few reigning monarchs, had invited her. The Queen's Household and the Foreign Office were obviously hesitant about Morocco but felt it would be counterproductive to visit only part of the Maghreb. Curiously, there had been even more anxiety and doubt about Algeria, which proved to be superbly organized, and Tunisia, which was in the economic doldrums. Morocco was not very important commercially, but there was a huge steel contract for a British company in the offing and bad diplomatic relations might cause it to sink disastrously out of sight.

The Queen knew all about the King's funny ways. As the Irish put it, she knew 'he was Himself'. Princess Margaret had warned her sister, 'Going to Morocco, you'll find, is rather like being kidnapped; you never know where you are going or with whom.' So she set out in a perfectly philosophical mood; but nothing could have prepared her for the idiosyncracies of her host, and his cavalier behaviour seemed particularly shocking after the grace of her visit to Italy, with those cries of 'Viva Regina', and the surprising welcome in Algeria.

But first she went to the Vatican, and her anxiety to get the meeting with the Pope just right was evident her conern over what to wear. Each of her three designers had been commissioned to design full-length grand black dresses and every member of her Household wore black as well. But the seamstresses at Ian Thomas's salon wept in front of the television set in London when they heard her slinky black taffeta wrongly attributed to Hardy Amies. For them it ruined the marvellous sight of the Queen leading her Household through the Vatican past luscious cherubs and Alberti frescoes to the white Papal throne. By the evening bulletins the grand, almost medieval dress was correctly attributed to the youngest of her designers.

Yet while the Queen looked wonderful, it was very clear that this was a meeting between the Heads of two great Churches. The waves of formidable, intangible power overawed the few privileged onlookers. The Duke broke the tension with a gruff remark about the photographers being an occupational hazard which the Pope did not quite understand. Then the Queen gave the Pope a book on Windsor Castle and said: 'How wonderful!' with her enchanting smile and that little-girl trick of folding her lips over her teeth, like a schoolgirl concentrating on her best writing. Her present from the Pope was a copy of Dante's *Divine Comedy* not, unfortunately, Henry VIII's divorce papers, which are still in the Vatican archives. Then the Pope blessed the royals, and also the workers with their cameras and notebooks.

Outside there seemed to be a huge sigh of relief as the Queen appeared looking extraordinarily starry and happy in her diamonds, her Garter Sash and her long dress at midday; the ascetics had been charmed; the domes were ringing to the cheers of the crowd – and the Queen seemed to twirl for a moment in the Vatican courtyard as the sun caught the jewels in the tiara. She was taken back into the material world – up the Appian Way in the aubergine Rolls driven by Harry Purvey, the royal chauffeur, who had brought it proudly from Buckingham Palace a week before. The tension was over and Harry gave a great chuckle as he slid the Rolls through the narrow archway. He was off to Naples. The day before the Queen's arrival he had called in to the Grand Hotel, where he drank a large gin and tonic to celebrate after a dummy run. Harry (now retired) is a bit of a lad and, in the telling, he had nudged and winked his way through the impetuous Italian traffic, earning the respect of the most macho drivers and Caribinieri alike. Harry and the car, a British diplomat said with a certain honesty, had been attracting almost more attention than the Queen herself.

In Tunisia there was a glimpse of the royal feet as the Queen removed her black patent shoes to go into a seventh-century mosque at Kairouan. They say you can judge a person's character by his shoes; predictably, the Queen's are neat black patent. At the door of the mosque the Household left a mixture of suede chukka boots and solid brown lace-ups. 'Somebody has come here in her slippers,' Prince Philip said of some comfortable white sneakers. There is a fetish amongst the royals about shoes, which seems to run through the family and the Court. It is a boiling hot day and everyone is covered in sand, but the Queen emerges cool in a coat of floating green chiffon, pleasantly flimsy for her. However, even she is not always able to choose whom she talks to at her own parties and sometimes gets stuck with the pushy or the sycophantic. Always close to her on this trip was a spaniel-eyed creature with moist lips; accredited, but not known in Fleet Street, although attached to royalist publications, and constantly ready to engage the Queen in conversation. He had engineered his way close to her and now tried to interest her in some little-known facts about the Knights of Malta. 'Are you doing the whole tour?' asked the Queen wearily and, on hearing his gushing 'Yes, Ma'am, if you please,' stepped neatly backwards and turned to another group, her way of disengaging from the unctuous.

Tunisia was pleasant. As they drove into town the Queen took off her shoes and stood on the seat of President Bourguiba's car being showered with jasmine and rose petals.

Before she left London, Algeria had been hit by the El Asnam earthquake, but President Chadli made it clear that the Queen must still come to Algiers – there would be great disappointment if she did not. The two-day royal itinerary changed; Prince Philip flew up early in the morning to the disaster area to meet helpers, and talked in a practical way about aid, both medical and financial. The Queen spent the first afternoon visiting victims of the earthquake in hospital in the centre of Algiers.

There had been concern that there might still be some danger of another earthquake as there were still one or two tremors – but this would hardly put the Queen off. Her concern had been that her visit should not hamper the rescue work or intrude in any way.

There were one or two moments away from the grief of El Asnam when the Queen had a sedate walk in the Casbah and enjoyed Roman ruins at Tipasa and being greeted by the country folk with offers of milk and dates. The brief visit had been extremely well organized, putting everyone in a good mood for Morocco, where there had been no disaster, and which must surely be even better!

At 11.30 am on Monday, 27 October, the Queen arrived from Algeria in Rabat, the capital of Morocco. Shortly after the official welcome, the tour started its decline and took on an *Alice in Wonderland* quality that had none of Lewis Carroll's zany charm.

Because of the antipathy between Morocco and Algeria none of the British Press was at Rabat for the welcoming ceremony. Instead they were unceremoniously abandoned for seven hours at Algiers' unsavoury airport with no food or telephones and disgusting lavatories. When they eventually arrived at the Rabat Press centre there was at first no sign of Michael Shea, but he suddenly arrived white-faced. The King, it seemed, had been behaving in a most extraordinary way from the moment the Queen arrived. He had decided to play golf rather than join her for a welcoming lunch and had dismissed two of her most formidable ladies-in-waiting from the room in the guest palace when he sailed in unexpectedly. Both Mrs Kathryn Dugdale and the Duchess of Grafton felt decidedly huffy, but behaved like the aristocrats they are and haughtily left the room. The fact that they had been allowed into the palace at all had been a breakthrough, as women play a very small part in the world of this ruler who believes himself to be the descendant of the Prophet. It is true that, according to Bazaar gossip, three coachloads of women had been moved to his palace after the Agadir earthquake; but not for the pleasure of their conversation. All this vexed the Palace greatly, but the tabloid reporters cheered up visibly and wrote stories to go with hysterical headlines such as 'Queen in rage over snub' and 'What an insult!'

Something was again clearly afoot when the Queen did not turn up until 9.35 pm for a State banquet in her honour scheduled for 9.00 pm. Actually, the original Buckingham Palace programme had said 8.30, but the King had quixotically delayed it by half an hour. However, the Queen looked serene enough and was met at the entrance not by the dark-browed King but by two of his children. At this stage the Press did not know that she had been kept waiting in evening dress and tiara for a full half-hour, on her own in her car in the courtyard of the guest palace. The King and his henchmen were unsmiling at the banquet, and the atmosphere became more unnerving when, just before the speeches, the room was twice plunged into darkness: not a glimmer from the chandeliers. When the King was later taxed with the Queen's long wait in the car he blamed her staff. But the Queen said firmly, 'It was my decision to remain in the car.' Unable to explain why he had ordered the Queen to wait before joining him at the banquet, the King had perhaps hoped that the Queen would order her Private Secretaries' heads to be chopped off. Worse was to come. The Queen was taken to a totally unexpected reception to meet Moroccan dignitaries in their fezes. The King's chief of protocol – the palely-sinister El Hafiz Alaoui – behaved as if this final unexpected twist to the evening was the greatest honour imaginable for the Queen. She left after midnight, looking pale and exhausted.

In the early hours of the following morning, a meeting unprecedented in the history of royal tours took place. Keith Graves, the BBC Television News correspondent received a call in his hotel room at two am, just as he was trying to get some sleep before the next morning's six o'clock start. 'Can you get round here?' a member of the royal Household asked urgently. 'Tell ITN's Tony Carthew we'd like to talk to him too; we'll send a British Embassy chap to collect you both.' In a tense mood, Sir Philip Moore was waiting for them. 'The Queen,' he said, 'has never been so angry.' Next morning, on the Press bus, the plant worked. Graves, loquacious as expected, passed on suitable snippets of the meeting; the Buckingham Palace gloves were off. Relations between the Palace and the Press are never very trusting, but there is nothing like the slightest implied rudeness to the Queen on a royal tour to inspire a closing of the ranks.

The Queen had been going to Fez but that was cancelled. It seems that the King had been displeased by the routine recce made by her staff months before. At the time he had said to the British Ambassador, 'When the Queen gets here, she and I will have a chat and fix things up.' The Foreign Office said that the trouble was the King was trying too hard to be hospitable. He was very sour when he saw the Buckingham Palace booklet with its timings and meticulous schedules. Needless to say, it was never to bear any resemblance to those bizarre three days.

Nobody knew, for example, whether the King was going to turn up at Marrakesh; after all, he had abandoned the Queen at lunch on the first day. But just before midday his Jumbo 747 appeared, dropped him off and then took off like an angry elephant, blowing away all the red carpets and bunting set out for the Queen. The military personnel prostrated themselves before their King. The Queen, absolutely composed and inscrutable, then joined him in a limousine for a fairly standard drive through the city and its outskirts, past huge crowds who looked delighted and held up embroidered kaftans with mock heads covered in flowers, to symbolize both their welcome and their prosperity. But the people's simple pleasure changed to disappointment as, quite suddenly, the rather sinister black cavalcade of cars increased speed, hurtling along rough roads and ballooning ochre dust in their astonished faces. Then without warning the cavalcade stopped. The Queen was unceremoniously hustled into a different car, and on the Press raced. This was to happen another half-dozen times. 'Security reasons,' the King said sulkily. The scary thought in everyone's mind was of kidnapping. But at last the crazed motorcade arrived at the Atlas Mountains. In boiling heat, exhausted, hungry and alarmed, everyone nevertheless cheered up at the sight of an elaborate tent laid out with embroidered silks and silver tea urns, and was pleased for the Queen.

The Queen was motioned to a seat of honour, alone at the front. The Duke of Edinburgh was decidedly put out, but the King looked crossly at him and told him to stay in his seat in the back row. But as soon as the Commander of the Faithful, Amir al-Mu'minin, as the King likes to be known, disappeared into his air-conditioned caravan at the back, the Duke raised a metaphorical two fingers and vaulted to the front row. Irritably, he beckoned to the men of the royal Household, who do not go for lightweight suits, to come in out of the hot sun, 'for God's sake', and not stand outside like dummies waiting for the King's permission to sit down.

Then, a most extraordinary scene unfolded. For the next hour the Queen was virtually abandoned – no King, no food. She opened and snapped shut her handbag several times; fiddled with her gloves and pursed her lips, looking in an absentminded way at the nervously fixed smile of Douglas Hurd, Foreign Office Minister in Attendance, who was seated on a far-away sofa. She sent for

Sir Philip Moore, and pointed irritably at the programme. Mopping her brow, she looked helplessly towards the Atlas Mountains, where a dramatic line of a thousand horsemen had waited patiently since dawn. Shea went over to the photographers: 'Keep your cameras trained; you may see the biggest walk-out of all time.'

Robert Fellowes, the Queen's Assistant Private Secretary, who always looks worried even when things are going well, studied the programme as the Queen tapped her foot. It seemed indecent to watch all the stress signals. Boiling with indignation, the men from the Palace were impotent. And still the King was reluctant to abandon his cool caravan. He did dart in and out once or twice, and the Queen, always correct, stood up each time he appeared; on one of these forays, this left her in an uncharacteristic pose, standing feet apart with her thumbs in the belt of her dress as she watched his disappearing back. The Moroccans explained that, of course, the King was supervising the food as he wanted everything to be perfect for the Queen. The Queen made it clear at this point that she wanted to leave. It was 3.40 pm; she was hungry, tired and hot. This posed a delicate problem. Not even the Queen of England could get away without the King's blessing. A Moroccan chauffeur would not drive even an English monarch into Marrakesh against his King's wishes. Even a Moroccan pilot could not suddenly take off from Marrakesh and get clearance for an unscheduled flight to London, and how much more difficult would this be for a British Caledonian crew?

So, the Queen stayed put, but asked her Secretary to let Hassan know in his caravan that she did not want to miss her appointment in Marrakesh with the ninety-six-year-old Field-Marshal Sir Claude Auchinleck. The King waved aside such notions. At 4.00 pm the Queen was offered some tea from a copper tray by a bowing servant and was presented with four Arab horses.

By the evening, reaction was coming back from London. 'Outrage', 'Shock', 'Horror!' There was concern too that the contract worth several million pounds involving a British firm of design and consulting engineers, W. S. Atkins Group of Epsom, Surrey, might be cancelled by the King, who was furious about the adverse publicity. But there had been a strong feeling of public revulsion in Britain; and a tendency to blame the Queen's Household, which was in some disarray. So the Palace machinery got to work. In London, as the anger escalated, Sir William Heseltine was saying that it was all a fabrication by the Press: 'Of course there had been no intentional rudeness to the Queen.' And in Morocco Michael Shea said, 'The Queen is very pleased with her gift – her Arab horses – and is enjoying her stay.'

'I never like "plants". I like to find my own stories,' wailed Angus McDiarmuid of the BBC, doyen of the reporting corps and on his last royal tour. Emitting doleful sounds, he shook his head as he saw his colleagues being ratted on by the Household – so friendly only twelve hours previously. The Press had been useful and the King's rudeness had been made public, but now it was time to mend fences with the Moroccans.

'How splendid – great success,' the Buckingham Palace courtiers intoned as they stood rocking on their heels. The man from the Foreign Office and the experienced Ambassador, Simon Dawbarn, said that they had always known that the programme would be on the flexible side. The Queen coped best. Many of her Household, trained civil servants, meticulous and bureaucratic, were totally thrown by the unexpected. Eccentricity has always been the prerogative of kings and aristocrats, so the Queen understood better than most – but she was cross with her staff. The tabloid papers kept a relentless vigil. A breakfast menu with the King which offered roast pigeon on a train from Marrakesh to Casablanca prompted the *Sun* to cry, 'Queen Gives King the Bird'. Headlines fanned the resentment at home, urging, 'Bring Our Queen Home from this Fly-Blown Desert Kingdom'. But she showed typical sang-froid and was determined to stay till the end. At times she flashed a cool, conspiratorial glance. For the photographers the Atlas incident had been a festival, to be able to focus on the Queen for so long. Normally only a few minutes are allowed. For the reporters, the King's antics had everyone doubled up with laughter or gaping in plain disbelief.

The last day was the worst. The Queen was holding a banquet on board the royal yacht. In the afternoon, Laura Dugdale, a niece of one of the Queen's ladies-in-waiting, left her ITN crew and nipped over to talk to her Aunt Kathryn, who agreed that it was all 'hilarious' as she puffed her ciggy on the deck before the Queen arrived. This was to be the Queen's first minute to herself and away from an erratic host who had been more of a jailer than a welcoming, kindly King.

'How's Norrie?' She asked as usual when she arrived, without
fuss, on the royal yacht. Norrie is the chief steward, who often
arranges the Queen's favourite flowers in her sitting-room and
who taught some of the royal children to water-ski. It is a relief for
the Queen to be home, to have a cup of tea and a chance to slip off
her shoes and talk freely. As always, immense trouble was taken
with the banquet on *Britannia*. The King was expected at 8.15 pm
– allow fifteen minutes or so.

Smiling guests went aboard. Sir Philip Moore gave a confident
jaw-jutting grin. There is a justified belief that the Queen's hospitality overawes many of her guests, even the most intransigent.
The Queen's Equerry, Lieutenant-Colonel Blair Stewart-Wilson,
always a calm, reassuring sort of person, smiled – everything was
going smoothly.

The first hint that the evening was not going as planned was
when the King's bodyguard arrived and tried to take up the spot
on the quayside where the Marines were to stand for Beating
Retreat after dinner – always a highlight. There was some skilful
manoeuvring and they were persuaded to take their places at a less
strategically-awkward spot. By 8.50 pm there was still no sign of
the King. Then a fleet of cars swished to the quayside – not bearing the King, but instead fifteen unexpected guests, members of
his family and some aides. Good manners on board the royal yacht
prevailed. 'Yes, of course, you are most welcome.' But the aperitifs and pleasantries were being stretched to their limit. Members
of the Household kept popping out on deck to look desperately
towards Casablanca, scanning the darkness for a limousine
beyond the light thrown on the quayside for the television. At
9.10 pm, ignoring '*L'exactitude est la politesse des rois*' and looking
considerably out of sorts, King Hassan strolled aboard *Britannia*.
The Queen, shimmering in cool diamonds, took her guests into
dinner. To be in time for Beating Retreat, they had to eat salmon
in pastry and roast duck rather hurriedly. By tradition, Beating
Retreat takes place at 10 pm wherever in the world *Britannia* may
be; it is as unthinkable to vary its time as to change the order of the
Queen's Birthday Parade. The person who bore the brunt of the
King's bad temper was the amiable Douglas Hurd, unfortunately
seated next to him. 'Hassan is a highly-educated man, interesting
too. But he gave me a very hard time at that dinner. Of course, the
adverse reaction in London had angered him and meant that he

nearly cancelled the steel contract.' Angry and withdrawn, the King bore with Hurd's pleasantries until suddenly, at 9.40 pm, he petulantly put down his gold knife and fork and said he wanted to leave immediately.

Now the Queen took over. No bustling courtiers were needed. The King, she said, would stay, and he would watch Beating Retreat. Incredulously the guests saw the bullying survivor of the Alawite dynasty leave his food and sulkily go out on deck to watch the ceremony which means so much to the Queen. She looked palely grand in white as she explained the ceremonial to the King in French. Behind that aristocratic glaze, you could sense that she could hardly wait for the moment to say goodbye. Nobody could miss her frosty, almost cursory, leavetaking as she shook hands with Hassan. He came down the steps, watched reverently by his soldiers, and turned at the foot of the gangplank to give the Queen a royal wave. But there was nobody there.

However King Hassan was to have the last, imperious, laugh. According to the programme, farewells would be said on the royal yacht after the banquet. The Queen and Prince Philip would fly from Casablanca without fuss the following morning. The next day there was, suddenly, all sorts of confusion, whisperings and panic amongst the officials at the airport. The King, it seemed, was determined to see the Queen off himself, a last-minute decision which meant that she could not possibly arrive at the terminal before him. The resulting delaying tactics, proof of Princess Margaret's theory, nearly gave the Queen's detectives heart failure as the Moroccan chauffeurs whisked her up deserted tracks and rough side roads and parked for fifteen minutes with only shrugs of dark-suited shoulders as explanation. This scary journey to the airport seemed the final indignity and left everyone slightly shaken.

The Queen relayed a tongue-in-cheek message: 'We have been especially touched by the way in which Your Majesty took such a personal interest in our programme ... ' As she and her party were going towards their aircraft, Sir Philip Moore was still wittering on. 'You know, in retrospect, there has been no question of the Queen taking offence; it really is not in her nature to get angry.' He warmed even as the engines revved. 'You see, it is possible there was confusion between a genuine desire to please and a general attitude and style of working; we were saddened that it over-

shadowed the whole success of the tour.' He stumped purposefully up the aircraft's steps, confident he had left a diplomatic message for the gullible. The journalists stood on the tarmac with the
statutory hand-out, describing the Queen's dress.

The doors of the British Caledonian 707 closed and, as it soared
out of Casablanca, the Queen and everyone on board cheered.
Douglas Hurd sat back and laughed. 'I wouldn't have missed that
trip for anything, though the King gave me a hard time.' A member of the Household said softly, 'It has been a bloody trip.'

But the steel contract was secure and a multi-million-pound
contract for hardware went to Davy Loewy in Sheffield the following December, beating tenders from all foreign firms. The
Press were conveniently blamed for a visit which should never
have taken place. 'Trade with the Maghreb' remained the Foreign
Office's weak excuse. The Queen, the only person who had
unnerved King Hassan a little, went to well-ordered Windsor for
the weekend.

CHAPTER 20

❀ ❀ ❀

Motherly and Protective

'IT'S THE QUEEN for you,' the little bellboy said in the large hotel in Edinburgh where Lady Elizabeth Anson was having a hard time working out the cost of a party with the banqueting manager. He had already been slightly fazed by this cheery, redheaded little aristocrat, because of her annoyingly good business sense. His look implied, 'Och, go on with you,' until Lady Elizabeth, a cousin of the Queen's, jumped up to take the call. 'Can you excuse me for a moment.' 'Oh, Liz, I just wanted to know how your mother is.' It was the Queen, concerned about Princess Georg of Denmark, who had been ill with pneumonia at the wedding of her son, Patrick Lichfield, Lady Elizabeth's brother.

Lady Elizabeth Anson, married to Sir Geoffrey Shakerley – photographer and sixth baronet – is related to the Queen on her mother's side. Princess Georg of Denmark (who died in 1980) was the daughter of John Bowes-Lyon, second son of the 14th Earl of Strathmore and brother of the Queen Mother. A royal favourite, Liz or Liza as she is called, once could not stop herself rushing up to the Queen at a formal party where, as usual, the Queen had walked along and there was lots of bowing and curtseying as a whole line of guests were presented – all very grand. But suddenly, at the end, the Queen seemed to be standing quite alone for a minute, looking vulnerable. People hesitated to join her. 'So I am afraid I just rushed across the marble floor, kissed her on the cheek and said how lovely it was to see her.' A nice moment, but other junior members of the royal family would be advised not to be too spontaneous. Angus Ogilvy, Princess Alexandra's husband, got a rather frosty, startled look when he tried to kiss the

Queen's hand when she visited Leeds Castle. He was one of the Trustees and was greeting her publicly on arrival.

Kissing on the cheeks for the Queen must be reserved for the drawing-room on private occasions or on Christmas Eve, though the Princess of Wales got a warm cheek-to-cheek from the Queen at polo before she was married. But on the whole there is a good deal of bowing and curtseying and falling into the furniture when the Queen is about. One guest said, 'You are always jumping up and down; even a fairly informal house party when the Queen is staying can be disconcerting.' Her own children bow and curtsey first thing in the morning or last thing at night. One of the first Christmases that Princess Anne's sister-in-law, Sarah, stayed at Windsor she was so overwhelmed that she even curtseyed to Angus Ogilvy.

A royal Christmas at Windsor is the closest they get to being a big real family – quite ordinary people. There are grandmothers, difficult aunts, small children, shy teenagers, rivalries, games; everyone gathers round the television for the Queen's Christmas Day Speech and in the evening there are charades. The Queen loves Windsor Castle and thinks of it as a pleasant country house. Her attitude there is bustling and proprietorial, often altering pictures and moving furniture around, much to the amusement of owners of not inconsiderable homes of their own. 'Do you see that armchair – well, it was my grandfather's; he loved it and I don't like it much myself,' and guests look with respect at a chair which framed the bulk of George V.

The Queen's taste is, of course, upper class. There are lots of family photographs in silver frames, drawings and watercolours of horses and flowers, little self-portraits and small paintings of the children: one by Prince Philip. When redesigning and altering the gloomy guest suites at Windsor, the Queen was advised by Sir Hugh Casson, who is President of the Royal Academy – a small, witty man who designed the apartments on the royal yacht thirty years ago. He trundles to Windsor occasionally with a van of about fifty paintings, some very modern and abstract which the Queen rather likes. Her choice is for grand modern fabrics, and some of the guest suites in the King Edward III Tower now have strong lilac walls and soft grey carpets. Everywhere there are lots of fresh flowers and soft lamps. Guests tend to be in a bit of a panic in case they are late, racing along from the Tower – quite a distance – to be exactly on time for drinks before lunch or dinner, skating along and then slowing down to saunter into the drawing-room to chat about the weather or the number of red berries on the holly in the grounds. Or there might be lighthearted chat about Princess Alice of Gloucester's Christmas card, a charcoal drawing of herself done by a young artist, Richard Stone, from West Bergholt in Essex, which she first rejected because it was 'too severe'. Then Stone, determined to get it right, produced a beaming study of Princess Alice – hers is hardly a sunbeam face – who, when she saw it, declared, 'Heavens, I look just like Margaret Thatcher ...' The royal family love any jokey references to the Prime Minister.

On one of her first Christmases, Princess Michael of Kent was dismayed by the size of the guest suite she and her husband had been given, feeling it was not quite large enough and obviously missing her own big bed draped lavishly with yellow Thai silk. But it was a great mistake. The Queen heard about it and there were pointed references the following year, hoping 'our Val', as the gracious Princess is known, would not be uncomfortable. A family friend said, 'The Queen has gone to such trouble; the décor is really jolly nice country house stuff.' Looking for ideas, the Queen paid a heavily disguised visit to one of the grey skyscraper hotels near Heathrow and later went to look at the more sybaritic Berkeley Hotel in Knightsbridge, where she wandered round the guest suites and looked at the swimming pool.

The extraordinary thing is that the Queen knows the colour and shape of every single scatter cushion at Windsor, Sandringham and Balmoral and loves being chatelaine of Windsor. There is a dinner service there which dates back to the time of George III, when it had 280 pieces; now there are 276. Though not aesthetically excited by her collection of paintings, she loves showing them to guests. Her memory is sharp; she knows exactly when a painting was last lent or cleaned.

On Christmas Eve the adults exchange presents by the tree. Thrift is admired: 'It's not quite oven gloves', but spending a large amount of money on a gift would be thought rather poor taste. Junior royals such as Prince Michael of Kent can be found in the John Sandoe bookshop off the King's Road: 'I am looking for a book for someone who loves horses and works with them,' and so Princess Anne's Christmas present is organized. On Christmas

Day, as one of the royal family, said, 'We don't have a minute ...
We go to two church services at St George's, then there is breakfast, drinks with the Dean, Christmas lunch, the Queen's Speech,
a brisk walk at "wellies time", tea and then dinner.' It is at Windsor that the Queen enjoys driving most, whisking along the roads
in her old estate car.

There can be little tensions. Princess Michael sometimes complains that they are short of money and once told friends that she
was allowed to root around the Palace basement for furniture. She
found wonderful Fabergé eggs – 'Dahlink, if I could get my
hands on one we'd be millionaires.' She is not very keen on Kensington Palace and is always pleading with the Queen that her husband should be on the Civil List. She thinks her husband is more
deserving than all the others – and more royal too. His beard
makes him look extraordinarily like Edward VII and he can also
be rather frosty. When the Princess was spotted on a yacht by
some trendy Australians who knew her from her days Down
Under they yelled 'MC (Marie Christine), MC,' and they
arranged to meet that night in a bistro, but it all got a bit roistering
and Prince Michael suddenly stiffened: 'I want to go now. I want a
car.' The order was conveyed. 'His Highness would like to go
now,' and a car and chauffeur were rustled up very quickly. He
sometimes leaves his wife chatting after dinnner with the chic
intelligentsia she likes to cultivate – the conductor Herbert von
Karajan and Bernard Levin – and goes happily to bed. Princess
Michael is now working industriously on charity committees,
though her sister-in-law, Princess Alexandra, still views her with
a certain reserve. But she has added a tremendous glamour to the
royal family, outdistanced only in the summer of 1981, when the
Princess of Wales stole all hearts.

The Queen may tease her and talk about 'Our Val' – they like
their *Private Eye* nicknames, calling each other 'Brenda and Keith'
or 'Brian' for Prince Charles and 'Yvonne' for Princess Margaret –
but when Prince Michael fell in love with the statuesque divorced
Austrian baroness, the Queen had to grant her permission under
the Royal Marriages Act of 1972. He could marry the Roman
Catholic divorcee, but the Queen did not go to the wedding in
Vienna, though Princess Anne was there and Lord Mountbatten,
giving family support. Princess Michael has her grand little ways
but there is great affection for her; she looked as if she could hardly

believe her luck as she waved and smiled from the royal proces-
sions in the early years of her marriage. 'Look at his lovely big
hands, he should make an excellent plumber,' she said delightedly
when her first baby, Lord Frederick, was born in St Mary's Hospital, Paddington.

The Queen loves babies and small children, though she will
never show this on public engagements. When Princess Anne's
first pregnancy was announced – a Silver Jubilee baby everyone
said, as he was born in 1977 – the Queen dryly imagined, 'We
might well expect it to have four feet.' Peter Phillips, the first
royal baby born to a commoner for more than five hundred years,
arrived on 15 November after a short, seven-hour labour, with his
father Captain Mark Phillips present but trying to read his copy of
Horse and Hound. His wife complained, 'Honestly, three-day
eventing at Burghley is a doddle compared to this.' The Queen
was so excited by her first grandchild that she was eight minutes
late for a Palace investiture and arrived beaming, just as she did the
day Prince Charles's engagement was announced. She sees her
grandchildren for long spells at Balmoral and Sandringham, but
she really does not have typical 'grandmother' holidays with them
in a house by the sea. Prince Charles has a cottage, 'Tamarisk', in
the Scilly Isles, which is used by some of the royal family for
simple holiday breaks with children – with walkie-talkies, just in
case ...

At a garden party at Buckingham Palace, the Queen spotted
Roy Mason, who was Secretary of State for Northern Ireland at
the time. 'But where is your wife?' the Queen asked. 'Well,
Ma'am, she is taking care of the grandchildren,' to which the
Queen replied, 'Well, isn't that what grannies are for?' She enjoys
her motherly and protective role and when a member of the exten-
ded family is worried or has a problem always says, 'Don't feel
you can't talk to me.' One relation mentioned concern about an
aunt who, it was feared, had cancer. The Queen insisted, 'Please
take her to my doctors – say I said so, and let me know what the
outcome is'. And she added, 'Never feel you can't ring me at any
time. Keep in touch.'

Prince Philip gets a bit impatient with his son-in-law at times, as
he does with his own sons – he thinks Prince Charles 'a bit of a
whipper snapper', it is said. When Captain Mark Phillips preferred
not to settle for a desk job at the Ministry of Defence, there was a

family conference and the Queen helped her daughter and son-in-law to buy 600 more acres to farm with the 730 acres at Gatcombe Park for a price of around £250,000. Together the two estates will have cost the Queen about a million pounds. 'Very kind of her,' Captain Phillips said gratefully. There is no doubt, a member of the royal family agreed, that Princess Anne and the Queen do have a rumbustious relationship – it is up and down but much calmer nowadays. Princess Anne has mellowed a little and there are plenty of visits from her mother which are never heard about unless snowy weather hems her in. (Early in the blizzards of 1982 the Queen, accompanied only by her detective and her dresser, was marooned for several hours at the Cross Hands inn at Old Sodbury in Avon because the snow made it impossible to go on.)

When the Queen was feeling fragile after the events of summer 1982 when there had been an intruder in the Palace, it was Princess Anne who rallied and went with her mother to Balmoral, although it meant further separation from her husband, and caused another cyclone of rumours about the stability of the marriage. But Princess Anne weathered this and said the Queen needed family about her. Behind the brusque personality there is a more sensitive heart than the Princess would have you believe.

And it would be dull if Princess Anne changed into a simpering, accommodating creature instead of being her courageous self who will prove a good friend to the Princess of Wales, not being at all competitive about fashion or envious of her pretty sister-in-law. (The outburst about the fuss over the Princess of Wales's first baby was not directed at her brother or sister-in-law but at the following press in Canada where Princess Anne was on a visit.)

The children all called the Queen 'Mummy' when they were small, 'Mother' now; and Prince Philip is 'Papa', or sometimes in public 'Sir'. He has taught the boys to swim, to ride, to play polo, to fly, to sail, so that now he has created three highly individualistic men, threatening even to nudge him from his position as royal family male lead number one. He may appear racy, relaxed, modern and witty but he is a sensitive man and has the same enduring and solid attitudes to family life as the Queen. They both relish being at the centre of this democratic dynasty, which spans out to encompass Princess Margaret's two children, Viscount Linley and Lady Sarah Armstrong Jones. The Queen has taken a very protective interest in them from the time the marriage to Lord Snowdon broke up and her sister had some psychiatric help. The two sisters have a very loving relationship, but a friend of the royal family's says: 'Allowances are always being made for Princess Margaret.' It grieved the Queen to see her sister chasing some sort of happiness by running round town with 'toy boys', getting overweight and in general behaving erratically. A Christian woman, a little prim, almost prudish about sex, she wishes her sister could have her own emotional stability.

In the fifties the Queen's own marriage was rocked by the break up of Princess Margaret and Peter Townsend. In a bitter and introspective mood, Princess Margaret turned her 'large purple eyes and generous, sensitive lips', as Peter Townsend described them, to her sister's marriage and there were innuendos about Prince Philip's infidelities. These revolved round his lunches in Wheeler's Oyster Bar every Thursday in Soho and evenings with his friend Baron, the photographer, at the Thursday Club. A friend of the Queen and Prince Philip says, 'Philip was just reacting to the strictures of royal life.' He had given up his career in the Royal Navy; they had postponed a further family and the Establishment had removed the name Mountbatten-Windsor from the royal family on 9 April 1952. It had survived barely two months since the Queen came to the throne on 6 February 1952. To this day Prince Philip is bitter about this slight, and he can also be 'very savage' at private dinner parties about the 'uppity' attitude of friends of the old King. The Queen, young as she was, realized the damage done. Eleven days before the birth of Prince Andrew on 8 February 1960 steps were taken to restore the name Mountbatten-Windsor to the children. The Queen was growing in confidence and no longer listening to 'whiskery old nanny goats who had been in the Palace for yonks', in the words of a friend at court. Prince Edward was born in 1964 and, like Prince Andrew, was to have a much more relaxed upbringing, more protected from the public eye.

The mid-fifties were a turbulent, questioning time for the Queen. There was criticism of her style of monarchy and her marriage was threatened. But the jolt did nothing but good. A friend of both said, 'All this is nonsense about girls. Prince Philip was having evenings with the boys – as if they were still in the Navy – telling stories and drinking too much. But other women – no.' The marriage has done better than survive. It is not a sugary relationship. People have seen the Queen and Prince Philip have a blistering row but then, like all good professionals, walk out amongst the eager crowds with smiles and waves. Siding with the Queen in a row once, a courtier got barked at ferociously by the Prince: 'Stupid man', and then they all roared with laughter. They complement one another; Prince Philip makes the positive judgements, the Queen is the cooling influence. When they celebrated their Silver Wedding in 1972 the Queen said with a smile at a Guildhall lunch, 'I think everyone will concede that today of all occasions I should begin my speech with "My husband and I".' She went on to say that she was like the bishop who, when asked about sin, replied he was against it. If anyone asked her the same question about marriage and the family her reply would be, 'I'm for it', and friends say she sparkled that day like a bride leaving the church after her wedding.

The Princess of Wales makes her father-in-law laugh. He used to watch her quizzically as she sailed along the corridors at Balmoral with her headphones on during her pregnancy – only the roller skates were missing. But although she is indulged by the Queen and Prince Philip they have found it disconcerting when she jumps up in the middle of a dinner party and goes to Prince Charles, jumps in his lap, puts her arms round his neck and gives him a kiss. In her chintzy sitting-room/office on the second floor of Buckingham Palace the Princess considers her verdict on the pros and cons of royal duties: seventy per cent is sheer slog and thirty per cent is fantastic!

Every autumn Prince Philip holds a 'family annual general meeting' at Balmoral. He will look at the way the younger royals acquitted themselves in a brisk, lighthearted way. A member of the royal family never cancels an engagement. If you've got a headache, take an aspirin! Within the household Prince Philip's is the most-heard voice and he is very much its head. All the children admire his ability as a pilot, wildlife expert and spokesman for conservation – and also as the owner of a nippy red helicopter and an electric vehicle which whisks him silently around London, surprising people when they see him jumping out of what looks like a milk float. He is always trying to economize and once suggested that the royal family should commute to and from Windsor using British Rail instead of fuel-guzzling cars, but somehow this never got any further. He has sophisticated computers and runs the Sandringham and Balmoral estates to make a profit.

On the way to or from their early-autumn holiday at Balmoral, the

Queen and the family often like to sail around the Western Isles and North coast of Scotland. The boys – Prince Andrew and Prince Edward – will be in jeans all day, consulting maps and discussing the best points for scuba diving; in the evening they are expected to help entertain guests, whose cabins will be on the same deck as theirs. Breakfast is help yourself, bacon and egg, kippers from a sideboard; lunch is informal and tea is at 4.30 pm in the guest sitting-room. In the evening everyone joins the Queen and Prince Philip for dinner. If it is warm Prince Edward might join the Queen and the ladies on deck, leaving his father and the men to their brandy and cigars. Everyone remembers how Prince Andrew had to be carried to bed in disgrace on the night of the Silver Jubilee Fireworks in 1977, when he had a couple of liqueurs too many to celebrate his mother's twenty-five years on the throne.

Afternoon tea with the Queen is a very private family time. 'Such a cosy meal,' the Queen says. 'We are not very interested in alcohol,' Prince Charles once said, 'but in our family everything stops for tea. I have never known a family so addicted to it.' This is the time when the Queen is relaxed in her sitting-room, as she boils the Victorian silver spirit kettle which Prince Philip had converted to electricity and dips the old silver spoon into the jade tea caddy.

Lady Diana Spencer was invited to tea with the Queen at Buckingham Palace the day before the engagement was announced. A trolley covered in a white gossamer lace cloth was wheeled in by the Queen's Page of the Presence. It was absolutely laden with thin bread and butter, egg and cress sandwiches, muffins, gingerbread and Windsor sables. The Queen always makes the tea, being very fussy about the right Darjeeling blend. She allows one spoonful per person and three minutes to brew if it is a small leaf, six for a larger one. The milk is in a silver cream jug shaped like a cow which has been in the royal family for six generations. No tealeaf must be allowed to escape; if it does, the Queen's tea will be left severely alone. Once, on an early-morning flight across the Atlantic, Prince Philip went into the galley to pour his wife an early morning cup of tea and then swore softly: 'Oh, ———, I've forgotten the strainer. Now I'll have to throw it all away.' The Queen, who likes her tea lukewarm, resists the cakes and wants to hear all the family news; grandchildren fiddle with one of the jigsaws or go out into the corridor where the growling corgis have been gobbling up the diced meat and biscuit laid out for them by the Queen on a sheet. They find the 'dorgies' more amiable, with their long, curly hair inherited from the dachshund strain and the same low, cuddly shape.

The Queen's love of tea was inherited from her mother. But the Queen Mother is not such a purist and has an electric tea maker by her bed at Clarence House. The Queen does not approve of this and likes to complete the whole ritual in the old-fashioned way. Once a friend calling on the Queen Mother found her pouring boiling water over a teabag to make herself a quick cup. 'Oh dear, don't tell my daughter,' she laughed, 'She is very Puritan about these things.'

The relationship the Queen has with her mother is 'marvellous', a friend says. She may pretend to get cross with the Queen Mother, who, she thinks, is hopeless with money and extravagantly generous. 'Oh Mummy,' the Queen will reprove. But the Queen Mother just opens her arms, swathed in the pale-blue osprey feathers of a new outfit, and says disarmingly – 'Oh, but darling! ...'

CHAPTER 21

❋ ❋ ❋

A Countrywoman at Heart

ON AN EARLY spring morning in Berkshire in the comfortable acres of West Ilsley, near Newbury, where the air is crisp and there is no sound except, perhaps, a flight of ducks passing over the red-stoned rectory, a woman in a brown tweed suit and head-scarf stands at the end of the gallop with binoculars trained as the first lot of horses strides out. Neither the Queen nor her trainer, Major Dick Hern, will speak. Not until all the horses have finished work will the Queen put her questions, but they'll be quick-fire – rattling off the breeding, the horse's temperament; or suggesting why one is playing up – because it goes back in history to the grandam, also difficult to handle. When the Queen is coming to visit her trainers – Ian Balding is the other – the stable lads try to look a bit smarter than usual. After all, 'the most important lady in the land is coming today,' but after that it is all professional. The Queen, her trainer, the lads, the jockeys are concerned only with the moment, and the promise in each horse to, perhaps, win the Derby, something the Queen has never achieved.

Major Hern is dedicated to his horses; his stables, owned by the Queen since December 1982, are well-run; he has a happy staff who respect his habit of taking an afternoon nap. He gives a party once a year for them, never swears at them but does get a bit up-tight under the pressure. There is a village of prefab houses for the stable staff and as they drive by in Land-Rovers and pale blue lor-ries marked 'Horses' they may see the Queen sitting out on the Herns' patio with binoculars on the white wooden table and roses on the wall. Major Hern is a bit deaf but he does not miss the horses' coughing. He has trained many winners for the Queen, the extrovert Willie Carson riding them in her colours – purple, gold braid, scarlet sleeves, black velvet cap and gold fringe. At the race-course, Carson says the Queen is often completely carried away, jumping up and down with excitement, and Carson feels quite unselfconscious when he talks to her. 'Oh,' he says, 'I'll chat away.' When he had been badly injured in a riding accident, she put a call through to his cottage, just down the road from the stables.

The Queen's racing manager is Lord Porchester, a lifelong friend who has helped to make her one of the most successful owner-breeders in British racing. It was Lord Porchester, son of the garrulous Lord Carnarvon who likes to talk on television about his romantic exploits, who was to turn the Queen's racing fortunes from indifferent in the 1960s to impressive in the seven-ties. Now she owns shares in four stallions, including Bustino and Shirley Heights, and is knowledgeable about breeding both horses and black labradors and everything is handled in a professional even competitive way.

For a brief time George VI's racing manager was Brigadier-General 'Mouse' Tomkinson. When he died in 1937 Captain Charles Moore was appointed – a witty and delightful Irishman who was devoted to the King and later to the Queen, making her laugh even when the horses were playing up. By 1963 his health had started to fail, and the Queen and Queen Mother went to see him at his Grace and Favour Home in Hampton Court. He shuf-fled downstairs in his dressing-gown, shaking his head and strok-ing his white moustache. When the Queen asked, 'Now how are you feeling?' the old man replied, 'Well, Ma'am, I feel like a rabbit who has been bolted by a ferret.' She turned to her mother and remarked, in a deadly serious voice, 'I may have been called many things behind my back, but I have never been called a ferret to my face before!' The Queen was to learn a great deal over the seven-teen years from another Irishman, Captain Sir Cecil Boyd-Rochfort, who was appointed royal trainer in 1943 and retired in 1968.

On the morning of the Coronation, when one of the ladies-in-waiting asked the Queen if all was well and whether she was feel-ing any apprehension about the ceremonial, the concern was ignored and the Queen replied airily that she was pleased because Boyd-Rochfort had just rung up to say that Aureole was going well. Aureole, one of the best horses owned so far by the Queen, was bred by George VI but was pipped by Sir Gordon Richards on Pinza in the Coronation Derby. Afterwards, talking to Sir Victor Sassoon, Pinza's owner, and his trainer Norman Bertie, in the Royal Box, the Queen said, 'Congratulations, Bertie, on winning the Derby,' and he gallantly replied, 'May I congratulate you on winning the world.' Everyone knew how much the Queen had wanted to win the Derby and how disappointed she really felt but she 'showed herself a marvellous sport,' Sir Gordon Richards said, when they had talked about the race. It was his first Derby win, after trying for twenty-eight years. When the Queen is watching a race, she sits forward, dark glasses on and reading the tactics as expertly as any of the trainers. Although racing is full of tensions and dramas, it is, for the Queen, complete relaxation. Her horses are captured with her cine-camera, though once she was caught out: she forgot to wind on and got a litter of puppies at Sandringham with a herd of elephants sitting on top.

Occasionally the Queen will go privately to Normandy to visit the principal studs in France with Lord Porchester. When Highclere won the *Prix de Diane* at Chantilly on 16 June 1974 it was the first French classic win for a reigning British monarch. The Queen had to get back to Windsor Castle immediately after she had led her winner in, but that evening, as Major Hern, his wife Sheilah and the winning jockey, Joe Mercer and his wife Anne were in mid-air on their way back to Shoreham in Sussex a message was relayed by the Queen's Flight saying that Her Majesty hoped that they would all come to dinner at Windsor Castle. The plane was diverted to London Airport, but they still thought it was a joke until a Palace chauffeur met them at Heathrow. When they got to Windsor late in the evening, the Queen, smiling, came down to meet the 'weary warriors', and the end of 'the greatest day in our lives' as Joe Mercer called it later, was a family party with the Queen, Prince Philip, the Queen Mother, Princess Anne, Lord Mountbatten, Lord and Lady Porchester and Michael Oswald with, as the centrepiece of the party, the gold trophy which had been presented to the Queen that afternoon.

Prince Philip may not like racing much, but he understands the Queen's fascination for it. She has owned the winners of five British classics, and he gave the Queen as a Silver Jubilee present a painting of three of her favourite mares with their foals in a paddock at Wolferton at Sandringham. It is very vivid and greenly bosky with red roofs of estate cottages in the distance. The Queen was the leading owner in 1954 and again in 1957, and third in 1977. She won the Oaks and the St Leger with Dunfermline in Jubilee Year. All her horses, stud and bloodstock, are her private property.

The Queen, guided of course by a very able racing manager, is always astutely alive to the business possibilities in the changing world of bloodstock, and sentiment is never allowed to intrude. A good example of this was the sale of her three-year-old filly Height of Fashion in the summer of 1982 to the Sheikh Hamdan Al Maktoum of the ruling family of Dubai for a sum rumoured to be significantly in excess of £1 million. This horse – by Bustino out of Highclere – ran in the Princess of Wales's stakes at Newmarket on 6 July and broke the course record for a mile and a half. She had pleased her owner earlier in the season by winning the Lupe Stakes (named after an Oaks winner) at Goodwood in May, when she won by two lengths. The Queen then smartly decided to sell Height of Fashion, but still having the benefits of the blood of her dam Highclere in the stud on Sandringham. No wonder Lord Porchester was relaxed, and entertained visitors from the racing press to champagne from crystal glasses that summer, sitting by the lake outside his house nestling in the Berkshire hills near Burghclere, Newbury.

In the past the Queen might not have sold a horse of this calibre, but she is shrewd about the economics of horse racing: the cost of keeping a horse in training was estimated by the Racehorse Owners Association in 1982 to be about £7,000 a year.

A less fashionable interest is pigeon racing; but pigeon fanciers and breeders find Her Majesty's pack highly competitive. Her interest stems from the Queen Mother, and from Edward VII, who was a great pigeon fancier and started the royal lofts in 1883. 'What she doesn't know about it isn't worth knowing,' says Mr Len Rush as he looks over the two hundred birds reared for Her Majesty in lofts at the back of his semi-detached house in King's Lynn. The Queen calls on him about once a year for coffee before the open log fire and a professional look at the grey birds with their ER gold ring. There is a natural acceptance of royalty around Sandringham, though the locals look at strangers with deep distrust. It is very informal when the Queen calls on her pigeons, with just a lady-in-waiting, who sits in the parlour with its Toby jugs and small statues of Red Rum and Nijinsky. The chauffeur and detective stretch their legs outside.

Somehow, the Queen confesses, she feels even more remote from London at Sandringham than at Balmoral, and it is at Sandringham that the royal family spends New Year. It has a happy country-house flavour, smelling of polish, with bowls of flowers and tapestry cushions worked by Queen Mary. At the entrance there is a footscraper, for use after a day spent tramping through the damp fir forests in January; when cheeky, fat pheasants, having dodged the royal guns, squawk their way home to the sound of curlews in the early evening air. Amongst the family portraits of royal ladies in creamy lace holding overblown pink roses and the veneered bookcases filled with beautifully bound copies of works by Charles Lamb and Pope which look as if they are rarely disturbed, there used to be a nodding corgi toy on a circular table. Beside the path to the royal church, near the summerhouse, there are the graves of Queen Alexandra's dogs, 'Facie and Punchie, my darling faithful little companions in joy and sorrow.' This is where the Queen has buried her dogs, including the favourite corgi Susan who was in her wedding carriage.

Every New Year the Queen goes to the Women's Institute meeting in Sandringham and, with the Queen Mother, will spend two hours talking about lacemaking or looking at the entries in a competition for the best cheese straws. On the last Sunday of the New Year break, she calls on the estate workers. Mrs Doris Waite, whose husband Fred was the family gardener at Sandringham until his retirement, remembers how they always had to wear formal clothes for church, the men in dark suits and bowlers. 'The Queen is a lovely little person,' she said, but Her Majesty's love of flowers meant that when there were visitors to Sandringham Fred had 'ninety-nine vases to fill with forced spring flowers.'

The Queen, a countrywoman at heart, loves jumping into a Land-Rover and driving to the stables with a crowd of children swaying in the back, brushing against muddy labradors. It is a good time for confidences. Viscount Linley will chatter about his carpentry and Prince Edward about his exams. 'My young friends were telling me ... ' the Queen will say later at dinner.

'Go and get some water,' Marie Mason, the head stable girl at Windsor said over her shoulder as she held one of the horses. Passing a bucket, without looking at the person next to her, she said,

'You'll find a tap over there.' When she looked round to see if
Lady Sarah Armstrong Jones had found the water, she was hor-
rified to see the Queen trotting towards her with a brimming pail.
Nothing could give the Queen more pleasure. She is happiest in
shabby country clothes, walking her land. She breeds labradors in
a stud at Sandringham, exercises them professionally, is not
squeamish if they have an injury and likes to remove their fleas
herself.

She loves being at Balmoral, where everything is rather tartan.
This is where she has her six-week holiday, walking and picnick-
ing. Her idea of heaven, she admits, is to picnic at Balmoral with
her mother and sister or join Prince Philip and the family at
lunchtime during the shoot or by the banks of the Dee. 'Have you
got a picnic basket for two?' one of the staff at Peter Jones's household department in the basement was asked over the phone. 'Yes,
we do.' 'Would you send it round, please, on account?' 'Where to,
Madam?' the assistant queried, and heard a slightly familiar voice
reply, 'Buckingham Palace, please.' Thinking it was a practical
joke, she asked, with mock seriousness, 'And who shall we send it
to?' was told, 'The Queen, thank you,' and down went the
receiver. The store checked immediately with the Palace and a
member of the Household said, 'Oh, she is naughty; we are meant
to do things like that for her.'

Visitors arriving at Balmoral from London may find the Queen
sitting in the sunshine on the lawn in front of the gaunt granite
turreted house the family loves so much, having a picnic lunch on
her own: 'The family have gone for a walk with their guns.' Even
though the visitor is on official business, everything is much more
relaxed than at the Palace, with plenty of salmon and roast beef to
feed hearty appetites after a day outside. Footmen in their red and
gold liveries still offer a sherry from a silver salver before lunch,
but nowadays these smooth-skinned members of the Queen's
Household are fewer in number and have to perform many more
tasks as inflation hits even the Queen. Her staff has been drastically
cut down to 346.

Footmen who want to go on working for the Queen must now
be messengers and porters and help hump trunks about the place –
no longer lurking discreetly in corners to glide forward with a
silently attentive step. The Queen's total Civil List payment is
£4,612,883 in 1982/3, and out of that the Palace wage bill came to

nearly £3 million. Monies from the Civil List are often thought of as salaries for the royal family, but they are sums repaid for public engagement expenses. It is reckoned that the total cost to the nation of maintaining the royal family is about £15 million a year.

The Civil List Payments are as follows:

	£	
Duke of Gloucester	83,900★	
Duke of Kent	113,000★	
Princess Alexandra	107,800★	
		£ 304,700
Queen Mother	306,600	
Duke of Edinburgh	171,100	
Princess Anne	106,500	
Prince Andrew	20,000	
Prince Edward	16,183	
Princess Margaret	104,500	
Princess Alice, Duchess of Gloucester	42,000	
		£ 766,883
		£1,071,583
HM The Queen		£3,541,300
		£4,612,883

★ These payments come out of the Queen's purse.

An estimate of the likely breakdown of the Queen's own Civil List expenditure, bearing in mind that the most recent published figures are ten years old, is as follows:

	£
Wages and Salaries	2,330,000
Household Administration	400,000
House Supplies	260,000
Royal Mews, Transport and Travel	130,000

Garden Parties, subscriptions and other miscellaneous expenditure	210,000
	£3,330,000
Less deductions including Treasury and Foreign and Commonwealth Office contributions towards particular staff costs	150,000
	£3,180,000
Add the cost of	
Royal Flight	some 3,000,000
Royal Yacht	2,700,000
Upkeep of Royal Palaces at Buckingham Palace and Windsor	5,000,000
Other members of the Royal Family	1,000,000
Total Civil List Expenditure:	£14,880,000

This works out at about £30 per hour and requires a contribution of some ½p a week from every man, woman and child in the UK. In view of this it is surprising that the aura of mystery surrounding the cost of the monarchy has been allowed to persist for so long.

The Queen's Civil List income was set at £475,000 at the beginning of her reign in 1952 and included for the first time a supplementary provision of £95,000 as an inflation allowance. The extraordinary thing was that before this gesture was made the Civil List had remained remarkably unchanged, at between £400,000 and £500,000 since the Accession of Edward VII in 1901.

Prudent housekeeping by the Queen meant that the bulk of this £95,000 inflation allowance was set aside each year, but this financial cushion was severely punctured in 1962 when continuing inflation meant that the Civil List Expenditure exceeded the annual £475,000 for the first time. The cushion was going down at such a rate between 1962 and 1970, but the first the country really knew about it was a public statement by Prince Philip on American television in 1969 announcing baldly that the monarchy would shortly be 'in the red'. This prompted a Select Committee on the Civil List set up in the summer of 1971 by Harold Wilson, who was then Prime Minister, and the findings formed the basis of the present income from the State enjoyed by the royal family as a whole.

There is a reticence bordering on coyness at Buckingham Palace about the royal finances. But the probing into the royal house-keeping and the increase in inflation in the 1980s resulted in a further pruning of the royal budget. In the winter of 1980 John Biffen, Treasury Secretary, said that in such hard times no one was immune from Government spending cuts – not even the Queen and that the search for economies applied to the money allocated to the royal family for public duties. But the Palace replied almost smugly that economies in the Royal Household's expenditure had been under review since the middle of the previous year – 1979 – and it was difficult to see where there could be further economies made. A reduction of twenty was made in staff in 1981 and this was right across the board.

Part of the efficiency campaign has involved cuts in stationery and office services, which have recently been reduced by £50,000. Prince Philip suggested the installation of word processors – the sort of gadget which appeals to him – to save on office staff. These would be particularly cost effective when there is an avalanche of mail because of an engagement, a royal baby or in sympathy. When Lord Mountbatten was murdered there were thousands of letters and the Palace had to call in extra help.

Buckingham Palace is where the Queen spends most of her working time from her return from holiday in October until Christmas when she goes to Windsor and then to Sandringham. Then it's back to the Palace until Easter, which is spent at Windsor. The early summer is spent at the Palace until August when the Queen goes for her long break to Balmoral. The upkeep of Buckingham Palace and Windsor Castle – estimated in 1982 at £2.1m and £2.9m respectively – is on the taxpayers' bill, so too is the cost of the Queen's Flight (£3m) and the royal yacht (£2.7m). These items in addition to the royal train and free postage will all be con-

sidered when the next major review of royal finances is undertaken. For the year 1980, Westminster Council's rates bill for
Buckingham Palace came to £101,609.82 and this was met by the
Treasury. But at Balmoral and Sandringham, the Queen's private
homes, she is responsible for all, as they are her private inheritance
but not subject to death duties.

When the Select Committee of 1971 began its investigations
into royal finances it met with courtesy and helpfulness until the
question of the Queen's private fortune arose. Here there is a reticence and Palace lips are at their tightest and most inflexible. The
Queen's personal wealth is stunning.

She avidly reads the *Financial Times* and the City pages, checking
her portfolio. Her brokers are James Capel and Rowe Pitman, and
her bankers are Coutts. The Queen and her large portfolio of
investments are watched with acute interest. The Queen pays no
income tax, or investment tax. The late Lord Rupert Nevill, an
experienced financier, was a trusted friend and adviser to the
Queen and Prince Philip. At one time the Queen had a considerable investment in United Biscuits, but her private wealth is
impossible to assess. In 1979, the Duchy of Lancaster yielded an
income of £625,000. The estate at Sandringham had fifty acres of
blackcurrant bushes and had been under contract to the Ribena
fruit juice company. Then there is the wealth of possessions in the
royal homes – the royal collection of paintings, the royal stamp
collection, the library, and most of the jewels, but the Queen does
not regard these as her own property to be disposed of as she might
wish – they are hers by right of being sovereign. The Queen found
it irksome when she heard phenomenal sums of money being
mentioned in connection with her possessions, so much so that
Lord Cobbold, who was then the Lord Chamberlain, spelt out her
view to the Select Committee in 1971:

Her Majesty has been much concerned by the astronomical figures which
have been bandied about in some quarters suggesting that the value of
these funds (her private wealth) may now run into £50 or £100 million,
or more. She feels that these ideas can only arise from confusion about
the statutes covering the Royal Collections, which are in no sense at her
private disposal. She wishes me to assure the Committee that these
suggestions are wildly exaggerated.

The Select Committee had given critics of the royal family and merely interested MPs a wonderful opportunity to question courtiers on their bookkeeping. The questions ranged from the exact output of mushrooms grown at Windsor Castle and sold in the open market, school fees for the Chapel Royal Choir and forage for ceremonial horses, and the cost of garden parties at Buckingham Palace and Holyrood House, the Queen's residence in Edinburgh and once the Palace of Kings in Scotland. There was great excitement because a party in Holyrood had cost £24,402 and that meant each guest was costing 77p (15s 5d) a head and this represented an increase of 21p (4s 1d) per guest from 1968. Knowing the pleasure garden parties give to the guests, the Palace replied that they were the Queen's way of saying thank you and 'the style and form of the monarchy'.

There is no Government funding for Prince Charles who lives off the Duchy of Cornwall revenues, which totalled £550,445 in 1981. Before his marriage he took half for himself and gave half to the Treasury. Nowadays, and with a young son as well as a wife to support, he takes three-quarters and his annual income is averaging £400,000 tax free. As for the Civil List allowance 'the money we pay to the royal family is the finest investment we make in this country', Nicholas Winterton MP for Macclesfield said, signing a Commons motion opposing any royal cuts suggested by John Biffen.

Buckingham Palace has about six hundred rooms which are thoroughly cleaned three times a year. The Queen has brought in outside contractors to fly all over the Palace with mops, dusters and vacuum cleaners instead of keeping a vast number of maids permanently on the payroll. More sophisticated telephones and do-it-yourself dialling to practically any part of the world has meant there is a smaller switchboard at the Palace now. More efficient methods of cooking have been introduced into the kitchens.

The Queen is naturally frugal and Prince Philip is mad about efficiency, so they have looked at every possible economy. During cold spells the staff at Buckingham Palace have sometimes shivered as heating is only allowed intermittently and the Queen herself often works by a one-bar electric fire. Working lunches are simple – 'no booze', a choice of salads, cheese and maybe one hot dish, and you pay for it: no more than £1 or £1.50. At Balmoral at dinner there is one glass of wine with each course; always, the Queen just drinks a great deal of Malvern water, attractive both for its non-aeration and price.

The royal finances are looked after by 'Royal Trustees', a board of

directors; but the Prime Minister and the Chancellor of the Exchequer also become 'very involved and concerned'. The man
who has most of the headaches concerning both the Royal Budget
and the Queen's private fortune is the Keeper of the Privy Purse,
Mr Peter Miles – a fifty-seven-year-old broker. Much of her
private income comes from 52,000 acres of the Duchy of Lancaster, which ranges from property in the Strand to grouse moors in
Yorkshire. She has a large portfolio of shares and Government
securities and makes substantial profits from horse breeding.
Michael Oswald is the manager of the Royal Stud at Sandringham
and Wolferton on the estate in Norfolk, with her yearling stud at
Polhampton near Kingsclere. Like other stud owners, she uses
some nominations from her stallions and sells others. Most are
assessed on the basis of four to five years and are capitalized
between four and five times the nomination fee. So a stallion with
forty shares and a fee of £10,000 could command a price some-
where around £45,000 a share. Her farms do more than supply
untreated Jersey milk to Buckingham Palace in special green
bottles marked with gold tops, or roast lamb from the rare Soay
sheep kept at Balmoral. They also contribute to the coffers.

CHAPTER 22

❈ ❈ ❈

The Queen's Musick

THE QUEEN LIKES light music, thrillers, jigsaws, comedies, documentaries; she adores ballet but simply cannot stand opera, especially Wagner. When she was very young she was taken by her cousin Lord Harewood to a performance of *Parsifal*. 'That damned George made me sit through the whole thing!' she seemed to say – and she hated it. She might later forgive her musical cousin his divorce and second marriage, but she has never forgotten those five hours locked in with Parsifal, Kundry and Amfortas. It left a deep impression and any enthusiasm for opera she might have developed was mutilated. Her cousin, only three years older, had a wonderful evening; he was later to become an effective managing director of the English National Opera.

There is a joke that the Queen will only go to an opera if it has a horse in it. Shortly after the Coronation, she went to see *Boris Godunov*, but even the appearance of a four-legged friend could hardly ease for her the length of the evening with the music of Mussorgsky, even though the role of Boris was being sung by the great Bulgarian bass, Boris Christoff. Many years later, in Silver Jubilee Year, 1977, the Queen was at Covent Garden again for another gala evening at the opera. Afterwards, a great queue of opera singers was presented backstage, and amongst them was Christoff, who had always longed to meet the Queen. At last he was introduced. 'Ma'am, you may remember Boris Christoff's great performance in *Boris* in the fifties.' The singer bowed before the Queen. She replied: 'Huh, I certainly do remember that evening!' Christoff beamed. 'I am so honoured, Your Majesty.' He had quite missed the nuance.

When Queen Victoria went to the opera she usually arrived late. The performance would stop, and the orchestra would play the National Anthem. Eventually, embarrassed by the sight of the audience on its feet and the artists silent on stage, Queen Victoria decreed that the National Anthem would only be played at the beginning or end of performances. Nowadays, if Prince Charles wants to see an opera he will slip quietly in to the Royal Box, not bothering with his black tie, and sit at the back. There will be a cold snack of smoked salmon in the dining room at the interval, but otherwise no fuss. He loves opera and one of the first occasions when the Princess of Wales – then Lady Diana Spencer – was seen in public after the engagement was at the Royal Opera House, in that dazzling black dress. She told Sir Claus Moser, Chairman of The Royal Opera, that the *décolleté* dress was a hurried second choice; the zip had broken on the one she had planned to wear. Nobody was complaining.

At the opera the Queen will earnestly read the programme. She studies the plot and there is a knitting of brows as she reads the story, which in most cases has as much subtlety as a pantomime with its goodies, consumptives, rich villains and unsatisfactory loves. But, typically, the Queen always does her homework. She will always have a word with the commissionaire on the way in. Sergeant Martin was once a celebrated figure at Covent Garden, with his military moustache and commanding manner. 'How frightfully well Sergeant Martin is looking this evening,' the Queen would remark, as if about a gamekeeper at Sandringham. After the performance, she would never dream of commenting on it as a whole because she would think that presumptuous on her part. Instead, she will pick out some little detail to talk about. Musical experts find this defence mechanism touching and delightful. She is careful not to spell out any praise or criticism. Once, when Maria Callas had given a superb performance in *Tosca*, wearing a red velvet dress for the occasion, the Queen did compliment her when the temperamental diva was invited to the Royal Box. 'What a pretty frock you are wearing.'

There are those who think she may not be enjoying a piece of music because she looks so solemn during the performance. This is because she is aware that she is always the focus of all eyes at the opera or concert hall and tends to sit forward with the spine rigid, in a very unrelaxed, uncomfortable position. She can hardly abandon herself to the music, dreaming away with her eyes shut, because the television cameras may close in on her face at any moment. Perhaps for this reason she does not enjoy long pieces of music. On a royal tour to Finland, there was a performance of music by Sibelius in the excitingly designed concert hall in Helsinki which was so brief that there seemed barely time for a quick burst of *Finlandia* before everyone was off again. 'How interesting,' the Queen said with a smile. Prince Philip looked searchingly at the organ pipes.

He hates background music, finds it irritating and will not have the radio on if he is shaving or driving. But he was once persuaded to go to a recording session in Edinburgh, as patron of the Scottish Baroque Ensemble. His patience was tested as they ran through Six English Lyrics by Malcolm Williamson, Master of the Queen's Music. But as soon as he was invited to look at the recording equipment away from the orchestra, the engineers watched the Duke quickly become absorbed in the technicalities and afterwards he told the Queen how much he had enjoyed himself.

It is while they are in Scotland, at Balmoral, that the royal family have the sort of musical evenings they really love – standing around the piano singing ballads. The Queen was playing Beethoven, Debussy and Chopin with 'real musical feeling' by the time she was fifteen, at a time when piano lessons were being endured by girls of the same age all over the country until the war. Her piano teacher was Miss Mabel 'Goosey' Lander – 'Goosey' because Lander rhymes with Gander, showing an unlikely royal addiction to Cockney rhyming slang.

Over the years there have been many enjoyable evenings at Kensington Palace with Princess Margaret seated at the piano, smoking through a jewelled cigarette holder, playing a seemingly endless series of Broadway melodies or singing 'Rose Marie' in a high, piping voice. She likes gala events, too, enjoying show people and the novelty of slightly disreputable, picaresque characters. Princess Margaret likes classical music too. When she agreed to be the first royal castaway on 'Desert Island Discs', her eight records were a catholic collection – *Swan Lake*, Brahms' Second Symphony, 'Rule Britannia' and a funny little 1948 dance tune called 'Rock, Rock, Rock'.

When Lord Drogheda was retiring as Chairman of the Royal

Opera in 1972, the Queen and the entire royal family turned up for
his farewell party. A great friend of the Queen Mother, sharing a
'heavenly sense of humour' and love of most music, Lord
Drogheda said how honoured he was that the royal family were
there and hoped for the sake of his successor, Sir Claus Moser,
that the Queen and Prince Philip would become regular visitors.
Adding that he was sure some very simple operas could be put on
to please them! This did not go down at all well – and a royal
rebuke followed. But the Queen's taste in music and her fondness
for Gilbert and Sullivan call for no apology. Any critical snobs
should be asked how they would acquit themselves riding
side-saddle in the Mall.

The cinema at Buckingham Palace shows all the latest films.
The Household and staff are invited by the Queen, and they watch
films such as *The French Lieutenant's Woman* or *Chariots of Fire* –
much admired for its old-fashioned values of sporting integrity
and patriotism. In *Absence of Malice*, a film about a journalist, the
Queen thought the language too tame for the story! When the
actor Tom Courtenay was invited to a lunch at Buckingham
Palace not long after his role in *Doctor Zhivago* he was desperately
nervous and sat in a corner hugging his knees. 'Look at him, look
at him,' said the Queen, teasing the dumbstruck actor. 'You
wouldn't think he wanted to overthrow society, would you?'

If the Queen has an evening off in London, she relaxes with a
copy of *The Field*, *The Daily Telegraph* crossword, *Sporting Life*, a
thriller of the turf by Dick Francis or a Hammond Innes adventure
story. There is a small kitchen attached to the royal apartments
and for the Queen it is a great treat to make scrambled egg and
watch television. Comedians like Ronnie Corbett and Ronnie
Barker always make her laugh – so, too, do Eric Morecambe and
Ernie Wise; they are always ridiculous but never too vulgar. 'Why
are you always introduced to me together?' she asked once at a
screening. 'Because we're only half a star on our own,' came the
reply.

A recent favourite is Paul Eddington in the role of a harassed
government minister being manipulated by civil servants in *Yes,
Minister*. Eddington was invited to one of the Palace lunches but
fell briefly from favour by talking about it afterwards. At these
lunches the Queen and Prince Philip relax guests by asking for
their help with names of new foals in the royal stables. The Queen

likes witty names for her four-legged creatures; especially successful was Lost Marbles – out of Amnesia by Lord Elgin.

An addiction to music hall is not a passion the Queen shares with
her mother and sister, who both love variety and old Flanagan and
Allen records. But all three have in common a love of the turf and
of dogs – big ones, small ones, but preferably with a pedigree.

Occasionally the Queen goes to the theatre, perhaps at Windsor, and prefers to see something light and amusing. She will also
go along to the Burlington House Antiques Fair for a sneak pre-
view after a private dinner party.

One might argue that she already has so many treasures – vast
collections of Gainsboroughs, Holbeins, Van Dycks and Reynolds
– but she does not see these as her personal belongings; they are for
the nation. Her private taste is shown in the abstracts by Alan
Davie in the guest suites and her own indulgence was a Lowry,
bought quietly one afternoon at the Royal Academy. The scene
she chose had none of the busy matchstick figures Lowry loved
but a fenced backyard – probably something the Queen has never
really seen – and an old 'banger' car being driven in.

For the Queen, off-duty in her country homes means walking,
swimming, deer-stalking – even a little Scottish dancing. Her gardens give her a great deal of pleasure and she knows most shrubs
by their Latin names, though she complains that her gardeners
bully her. 'I wanted some laburnum at Buckingham Palace but
they wouldn't let me have it,' she grumbled. The garden designed
by her father at Royal Lodge, Windsor, is still exactly the same
today with its clumps of rhododendrons acting as windbreaks and
creamy white, yellow and pink azaleas.

Difficult jigsaws are a deft distraction, helping the Queen to
unwind. She can often be seen talking to someone, her eyes fixed
compellingly on the speaker, and surreptitiously moving a piece
of the jigsaw on a table behind her without even turning round.

CHAPTER 23

❊ ❊ ❊

Intruder at the Palace

THE SUMMER OF the Queen's thirtieth year on the throne will surely stay forever in her memory, both for its awfulness and for its blessings, too. July was a rotten month for the Queen. A close personal friend, Lord Rupert Nevill, died suddenly; an intruder broke into her bedroom; her faithful detective, Commander Michael Trestrail, was forced to resign by the blackmailing threats of a homosexual prostitute; a troop of her personal guards from the Blues and Royals Regiment of the Household Cavalry was blown to pieces by an Irish terrorist bomb while riding in full dress duty near Knightsbridge barracks; and for the first time in her life the Queen had to go to hospital – for a wisdom tooth operation.

Traditionally, the month of July is for royal engagements which are summery and convivial, with lunches and garden parties at Buckingham Palace and usually a day or two at Goodwood for the Queen. July 1982 began harmlessly enough with a visit to Fife in Scotland for the Queen and Prince Philip. There William Hamilton, Fife's Labour MP and most vocal critic of the monarchy, met the Queen. His snipings against her have always earned him more attention than any work done for his constituents. Prince Philip congratulated the sixty-five-year-old MP on his recent second marriage and this should have rather disarmed the elderly bridegroom. However, it did not stop him from complaining afterwards that the Queen's handshake, when they met in the council offices, had been 'very frigid'.

When the intruder, thirty-one-year-old unemployed labourer Michael Fagan broke into the Queen's bedroom, only her impressively cool ability to keep him talking saved her from what might have been an even more horrifying encounter. The events that morning were almost comic in their ineptitude and the revelation of such lackadaisical security for the Queen appalled the country. Fagan had scaled the spiked Palace wall at 6.45 am, slipped behind a temporary canvas awning near the Ambassadors' Entrance and climbed through an unlocked window into a room with the immensely valuable royal stamp collection. He did not spend long enjoying the philatelic treasures. He found the door was locked so he climbed out of the same window, pressing on in his determination 'to see Her Majesty' ...

In his excitement he had set off a flashing light alarm in the security control room in the Palace. When it went off a second time the police sergeant on duty switched if off again, grumpily reassuring himself: 'That alarm is always going off for no apparent reason'.

The Queen was sleeping peacefully, the servants were beginning their routine at the Palace. A maid was cleaning in a room near the royal bedroom but had thoughtfully closed the door so she would not disturb the Queen's rest.

Meanwhile Fagan got nearer to his dream of seeing the Queen as he shinned up a drainpipe. Removing his sandals and socks he found a window which had not long been opened in the office of the Master of the Queen's Household. It was muggy, hot weather, and a housemaid had opened the window shortly after 6 am to air the office before Vice-Admiral Sir Peter Ashmore's arrival.

The Queen's corgis, usually so watchful and snappish, had been taken out for their morning run in the Palace gardens by a footman. The armed police sergeant, always slipper-shod for silence through the long night watch outside the Queen's bedroom went off duty when his shift finished at 6 and the royal bedroom was unattended. One of the Palace staff should have taken over immediately. It was now 7 am. The intruder was elated at his nearness to the Queen's apartments. 'I just kept following the pictures as a guide', he said later. He loped along the corridors, ignored by the royal servants. They thought he was a barefooted workman who had arrived early.

At 7.15 am Fagan entered the Queen's bedroom. He slipped first into an ante-room where he smashed a glass ashtray, which he claimed later he intended to use to slash his wrists in the presence of the Queen. The slamming of the bedroom door first alerted the Queen. 'I realized immediately that it wasn't a servant because they don't slam doors,' she told detectives later.

Fagan was visible to the Queen when he pulled the bedroom curtains, dragging them open by hand instead of using the cord. The Queen sat bolt upright in bed: 'Our eyes met and both of us looked dumbfounded.' The Queen recovered quickly from the shock and briskly snapped at Fagan: 'Get out of here at once,' in a voice which would strike awe in the most reckless. But Fagan took no notice and approached the Queen's bed, with blood dripping from his right thumb, and there he sat talking.

For ten minutes he remained there. The Queen's ability to keep a conversation going calmly is an art she has perfected over the years when meeting the tongue tied, the inhibited and the shyly inarticulate. One word said too hastily, or even the wrong intonation, could have thrown the man sitting on her bed into a frenzy. The Queen reached for a telephone. Her earlier pressing of the night alarm bell had gone unnoticed. There was nobody in the corridor or the pantry anyway. Having dialled 222 the Queen said in a perfectly normal voice: 'I want a police officer.' The Palace operator on duty knew the Queen's voice well after years of putting calls through, and all the operators enjoy connecting her to the Queen Mother, when they can say 'Your Majesty?' 'Her Majesty, Your Majesty.'

The operator telephoned the Police Lodge and the call was logged at 7.18 am. Six minutes elapsed; Fagan talked about his family. The Queen talked about her own – mentioning that Prince Charles was about Fagan's age.

The Queen made another call to the switchboard enquiring coolly why there had been no response. It was later established that there had been a series of blunders, both slack and bizarre. Fagan then asked for a cigarette. The Queen does not smoke but on the pretext of getting him some cigarettes she managed to get the attention of a stalwart young chambermaid, Elizabeth Andrew, who, when she saw the Queen's improbable bedside guest, the barefoot Fagan curled up at the monarch's feet, said: 'Ooh, bloody 'ell Ma'am, what's 'e doing 'ere?'

The Queen much enjoyed this moment and later did very good impersonations of the girl's Middlesbrough accent. It was the only light moment.

The Queen and her chambermaid together then managed to usher Fagan out of the bedroom, saying that they could get him some cigarettes in the pantry nearby. Paul Wybrew, senior footman, got to the pantry seconds later and grabbed Fagan firmly by the arm, but gave him some cigarettes.

By now the corgis were back and the Queen had some difficulty restraining them and keeping them away from Fagan, who had now become rather agitated. There was still only the twenty-three-year-old footman to cope with the intruder – and the Queen was getting rather testy.

Suddenly she saw a swarm of perspiring policemen surging up the grand staircase to rescue their monarch. The young one leading the field remembers how he got to the top of the stairs and, seeing the Queen's head poking out from the pantry, automatically started to straighten up his tie. 'Oh, come on,' the Queen snapped, 'get a bloody move on.'

Fagan was led away and later appeared in Bow Street Magistrates Court where he was committed to the Old Bailey for trial. He was charged with stealing half a bottle of wine from Buckingham Palace on 7 June, almost five weeks before the bedroom incident. He appeared in the dock at the Old Bailey on 23 September and was cleared by a jury of any wrongdoing, though he freely admitted breaking into Buckingham Palace twice. The hearing took four hours. He told the jury of seven men and five women: 'It might be that I've done the Queen a favour. I've proved that her security system was no good.' He was remanded in custody to await trial on a charge of assaulting his stepson.

Heads rolled as security at the Palace came under the spotlight. Mrs Thatcher brought forward her usual Tuesday evening meeting with the Queen by twenty-four hours to stress her regret and concern and to apologize.

In the House of Commons the flustered Home Secretary, William Whitelaw, was trying to explain the apparent incompetence of his security men at Buckingham Palace and did not impress the MPs when he said, 'No one was more shocked and staggered than I was by the Queen's ordeal ...' There was also the underlying embarrassment that the monarch should be so vulnerable under a Conservative Government.

The Queen watched the search for scapegoats and was not impressed by the initially complacent response to the incident by the Government. Although outwardly unperturbed – only a few hours after the incident guests at an investiture were unaware of her ordeal – the Queen argued, quite properly, that it had been extremely fortunate that the intruder had not been a terrorist.

The most unfair face-saving attempt by Scotland Yard was the threatened sideways move of the policeman who had been going home on his motorcycle after night duty and reported to the Palace guard that he had spotted an intruder climbing over the Palace walls. He got a black mark for his failure to follow the incident through – but in the end his initiative was appreciated.

An investigation was launched by Assistant Commissioner John Dellow and the A1 Royal Protection Squad into how on earth the Queen's plea for help could possibly have been so misunderstood. The Queen who normally does not show anger or emotion – she has only once been seen publicly with tears in her eyes and that was at Aberfan where so many children tragically died – kept her mask of self-control. But some weeks later, even at the happy family gathering for the christening of the Prince and Princess of Wales's first child, Prince William, she was tense. A member of her Household explained, 'The Queen is very strained, almost in a state of shock.'

She cancelled a visit to Goodwood and was ordered to rest by her doctors who believe in the theory of Hans Selye, a psychologist who argues that shock can often take its toll in some form of physical illness. Prince Edward tried to cheer his mother up, saying that the security would become so intense around the Palace that if a member of the royal family was spotted outside – at Badminton or Windsor – the cry would go up that 'one of them has got away!'

Publicly the Queen had recovered her composure – entertaining guests at Palace luncheon parties with a sanguine re-telling of the incident. But, secretly, she was bristling at the intrusion into her own privacy, and hating the unwelcome and open discussion, verging on the prurient, about why Prince Philip had not been around on the morning of the incident. He had evidently been in a separate bedroom – by no means uncommon in aristocratic homes – as he had to be up early to take part in horse-driving trials in Scotland. It was felt that perhaps it was a good thing that the Duke and Fagan had not met head on. When the forensic experts checked the Palace there were one or two appreciative smiles when corgi hairs were found on the royal blankets!

Looking a little pale the Queen mingled serenely with some 7,000 guests at a garden party later in the week. Animated and interested, she chatted about the family's pleasure in the 'second heir' – 'we are enjoying him very much!' The Queen chatted about education, racing pigeons, Korea and the Falklands and everybody marvelled at her smile as they ate their cucumber sandwiches and chocolate cake and the brass band played. Two days later the Queen was in hospital.

If the Selye theory is right, the Queen had been in pain from the wisdom tooth all week. It was not apparent as she went to the Open Air Theatre in Regent's Park where she enjoyed Shaw's *Dark Lady of the Sonnets*, ironically a play about an intruder at the palace. Nor did anybody notice any signs of pain when she visited the Royal Engineers Postal Branch at Mill Hill. But by Friday the pain was so bad that her dentist, Nicholas Sturridge, advised surgery. The Queen was driven to the King Edward VII Hospital for Officers in a Rover with her trusted private detective, Commander Michael Trestrail, solicitous and watchful as ever, in the passenger seat next to the chauffeur. The operation was performed by Mr Herbert Cook. The Queen fortunately seemed to recover quickly from the general anaesthetic and rested in the four-roomed Suite 20.

She left hospital on Sunday looking drawn and pale with a slight swelling in her left cheek where the tooth had been extracted, and drove to Windsor to rest.

Commander Michael Trestrail had been the Queen's personal bodyguard for nine years. The first question marks over his impeccable record came when the intruder was found in the Palace on 9 July. The Queen's safety in her own rooms was not his province, but events were to build up catastrophically for him.

He had always provided just the sort of police protection the Queen liked: subtle, swift and courteous, but never obvious. Lean and looking very much part of the administrative side of the Household, Michael Trestrail's appearance on a royal tour – running down the steps of aircraft or *Britannia* – meant the Queen would be appearing in seconds. He would carry her umbrella, or her handbag and often a rug. He mixed urbanity with the darting eyes of a good policeman. He wore a taut expression – the natural shape of his mouth always gave him a look of suitable dignity and seeming appreciation of the formality of occasions. Only later, at a banquet or lounging around when the Queen was enjoying a break for tea, would he crease with laughter at some amusing incident. He never threw his weight around but would intervene if he saw foreign police being unnecessarily hard on the photographers. In turn he won the respect and co-operation of the host country's security men.

He adored the Queen. His own mother had died when he was very young. He always remembered his staff. The last Christmas before his resignation he mentioned to the Queen how a couple of young policemen had done very good work and, to their complete surprise, the Queen singled them out for a special word of thanks.

He is a cultivated man and the Queen would discuss plays and films with him. 'We thought the dialogue was a bit false, a bit too toned down,' he said at the Hatchards Author of the Year party when the Queen was a guest. 'We know people don't talk like that,' he said, and he was not putting just his own point of view.

He protected the Queen with vigour and, she thought, distinction during his nine years' stewardship of the royal life.

It was when the Queen was at an unaccustomed physical low ebb, with delayed shock from the events of the previous week, that she heard that Commander Trestrail had resigned because of his homosexual relationship with a male prostitute. He had offered to resign after the intruder incident, but the Queen would not hear of it. His last job as the Queen's personal detective was when he escorted her to hospital.

The publicity over the security at the Palace had prompted a male prostitute, thirty-six-year-old Michael Rauch, with whom Trestrail had had a casual relationship, to approach a newspaper, the *Sun*, hoping he would be well paid for an account of the liaison which had ended three years previously. The newspaper alerted Buckingham Palace and Rauch went to Scotland Yard on the Saturday morning. Commander Trestrail who might normally have spent the day at home in his flat in Twickenham looking after his garden or preparing a meal for friends, was summoned to the Yard and confessed – unaware that Rauch was in a nearby room.

He revealed that he had also been sent blackmail letters demanding £2,000. Such circumstances are always regarded as creating a security risk irrespective of the integrity of the individual – the old fear that secrets get passed to lovers. In fact he never had access to State papers.

The Queen tried to persuade her detective to resign on health grounds as a face-saving exercise. Her view, openly expressed, was: 'He has done his work excellently', but even the Queen could not save him. The Home Secretary was hastily revealing full details and by the following Monday Commander Trestrail was a broken man. He told friends he felt 'leprous'. Highly placed people at the Palace wrote him sympathetic letters.

The relationship between the royal family and their detectives has to be close; they rely a great deal on the skill of the detectives. Although it is a friendly relationship, like the affection you feel for the doctor who makes the pain stop or the pilot who gets you through the electrical storm – it still is servant and master.

Commander Trestrail apologized through his solicitor Sir David Napley to the Queen and the royal family for the distress he caused them. The Queen did not see him again – instead the rug for her knees would be handed into the car by his replacement, Superintendent Chris Hagon. The Queen is tolerant enough and will allow for emotional stresses or human error – but only occasionally. Once you fall from favour you are out, finished ...

Hagon was not seen walking a respectful ten paces away from the Queen at the garden party in that first week after the Trestrail furore. Instead he stayed in the Palace ploughing through paper work – relaxed and knowing that none of the guests would be likely to go berserk, throw off their finery and lunge at the Queen. Chief-Inspector Brian Jeffery, a tall, well-dressed, easy-going character whose normal task is looking after the Duke, protected the Queen that day as well. The Queen looked strained and tense and there were fewer smiles. She was distracted and visibly distressed about the bombs which had ripped into the Blues and Royals on the previous Tuesday.

The final blow, and one which made the Queen burst into tears, was the news of the death of Lord Rupert Nevill, a friend, and valued courtier, almost like a brother to her and also trusted adviser and Private Secretary to Prince Philip.

After Lord Rupert's death the Queen, for the first time in her
reign, was ordered to rest by her doctors. Most women could not
have coped half as well as the Queen with the intruder, but such a
chapter of tragedies had taken its toll.

However, the summer had its happiness, too. At 9.03 pm on 21
June 1982 in a hospital room in Paddington, the Princess of Wales
gave birth to her first child, a boy weighing 7lb 1½oz. It had been a
long, hard day for the Princess and for the Prince of Wales who
had driven his wife to St Mary's Hospital just after five that Monday morning. He stayed at the hospital all day and insisted on
being present at the birth. Later, rather stunned by his wife's
achievement and the expertise of George Pinker, the Queen's Surgeon Gynaecologist, Prince Charles spoke to crowds outside the
hospital. When asked if he wanted a large family he burst out:
'Bloody hell, give us a chance.' The baby destined to be king and
second in line to the throne was just hours old, 'cried lustily' and
had blue eyes and blond hair.

The Queen was amongst the first to see the new baby and was
solicitous about her daughter-in-law. The Queen and Prince
Charles arrived at the Princess's top-floor room chuckling. In his
excitement Prince Charles had pressed the wrong lift button. The
Queen and the Prince had travelled speedily to the hospital basement where the doors had opened on a policeman, his jacket un-
buttoned, his tie loosened and his head encircled in a film of smoke
as he enjoyed a furtive cigarette.

The birth of Prince William has strengthened the bond between
the Queen and the Princess who share exactly the same views on
family life. The Princess has a tonic effect on the Queen, makes
her laugh and relax. The Queen's apartments are 'open house' to
the Princess who in turn makes sure that her London and Gloucestershire homes have specially large teacups for the Queen who
does not like her Darjeeling in fiddly little cups.

The christening was in the Music Room in Buckingham Palace
on 4 August, the Queen Mother's eighty-second birthday. The
baby, forty-four days old and wearing the christening robe of
Honiton lace first used in 1842 for another Prince of Wales – later
Edward VII – yelled and could only be comforted by his mother's
little finger. The Archbishop of Canterbury, Dr Runcie, poured
water over his head from the silver font – known as lily font – but
the water was not from the Jordan as the royal supplies have run

out. Afterwards, at a happy family party, the Queen Mother held the baby with the expertise of a young mother. Everyone wondered why the Queen did not hold the baby, but she wanted the Queen Mother to be the other centre of attention.

'Yes, he's a good speech-maker,' the Queen remarked, trying to ease the embarrassment of the Princess of Wales who was going as pink as her baby as he cried loudly.

After the champagne with the godparents, who were the former King Constantine of the Hellenes, Sir Laurens van der Post, Lord Romsey, Princess Alexandra, the Duchess of Westminster and Lady Susan Hussey, the 'second heir' to the throne, Prince William Arthur Philip Louis, was taken home to Kensington Palace and fed by the Princess.

Another joyous occasion was when the Queen went to Portsmouth on 17 September to welcome home not only her helicopter pilot son but 'all his mates' on board the carrier HMS *Invincible*.

After five and a half months in the Falklands, Prince Andrew jumped in the air, threw up his cap and with a red rose in his mouth said what he was really looking forward to was a 'pint of milk'! The Queen looked very happy as she filmed some of the banners on the quayside saying 'Welcome Home Our Heroes' and 'Mum's Little Pirates'. She was moved and kept brushing something imaginary away from her right eye and hastily recovering and pointing things out to Princess Anne. Prince Philip in his uniform of Admiral of the Fleet was enjoying a moment many fathers would envy as Prince Andrew, the son most like him, took him on a tour of the *Invincible* and introduced the rest of 820 Squadron. The Queen was anxious that her presence should not dim the pleasure of the homecoming for everyone else. There was a quick walk amongst the families and, carrying a basket of red roses, the Queen asked them: 'Aren't you pleased?'

She was asked the same question. 'I certainly am. Isn't it marvellous?' she replied. And the irrepressible Prince Andrew followed behind – full of high jinks, being hugged by the girls in the crowd while their sweethearts on *Invincible*, waiting to come on shore, pretended to shake their fists at him.

Prince Philip looked on with an expression like the Queen's when she watched Prince Charles leaving St Paul's on his wedding day, as if to say 'Well, I never!' Eventually the most notable sub-lieutenant in the Falklands war – or 'H' as they called him in the Squadron, short for HRH – left with his family in the royal barge to try and live a normal life. Well, not exactly. As he said himself, he was not sure he could get used to being a Prince again.

CHAPTER 24

❀ ❀ ❀

We Want the Queen

AT THE SUGGESTION that, in her late fifties, the Queen may be thinking of stepping down from the throne, the men at the Palace appear to be astounded. The Queen, they say, with absolute certainty, will not be retiring; it is an absurd notion. Laughing at the very idea that the Queen might like to hand over to Prince Charles now that he is married, settled and in his mid-thirties, one of the Household expostulated, 'Good God, you don't give up so your son can have a job!' But this is merely a Palace opinion, and whether it is a true reflection of the Queen's thinking or an inflexible view expressed by more senior members of her Household is not clear.

A few years ago the Queen suggested to a group of politicians and academics at a private dinner party that the ideal time for her to abdicate would be 'when Charles could do better'. The Duke of Edinburgh gruffly complimented her: 'You may be right; the doctors will keep you alive so long,' and the discussion evaporated in laughter. There are gloomy prophets who feel inexplicably that Prince Charles may never come to the throne, but this is utterly without basis or logic. The Queen is a religious woman who has always felt deeply about the spirituality of hereditary monarchy and is inspired by its mystical quality, and she might well argue that retirement is not for her to choose. If Kings and Queens could retire when they liked, monarchy's intangible, supernatural authority would be dispelled and cease to be above government. This would indicate that only the *force majeure* of illness or death could relieve the Queen of her crown. Yet Prince Charles is such an eminently suitable heir apparent.

There is an argument that, if he succeeded to the throne now, there would be the impossibly delicate position of having both a Queen Mother and a Queen Gran. The Queen Mother holds such a special place in everyone's heart, and her daughter would be the last person to disturb this family balance. On the other hand, the Queen Mother's eventual death does open another option, a gloomy one which nobody really wants to contemplate as she is one of the best-loved members of the royal family.

Before the royal family is the appalling, nagging 'Edward VII situation', as the Queen sensibly refers to her great-grandfather's long wait before he could become King. Despite her belief in the sanctity of monarchy (its continuity has only been broken once in the last thousand years, from 1649 to 1660) she is intuitive and modern in her outlook. Neither she nor Prince Charles need reminding of Queen Victoria's sixty-four-year reign which, at her death at the age of eighty-two, left a bewildered 'Bertie' trying to clamber up to the throne.

The Queen has always stressed that in the grooming of her eldest son for monarchy he should first of all be brought up to be a good man, 'Because if he is not a good man, how can he possibly be a good King?' There is a deliberate attempt by the Palace to cultivate an image slightly behind the times, just a little old-fashioned. This is intended to ensure a feeling of continuity with no sudden swerves or jars. Yet over the last few years there has been an almost imperceptible winding-down of the Queen's programme; Prince Charles is taking on more and more public appearances. It is perhaps the beginning of a relationship whereby the Queen becomes the president of the firm and Prince Charles, as the energetic managing director, gains experience. She will still do the State Opening of Parliament, Commonwealth Conferences and some important royal tours abroad but not the arduous long-haul eight-week visits. In Britain, she might go to Birmingham for a couple of days, whereas Prince Charles would take on the whole of the north-east, hopping by helicopter from one city to another in the same time span.

The Queen is at heart a countrywoman and this has taught her poise against the elements. She knows when to take cover, and would abdicate instantly if the people wanted a republic. But it is the very character of the British to know, deep down, that much of the stability of the country rests on the institution of monarchy.

The Queen represents something of value, standing for decent, caring humanity. Anyone wanting to dismantle it in the belief that they could substitute a better alternative would be dangerously arrogant.

Again and again the country has shown in its quiet way its addiction to the monarchy. 'You have the Queen,' an American remarked. 'We have only the flag.' Other countries, though materially successful, seem drab against this lustre, which would not survive without the integrity of a small, fineboned woman who dedicated her life, 'be it long or short', to her people. Even John Grigg, once Lord Altrincham, grudgingly retracts some of his criticism of the Queen made nearly thirty years ago, in the face of the royal family's now surging popularity. Some of the family may be more glamorous, more energetic, wittier, make better speeches, but it is the Queen who is appreciated for her 'pure, honest gold'. Her personality, he says, is 'very glamorous; her political savvy in dealing with her Prime Ministers and Commonwealth Heads of Government has been remarkable, and her stability of character a bonus.' He remains critical of some of the Queen's Household, thinks she is still surrounded by unimaginativeness and fears that Prince Charles is turning to the same sort of old-fashioned advisers. Certainly a black secretary was hired recently for the Prince of Wales's office, but Grigg argues that this was no more than a token gesture: 'A black typist but nobody of officer level to keep the monarchy in touch with the Third World.' When Charles III comes to the throne, he might be in his thirties or he might be fifty-five. But he will have had the benefit of guidance from the monarch which she herself was denied by the death of the King in his fifties.

'Charming little creature, I do hope they don't work her too hard,' Lord Pethwick-Lawrence muttered solicitously in St George's Chapel, Windsor, as he watched the young Queen in black at her father's funeral. It has been a lifetime of hard work and dedication, and the result has been a natural beauty and composure which shines through. At her Silver Jubilee, the Queen, who seems now positively to enjoy her role, reminded the nation of her promise made six years before her Coronation: 'When I was twenty-one, I pledged my life to the service of our people and I asked for God's help to make good that vow. Although that vow was made in my salad days when I was green in judgement, I do not regret or retract one word of it.'

Nowadays the Queen looks slim, is relaxed; she has a serenity about her. There is still never a complete day off – the red boxes must always be read on any holiday. Two hundred letters addressed to her are delivered at Buckingham Palace ('the office', as she calls it) every day, and 2,200 Orders, decorations and medals are presented every year. But there is more time to enjoy her family, slipping off to Gatcombe Park to stay with Princess Anne and to see her first two grandchildren, and then, like any grandmother dividing her time diplomatically, going to lunch with Prince Charles and his young wife at Highgrove. The Princess of Wales is seen as the perfect choice for a future Queen of England, with a gentle, spontaneous charm which is neither sickly nor overwhelming. The Queen is delighted with her, and the Princess says, 'I have the best mother-in-law in the world.'

The special values of both youth and scientific development are impressed on the Queen by Prince Philip, who still has a restless, questing streak. He darts about the world, doing 75,000 miles a year. But wherever he is, as a wildlife expert, a conservationist, a businessman, God to the Iounahan tribe in the West Hebrides or discussing as lay philosopher Karl Marx, sex and education, he sends his wife the same message: 'The Lord watch between thee and me when one is absent from the other.' His dynamism – he is a man full of ideas and activity – must also put the Queen in a dilemma about retirement. The marriage is mellow; she relies on him greatly, and he is gentle and protective with her. She is proud of him and secretly likes his outrageous outspokenness. 'What a po-faced lot these Dutch are,' he remarked irascibly in Holland, making the chauffeur very huffy on the way from the airport. Yet the relationship has subtly changed with the death of Lord Mountbatten. Prince Philip was deeply shaken by the death of the man who was his uncle, his friend and above all a father figure, who saw him through the insecurity of early years.

It was the Queen, sitting opposite Prince Philip on the funeral train to Broadlands, who kept a light, sensitive patter of conversation going so that any show of public grief could be held back until the train had pulled away from the platform and the silent crowd at Waterloo. They are at a stage in their marriage when it is usually the woman who feels she is spinning aimlessly as the children leave home, while the man has developed his career to its peak. But in the Queen's marriage, the positions are to some extent reversed. It is she who has had to discipline herself since childhood to cope with loneliness and a sense of isolation, but now in late middle age can breathe a sigh of relief and enjoy what she has achieved.

On the day of the royal wedding, in spite of the glamorous young couple standing on the balcony of Buckingham Palace giving each other a kiss, the thousands of upturned cheering faces started an insistent chant after the Queen had gone inside: 'We want the Queen, we want the Queen,' they shouted until they saw her again, poised, delicate in pale blue. 'The Queen,' they roared.

The Queen watched. She looked happy – a bit surprised but apart and restrained. She never makes you weep but turned everyone a notch more monarchist that unforgettable July afternoon. Inside the Palace they pay her an even greater compliment. They say they have never felt sorry for the Queen, for the burden she has to bear, because she has been moulded, almost typecast, for her special destiny: a good destiny, and a long one over a fortunate people. If you ask one of the Queen's most senior courtiers how long this destiny will last, he replies with a chuckle, 'We have beheaded monarchs, usurped monarchs, but we do not have retired monarchs.' But then courtiers share Bagehot's view that it is best not to know too much about royalty. Its mystery is its life. We must not let in daylight upon the magic.

Index